DELPHI™
The Official Guide

Published by
General Videotex Corporation
Cambridge, Massachusetts

General Videotex Corporation
1030 Massachusetts Avenue
Cambridge, Massachusetts 02138

Manufactured in the United States of America

10 9 8 7 6 5 4 3 2 1

Every effort has been made to make this handbook as complete and factual as possible. However, information contained herein is subject to change without notice and should not be construed as a committment by General Videotex Corporation, which assumes no responsibilities for any errors that may appear.

Library of Congress Cataloging-in-Publication Data

DELPHI: The Official Guide

Includes index
1. DELPHI (Videotex system) I. General Videotex Corporation
II. Title

ISBN 0-9625623-1-9

DELPHI is a service of General Videotex Corporation.
Other trademarks appearing in this book are trademarks of their respective companies.

All photographs, menus, screens, and data reproduced in tables and/or figures in this books are copyrighted in content and/or form by their respective providers and are reproduced by permission.

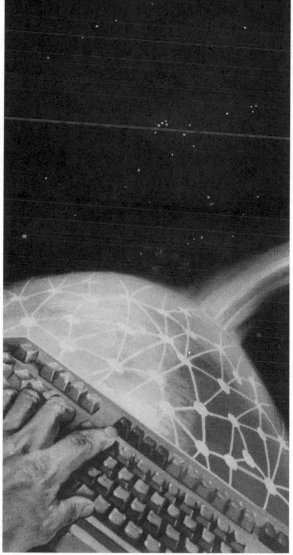

Retail Therapist

More savings — less guilt...

Suffering from recession depression? Anxious over high prices and low quality? Guilt-ridden if you spend too much? Now your computer can cure you of the shopping blues with Comp-u-store® OnLine.

Comp-u-store OnLine guides you to **over 250,000 top-name household and personal items** with "therapeutic" prices — **10%-50% below the manufacturer's suggested list cost**.

Now you can analyze product features and prices for the best value around. Purchase audio equipment, furniture, jewelry, toys, tools, and much more — all from leading brands, like Maytag, Panasonic, GE, Black & Decker, and Nintendo, to name just a few.

Thanks to our **Low Price Guarantee**, you won't miss a sale. If you find a better deal on the same item you purchased through Comp-u-store OnLine, the difference in price is refunded to you.* How's that for less stressful shopping!

Plus, Comp-u-store OnLine eases your mind with **Automatic Two-Year Warranty**, ensuring your OnLine purchases are automatically covered for **two full years** from the date of purchase — Free.*

And...if you need "live" counseling, one convenient call to **1-800-843-7777** will connect you to a professional Shopping Consultant.**

So, turn your computer into a retail therapist. **Type SHOP COMPUSTORE at the MAIN Menu, find us on the Shopping Menu,** or call us now at **1-800-843-7777**, to analyze 3 months of savings for only $1.

Then, unless you notify us otherwise, we'll continue your benefits for a full year and bill you only $39. If, for any reason, you're not completely satisfied, you can cancel your membership during the first year for a <u>full refund</u> — no matter how much money you've saved. Even Freud would've envied that! So, get hooked onto Comp-u-store OnLine, and see why our value, quality, and convenience make it crazy for you to shop anywhere else.

Introductory Offer: 3 Months For $1

* Conditions of our Low Price Guarantee and Automatic Two-Year Warranty Protection can be read online.

** Hours: Monday - Friday, 9 a.m. - 11 p.m.; Saturday and Sunday, 9 a.m. - 6 p.m. (ET).

Comp-u-store OnLine is a service provided by CUC International Inc.

© 1992, CUC International Inc.

DE6AS1

Contents

Foreword

Welcome to DELPHI!

This is an exciting time to be part of DELPHI. There are rapid changes taking place with the integration of thousands of services and millions of people through the Internet. DELPHI is the first major online service to offer you full access to this incredible resource. You can now connect directly to universities, colleges, government agencies, and powerful research services.

DELPHI's Internet connection works in both directions; if you have access to the Internet at your company, school, or through a regional service, you can now connect to DELPHI with just a few keystrokes. You'll enjoy DELPHI's expert Internet support forum and hundreds of high-quality information resources like Reuters newswire, Grolier's Encyclopedia, multi-player games, travel reservations, personal networks, and special interest groups.

This edition of the DELPHI: The Official Guide has been updated to include information about the Internet and other new features. Because DELPHI is growing rapidly, there will likely be additions to the service even before this book is off the press. Be sure to check online for the latest news and announcements. If you have a question or are looking for something specific, just ask. DELPHI members are always happy to help.

Once again, welcome; we're pleased that you've chosen to be part of DELPHI.

Dan Bruns
President & Chief Executive Officer
General Videotex Corporation

Introduction

YOUR DOORWAY TO TELECOMPUTING

A personal computer is a powerful tool, able to perform an amazing range of tasks. You may have found yours to be useful for business, entertainment, education or other applications at your home or office.

But until you connect your computer to the outside world, using your telephone line, you will only scratch the surface of your machine's capabilities. Going online gives you access — access to databases filled with vital information, access to thousands of public domain and "shareware" software programs, access to the knowledge and experience of a worldwide community of fellow computer users. You will also find constantly updated news and financial information, interactive games, and links to FAX and Telex machines.

There is no easier way to connect yourself than by using your computer and modem to call DELPHI.

HOW THIS BOOK IS ORGANIZED

Getting Started (The Introduction and Chapters 1 and 2) is your guide to getting "up and running" on DELPHI with ease and efficiency. Chapter 1 shows you how to connect with DELPHI—what you'll need and how to use it—and contains step-by-step procedures for dialing up and logging on to DELPHI. Chapter 2 introduces the basic commands you'll use in communicating with DELPHI. You'll learn how to move around the system, using simple English and Control-key commands. Making menu selections, moving from menu to menu, responding to prompts, learning to initiate and suspend activities, and more are covered in Chapter 2.

Chapters 3 through 19 provide a comprehensive guide to DELPHI's services and features. You'll find detailed information about what's available in each DELPHI Main Menu selection, as well as suggestions on how to get the most out of each area. Menus, commands, and options are covered step-by-step, with a table of contents at the beginning of most chapters for quick reference.

WHAT IS DELPHI?

DELPHI is a full-service communications, information, and entertainment network that takes your home or business computer far beyond the capabilities of its software and peripherals.

A simple telephone call connects your computer with DELPHI. Once you're connected, you'll have full command of an incredibly vast array of information and services, thanks to videotex—easy-to-use interactive computer services.

It's all made possible by advanced telecommunications, computer equipment, and software—but don't let that intimidate you. DELPHI was designed with *you* in mind. You don't have to speak "computerese" to use DELPHI. Simple English-language commands put you in charge; you can concentrate on what you want to do, rather than trying to figure out how to do it.

DELPHI can be used by anyone, anywhere—with any kind of computer or terminal. All you need to connect with DELPHI is a terminal or a computer with communications software, a modem, and a telephone line (your existing telephone line will do just fine).

DELPHI's ease of use doesn't detract from its power, though. Even if you're a sophisticated computer user, you'll find that DELPHI puts more into your computer than you ever imagined possible!

DELPHI Services

Among DELPHI's many services for personal computer users you'll find:

- E-Mail service (and the post office is *never* closed)
- online shopping services, providing computer supplies, coffee, and more
- computer, personal, and hobby Special Interest Groups
- downloadable Public Domain and Shareware programs for all types of personal computers
- real-time conferencing
- exciting multi-player games

- the educational resources of our Reference and Education menu, with Grolier's encyclopedia
- up-to-date news, weather, and sports reports and features
- vacation and travel information and reservations
- online file creation and management
- and a host of fascinating features and benefits

Here are just a few of the many business and financial services you have access to as a DELPHI member:

- instant messaging and document transfer (no more "telephone tag," and no expensive overnight delivery services!)
- access to stock and commodities market information
- special-interest groups and databases
- access to Dialog's Research Library, the world's premier knowledge base
- the latest financial and economic news—foreign and domestic
- online consultants, financial news, and assistance
- travel services, including the Official Airline Guide (OAG) and EAASY SABRE
- international Telex and international and domestic FAX communications
- and a wealth of knowledge and computing power, from a comprehensive collection of online services.

Benefits of Using DELPHI

What does this mean for you? It means that you will be able to take your computer to the limit—and beyond—while realizing invaluable benefits, tangible and intangible.

Is time important to you? With DELPHI, you no longer have to depend on someone else's schedule; communications and research services are available 24 hours a day, 365 days a year. You'll *save* time, too; communications of all kinds are instantaneous, as are business and personal information gathering and transactions, such as DELPHI's educational resources, databases, shopping and travel services—a few simple keystrokes can save hours of research time, telephone calls, and running from place to place.

DELPHI services are convenient. You can conduct business, do research, shop for computers and supplies, visit with friends, and more—without leaving your home or office.

DELPHI can save you money! Using Conference to communicate with associates and friends during evening and weekend hours is lower in cost than most long-distance voice telephone services. If you have a lengthy document that needs to be delivered tomorrow, you can send it to another DELPHI member at a cost far less than next-day delivery services. And DELPHI's research services, databases, groups, and other services put information on almost any topic at your fingertips—again at a cost far below that of conventional information sources.

Using DELPHI can make your work, hobby, or personal activities more efficient in many ways. And, no matter how you use it, you'll find that DELPHI is just plain fun.

Special Terms of Reference Used in this Book

A *command* is anything you type to instruct DELPHI to take a specific action. Examples of commands are EXIT and DELETE. Certain control characters are also commands. Commands may include a modifying word called a *qualifier*, which directs the command to operate in a certain manner.

A *menu* is a listing of available commands and other choices.

A *selection* is a choice that is available on a menu. If you choose an item from a menu by typing the item's name, you have made a selection. A selection may also be an item upon which a command acts.

Option is used interchangeably with selection, but usually refers to choices that are *not* commands. An item on a list of choices, which are not commands, is an option. So is a command qualifier.

A *prompt* is a signal that DELPHI is waiting for you to make a selection, enter information, or type a command. Each menu has a prompt, and there are special prompts that request special kinds of responses from you.

A *response* is your answer to a question from DELPHI, direct or implied. You may, for example, be prompted to enter "Yes" or "No," or to enter a date. Your answer to a direct question is your response. All prompts are in themselves implied questions; thus, commands are responses, as well.

Input is normally text that you type to compose a message or description. Input may also be information or directions that you type in response to a prompt.

The word *entry* may refer to text that you type to compose a message or description, or to a file or group of files in a database.

When referring to commands and your input, this book uses the following conventions:

Commands. Commands are printed in **boldface,** with all capital letters, so you can easily distinguish them from surrounding text. Example: To leave this area, type **EXIT.**

The «RETURN» Key. The key used to send commands or text to your computer or to DELPHI is referred to as the RETURN key, and is represented by this symbol: **«RETURN».** (This key may be marked **ENTER, NEW LINE, XMIT, CR,** or simply with a hooked arrow on your computer or terminal.)

Type or Enter. When you see the word "type" or "Enter," it means that you should enter (type on your keyboard) the designated command or text and press «RETURN». The command will be printed in boldface. For example,

　　　Type **GR SC** (Type GR SC and press «RETURN»)
　　　Enter **EXIT** (Type EXIT and press «RETURN»)

<text>. Text enclosed in greater than/lesser than symbols (like this: <text>) means that you should fill in the *kind* of information enclosed by the symbols before you press «RETURN». For example, type **PAGE <membername>** means that you should enter the command **PAGE,** followed by a membername, such as BOBADAMS or BUCKETHEAD (*not* the word "membername").

Entering Numbers. A number sign (#) or a lowercase x indicates that a number or numbers should be used or will be displayed with the command or option under discussion. nnnn is also used to represent numbers.

Chapter 1
Getting Started

What You Will Need

To access DELPHI, you need a telephone line and a computer with a communications software program (sometimes called terminal software).

Computer Hardware

Any brand or model of personal computer can be used to connect with DELPHI, as long as it can be connected to a modem and has the appropriate communication software. The modem settings, dial-up procedures and DELPHI commands discussed throughout this book are the same for all types of computers.

Modems

A *modem* is a device that enables communication between computers via ordinary telephone lines. Modems may be internal (on a card inside your computer) or external (a stand-alone device). The modem at your computer communicates with a similar modem at DELPHI's central computer, thus allowing two-way data transfer.

The speed at which a modem transmits and receives data is sometimes called its *baud rate,* although the technically correct term is "bits per second," or *bps*. DELPHI can communicate with your computer or terminal at 300, 1200, or 2400 bps. Users of 300 bps modems should investigate upgrading — you'll get much more for your money while online. Although you can connect at 9600 bps through some SprintNet and Tymtnet numbers, it is not officially supported at this writing. Watch for announcements online about changes in pricing or policies affecting 9600 bps access.

Software

You will most likely need to obtain communications software before your computer can use a modem to communicate. Sometimes called terminal emulation software, communications software routes data to and from the modem and instructs the modem to use proper *protocol* in communicating with DELPHI. (Simply put, protocol is an agreed-upon procedure for *how* data is to be transferred.)

At the very least, your communications software should allow you to select the communications speed (300, 1200, or 2400 bits per second) and to set these basic communications parameters: parity, data bits, and duplex. The recommended settings for these are shown in Table 1.1. If your software does not offer these options, don't worry; the parameters at which DELPHI operates are standard defaults for almost all communications software.

These settings are recommended for communicating with DELPHI:

Parameter	Value
Data Bits	8 bit ASCII
Parity	None
Duplex	Full-duplex
Stop bits	1
Auto-linefeed	No
Carriage-Return linefeed	No
XON-XOFF Handshaking (Flow Control)	Enabled(On)
Asynchronous	
Local Echo	Off

Table 1.1 DELPHI Terminal Configuration Guide

Communications Software Options. Better communications software packages offer many powerful features, such as the ability to log onto DELPHI automatically or send entire commands with one keystroke. Your software selection should be determined by the type of computer you own, your budget, and the features you desire.

There are several fine Public Domain and Shareware communications software packages available either for free or at an extremely low cost. Friends who own the same type of computer, your local computer user group, and computer magazines are good sources of information on PD and Shareware software.

Joining DELPHI

If you are not already a member of DELPHI, you become one by telephone or by signing up online. DELPHI accepts Visa, MasterCard, and Discover credit cards. You can authorize direct debits from your checking account (EasyPay). You can also be sent a monthly invoice. Direct billing carries a small surcharge.

You must provide the following information to signup: your name, business and/or home address, business and home telephone numbers, your employer name and telephone number, and your credit card number with expiration date.

You should also think of what you would like to use as a membername. Your membername identifies you to others for electronic mail and conference, and serves as your account number for member services and billing.

A membername can be from three to 12 characters in length, composed of letters and/or numbers in any combination, with no spaces or other punctuation. It can be a nickname, your company name, your initials, anything you like. Some membernames indicate professions (AUTHOR), while others reflect hobbies or personal interests (MODELMIKE).

One last piece of information you should have ready is your mother's maiden name. DELPHI Member Service representatives will ask you for this name when you call with questions.

Online Signups

If you are not presently a DELPHI member, or wish to open a new account, you may use the special signup offer at the back of this book. Follow the procedures outlined in this chapter to connect with DELPHI (either directly or via one of the major telecommunications networks), then log on with the membername and password provided.

When you use the online signup, DELPHI will request your personal and billing information and explain DELPHI signup options and billing procedures.

After you've completed the signup, and have provided a valid credit card you will usually be able to use your membername after 7 p.m. the same day as long as you have registered before Noon (Eastern Time). Otherwise, the new membername and password will be activated after 7 p.m. the next business day. Either way, a DELPHI representative must contact you first at one of the telephone numbers you provide during the signup procedure.

Signing on to DELPHI

Signing on to DELPHI is simply a matter of using your communications software to dial your local access number, identifying yourself to the network (if you are using a network), and then logging on to DELPHI by giving your membername and password.

Direct-dial access is available in Boston and Kansas City. If you don't live near Boston or Kansas City, you can connect to DELPHI using data communication networks called SprintNet and Tymnet. These networks have access numbers in over 600 cities and towns across the country, so it's likely you'll be able to connect with just a local phone call. Access from Canada is supported by both Tymnet and Datapac. If you have access to the Internet through your company, university, or organization, you can telnet to DELPHI using the address "delphi.com."

Instructions for Direct Dial Access

1. Dial (617) 576-0862 (Boston) or (816) 421-6938 (Kansas City).
2. Enter two or three «RETURN»s when you are connected (indicated by a high-pitched tone from an acoustic modem, the CARRIER light on a direct connect modem, or the word CONNECT on your computer screen.)
3. Enter your membername and press «RETURN» at the Username prompt.
4. Enter your password and press «RETURN» at the Password prompt (the password you type will NOT appear on your screen).

Instructions for SprintNet Access

U.S. Sprint Data, or SprintNet (formerly known as Telenet), provides local connect numbers nationwide and is specially designed to link computer users with services like DELPHI.

Access numbers. See Appendix C of this book to obtain your local access number or contact SprintNet (at 1-800-877-5045, extension 5). Be sure to specify the modem speed you'll be using.

SprintNet logon procedure. Here are instructions for logging on via SprintNet:

1. Dial your local SprintNet access number.
2. Once connected, press @, then uppercase D, and «RETURN».
   (at 300 and 1200bps, press «RETURN» first, then D, «RETURN».)
3. When TERMINAL= appears, press «RETURN».
4. When @ appears, type C DELPHI and press «RETURN».
5. Answer the Username and Password prompts with your membername and password (remember to press «RETURN» after each entry).

Instructions for Tymnet Access

Tymnet, like SprintNet, is specially designed to link computer users with services like DELPHI.

Access numbers. See Appendix C of this book to obtain your local access number or contact Tymnet (at 1-800-937-2862). Be sure to specify the modem speed you'll be using.

Tymnet logon procedure. Here are instructions for logging on to DELPHI via Tymnet:

1. Dial your local Tymnet access number.
2. For 2400 bps access, wait five seconds after connection, then type the letter **O**, but do NOT press «RETURN». For 1200 bps access, wait until a group of X's appears, then type the letter **O**, WITHOUT pressing «RETURN». For 300 bps access, wait until you see the prompt, "Please enter your terminal identifier," or a string of random characters. Then type the letter O. Do NOT press «RETURN».
3. When the prompt "Please Log In" appears, enter **DELPHI** and press «RETURN».
4. Answer the Username and Password prompts with your membername and password (remember to press «RETURN» after each entry).

Instructions for Datapac Access

Many Canadian users will find it convenient to access DELPHI via the Datapac network. (Certain Canadian cities offer Tymnet numbers for direct access at substantial savings; check with Tymnet for more information.)

Access numbers. To obtain your local Datapac number, contact DELPHI Member Services, or call Datapac (check directory assistance for the Datapac voice phone number nearest you).

Datapac logon procedure. Here are instructions for logging in via Datapac:

1. Dial your local Datapac number.
2. When connected, enter one period . for 300 bps or two periods .. for 1200 bps.
3. Enter Set 2:1, 3:126 for full duplex allowing deletes.

4. Enter p 1 311061703088 and press «RETURN». for SprintNet access or enter p 1 3106,DELPHI and press «RETURN» for Tymnet access.
5. Answer the Username and Password prompts with your membername and password (remember to press «RETURN» after each entry).

The Guided Tour

On your first visit to DELPHI, you'll be asked to change your password.

Your password is your private key to DELPHI. It prevents unauthorized use of your membername. A password must contain at least eight characters (letters and/or numbers in any combination), and should be long and cryptic enough so that no one can guess what it is.

Never reveal your password to anyone. Doing so will enable that person to use your DELPHI account at will, leaving you liable for whatever charges might accumulate on your account. If someone asks for your password online or by phone, please report this incident by sending electronic mail to membername SERVICE, DELPHI's Member Services department.

No one at DELPHI knows your password. If you forget your password, no one can tell you what it is; all that can be done in that case is to have Member Services change your password and mail it to the address on file. For your own protection, it is advised that you change your password at least once a month.

After you change your password, you will be told where on DELPHI you can go to establish settings on how you want DELPHI to interact with your computer. That is, how text should be displayed on your screen and so forth.

DELPHI Member Services

Member Services is your link to DELPHI. When you have questions about your account or about DELPHI in general, contact Member Services using one of the following methods:

DELPHI Mail. To contact DELPHI Member Services online, send electronic mail to membername SERVICE. Use this for questions about your account, or to report a problem with DELPHI.

Feedback. The Feedback selection on the Using DELPHI menu is for general comments and suggestions to the DELPHI Product Development Group. DELPHI appreciates your suggestions and opinions.

Service Forum. On the Using DELPHI menu, the Service Forum is where you go to ask questions, read answers to other's questions, and learn more about DELPHI.

Telecommunications Device for the Hearing Impaired. By calling 1-800-695-4115, the hearing impaired can communicate with DELPHI's Member Services via their computer. Support is available during normal Member Services Department hours (scc below). If you would like to leave a message during the off hours, you may do so.

Telephone. If you have trouble logging on, or are experiencing a problem online, you can telephone Member Services directly.

DELPHI's Member Services Department is available on the following schedule:

Monday through Friday: 8:00 a.m. until 11:00 p.m. (Eastern Time)
Weekends: 12 noon until 8:00 p.m. (Eastern Time)
1-800-695-4005 (617/491-3393 in Massachusetts and outside the U.S.)
(These hours are subject to change.)

Chapter 2
DELPHI Menu and Command Basics

MENU BASICS

DELPHI services, commands, and options are organized into a number of related menus. As discussed in the Introduction, a menu is a list of selections, or choices. Some selections are commands, while others lead to additional menus or to special prompts. Each menu consists of selections—usually listed in one or two columns—and a prompt.

The DELPHI Main Menu: Your Gateway to DELPHI

The Main Menu is your gateway to DELPHI. Each selection represents a major DELPHI service category. Thus, the Main Menu serves as a general "table of contents" for DELPHI. The Main Menu selections do not, of course, show everything available on DELPHI; each selection leads to a sub-menu or selection menu.

Selecting a Main Menu item will usually take you to another menu, which in turn will lead you either to a service or to additional options in other menus. This hierarchical structure is similar to the "directories" or "folders" used to organize hard disks on personal computers. You can move through DELPHI's menus one step at a time, as outlined below, or jump more quickly by combining commands as described in this section.

Selecting Menu Items

Selecting a menu item (command or option) is easy — just type its name.

If you misspell a selection, DELPHI will merely tell you it doesn't understand your request, and give you another chance to enter your selection.

If you enter the wrong selection and find yourself in unfamiliar territory, you may back out to the previous menu by pressing **Control-Z** or typing **EXIT**.

Shorthand selections. You do not have to type the entire name to select a menu item. Any multiple–character selection may be entered in "shorthand" format, consisting of enough letters of the command to distinguish it from other selections. (Usually, only the first two or three letters of the selection are required.)

The same is true of options at selection menus. If you wanted to select the topic NEWS FROM DELPHI from the USING DELPHI menu, for instance, you could type **NEWS**, or even **NE**.

Combining selections. Selections may be combined to save time. If you already know what you want to select at the next menu or sub-menu that your first selection will display, you can combine the two selections. Entering the first selection followed by the selection from the second menu will bypass the second menu entirely. (You must enter a space between the two selections, and press «RETURN» after entering the second selection.)

To illustrate, imagine you want to go to the PC Compatibles/IBM menu from the DELPHI Main Menu. To do this, you would first type **COMPUTING** (to select the Computing menu at the Main Menu), then **PC** (to select the PC Compatibles group at the Computing menu). This can be shortened to **COM PC,** which will take you directly from the DELPHI Main Menu to the PC Compatibles group menu, and you won't waste time looking at the Computing menu.

You can add even more commands if you like. For example, **COM MAC DAT** will take you to the Macintosh group's database section.

Note that the above examples assume that you are starting at the Main Menu. If you are in one area and want to move quickly to another, simply precede the combined selection with the word **GO.** If you were reading the news in the UPI section and wanted to go to the Atari group, for example, you would type **GO COM ATARI.**

If you would prefer to start your DELPHI sessions somewhere other than the Main Menu, you may use these techniques to set a new Default Menu in Using DELPHI's PROFILE selection.

COMMAND BASICS

There are a number of basic commands you can use at virtually any menu or prompt on DELPHI, whether or not they are listed on the current menu. These basic commands allow you to move around DELPHI and access most services with ease. Among them are the commands you'll need to use most frequently.

All DELPHI commands consist of either a Control-key command or one or more characters followed by a «RETURN».

Single-key (Control-key) Commands

Control-key commands (sometimes called "control-characters" because each consists of a control character) can be used at any prompt. If you enter an invalid Control-key command, DELPHI will ignore it.

Control-key commands are important when you are entering a message, because they are the only commands you can use during message entry. They are also important when you are participating in a conference.

Control-key commands arc issued by holding down the Control key on your keyboard and pressing another key (use the Control key as if it were a shift key). The Control key on your keyboard may be marked CONTROL, CTRL, or <. When this manual refers to a specific control-key command, it will do so like this: Control-Z.

There are two kinds of Control-key commands on DELPHI: Interrupts and Action.

Interrupts

Interrupt Control-key commands are used to tell DELPHI to stop or pause what it's doing. These are **Control-C, Control-O, Control-S,** and **Control-Q**.

Cancelling with Control-C. If you wish to cancel a current activity and return to the prompt from which the previous command was issued, press Control-C. Operations such as uploads and downloads, file displays, and sending mail (indeed, virtually all activities on DELPHI) can be cancelled with Control-C.

Control-C also cancels any input or commands you may have entered as part of the operation. Control-C acts the same way with online forms, so if you make a mistake in filling out a request or order form, the form won't be sent.

Stopping output with Control-O. If you are reading text online (a file, menu, other list), and wish to stop the text output, press **Control-O**. If you are logging on via SprintNet or Tymnet, press the **BREAK** key. This command skips through the remaining text, and takes you to the next prompt (i.e., the prompt you would see if you allowed the text to scroll to completion). This sometimes requires a brief wait. (NOTE: Use the letter "O," not zero.)

Pausing with Control-S and Control-Q. Sometimes you will want to pause the text you are seeing online. To do this, press **Control-S**. To resume displaying the text, press **Control-Q**.

(NOTE: if you press Control-S when DELPHI is not doing anything, such as at a prompt, you will have to press Control-Q before DELPHI will respond to further commands.)

Action Control-key Commands

Action Control-key commands are used as responses to prompts, or to issue specialized commands. These Control-key commands are **Control-R**, **Control-U**, **Control-X**, and **Control-Z**.

Redisplaying a line with Control-R. If you have entered and deleted a lot of characters (as in Conference or Mail) and wish to see your line in "clear" before you send it, press **Control-R**. This redisplays the current input line. You may then send, cancel or add to the line.

Control-R will also redisplay a command given at a prompt. (The prompt as well as the command is redisplayed.)

Cancelling with Control-U. If you make a typing mistake or change your mind when entering a command, a line in conference, or a line in a mail message, press **Control-U**. This is the equivalent of saying, "Forget that line." Use Control-U when you wish to cancel a command at a prompt, or "erase" a line in a message or conference.

Clearing with Control-X. Control-X clears anything you've typed ahead. Control-X is handy when you've typed ahead some commands, but changed your mind. It can also be used to erase a command or a line in conference or a mail message.

Exiting and sending with Control-Z. Use Control-Z when you wish to exit the current menu and move to a higher (or previous) menu. Control-Z is the "shorthand" equivalent of entering EXIT and pressing «RETURN». (NOTE: You cannot use Control-Z to log off DELPHI; you must type **EXIT** or **BYE**.)

Control-Z is used to send or post messages in Electronic Mail, Group and Club Forums, and other kinds of messages. Use Control-Z to tell DELPHI that you have finished entering your message, and wish to send it.

You can also use Control-Z to tell DELPHI that you've finished a process, such as entering text or uploading an ASCII file.

(NOTE: Some terminal programs use control-key characters to issue their own internal commands. If a control-key command makes your terminal take some action independent of DELPHI, your terminal program should be reconfigured to use a control key that DELPHI doesn't need.)

Shortcuts

Shorthand commands. As with menu selections, you need only type the first few letters of a multiple-character command. For example, rather than type **EXIT**, you can type **EX** to obtain the same results. This is true of both system-wide and Immediate commands.

Combining commands and selections. Although you cannot combine two commands, some commands may be combined with selections in certain areas. In Workspace, for example, you may delete a file by typing **DELETE** and responding to the prompt for the filename, or by typing **DELETE <filename>**.

Control-key commands may not be combined with selections.

Typing ahead. If DELPHI is busy sending information, but you know what you want to do next, you may type the next command before DELPHI completes the current operation.

For example, you may wish to go to the Writers' Group, see who is currently in the group area, and then go to Electronic Mail. As a shortcut, you can type **GO GR WR**, then, before you even see the group's first-level menu, type **WHO** and then type **MAIL**. The commands you've typed ahead (WHO and MAIL) will be acted on automatically, and you need only watch while the group menu is displayed, followed by a list of members in the group, and then the Mail menu. You may type four or five commands ahead in this manner.

Cancelling a typed-ahead command. If you change your mind before DELPHI acts on all the commands you've typed ahead, press **Control-X**. Everything you have typed ahead, and which has not yet been acted on, will be cancelled. Be aware that if commands are typed after a **Control-S** and before a **Control-Q**, or while DELPHI is otherwise busy, they will eventually be acted upon. DELPHI will act on a command as many times as the command is typed.

Cancelling other commands. If you enter the wrong command, you can cancel or back out of the function or operation it initiates by pressing **Control-C** or **Control-Z**.

Systemwide Commands

In addition to the commands available at various menus, DELPHI offers several commands that can be used virtually everywhere on DELPHI—at any menu prompt and at most other prompts. These are called systemwide commands and are sometimes not displayed on a menu.

BYE logs you off DELPHI. You may type BYE at any menu. BYE does not, however, work in a conference or at an input prompt (i.e., while you are entering a message or filling out a form) or in Mail. (See /BYE below).

EXIT is used to exit a menu or service. Typing EXIT will return you to the next-highest (or previous) menu. If you type EXIT at the Main Menu, you will be logged off DELPHI.

EXIT will not, however, work in a conference or at an input prompt (i.e., while you are entering a message), nor will EXIT work at certain prompts that require a Yes or No response, such as the More? prompt DELPHI uses when it is displaying text. At these prompts, you must use Control-Z.

HELP is used to access DELPHI's online help system. It can be typed at most prompts and menus. (See /HELP below.)

MENU will display or redisplay the current menu.

If you type **?** at an option prompt, you will see a one-line explanation of what is required, or a list of options. At other prompts, **?** is the equivalent of typing **HELP** — it will display help instructions. If you have not yet seen the menu, the first **?** will display the menu and a second **?** will show help instructions.

Immediate Commands

Immediate commands (which are always preceded by a slash [/]) can be used at most prompts on DELPHI, and are especially useful when you are participating in a conference, where only Immediate commands and Control-key commands can be used.

To see an abbreviated list of Immediate commands online, type **/HELP**. To see a list of all Immediate commands, type **/HELP FULL**.

We'll detail the most frequently used Immediate commands here.

/BUSY shuts off pages and conference messages (/SENDs) from other members within a group or the main conference area. A member who tries to page or send to you will be advised that you are not available, or that DELPHI couldn't send to you. Setting /BUSY will also disable automatic mail message notification, so you will not receive the one-line "New mail received from <membername>" message.

Use /NOBUSY to allow pages, messages, and mail message notification.

/BYE is like the systemwide command BYE, except that it is for use within certain areas on DELPHI where systemwide commands will not be recognized as commands. /BYE will log you off DELPHI from a conference in which you are participating, or from message entry (such as in a Group Forum; not in Electronic Mail).

Note: Logging off during message entry will result in the message you are entering being cancelled.

/EXIT works the same as EXIT at menu prompts. You will move to the next highest menu. /EXIT also exits a conference in which you are participating. If used during message entry, /EXIT will terminate and post/send the message.

/HELP displays a list of major immediate commands, with brief explanations. Use /HELP FULL to display a list of all immediate commands, with brief explanations.

/LENGTH xx sets screen length (the number of lines displayed before a More? prompt) to number specified (xx).

/TIME displays the current time (Eastern Standard or Eastern Daylight Time), in this format:

```
14-JUL-1992    20:55:22
72 MINUTES (1hr 12m 30s)
```

(The first line of the example shows the date—July 14, 1992—and the current Eastern time—8:55 and 22 seconds p.m. The second line shows a connect time of 72 minutes.)

/WHOIS <membername> displays the specified member's profile (if any) as entered in Member Directory

Responding to Special Prompts and Questions

Sometimes DELPHI will need a specific answer from you before it can continue a process. Some responses must be in a certain format, and some responses have a default value which is automatically entered when you press «RETURN».

The prompts at which these occur are called "fill-in-the-blank" prompts, requesting a "Yes/No" answer or a date. You may type a **Y** for yes or **N** for no in almost all cases.

If you are required to enter the date and time at a prompt, it must be in one of the following special formats.

MM/DD/YY. This format asks for the number of the month (MM), the date (DD), and the last two digits of the year (YY). Thus, to specify July 21, 1992, enter: **7/21/92.**

If you do not enter the year, DELPHI assumes you mean the current year. If you leave out the month, DELPHI assumes you mean the current month. At some date prompts, pressing «RETURN» defaults to the current date.

DD-MMM-YYYY. This format requires you to enter the date (one or two digits), the month (the first three letters), and the year (all four digits of the year).

Thus to specify August 21, 1992, you would enter: **21-AUG-1992.**

If you do not specify the year, DELPHI will assume you mean the current year.

Chapter 3

Business and Finance

DELPHI's *Business & Finance* section provides the services you need to stay on top of your business world. Far more than just a collection of stock market information, Business & Finance enables you to check stock and commodity prices, receive investment advice, manage your personal or business finances, and more.

UPI Business News

A comprehensive service, UPI Business News carries general business news, Wall Street news, commodities reports, and market indexes. (All update times are Eastern Time.) Each of the news categories listed on the menu contains one or more articles. To see what is in a category, simply type the category's name. (For example, to view articles in the General Business News category, type **GEN**.)

When you select a category, the headlines of the first few articles currently available in that category are automatically displayed. (This is assuming your screen length is greater than 20.)

Each item in the list has a relative number, a date and time of posting, and a headline.

To read an article, just type the article's number. DELPHI will display the specified article with More? prompts. Typing **READ** or pressing «RETURN» after reading an article will display the next article.

If you wish to read more than one article, enter the numbers of the articles separated by commas. You can read a range of stories by entering the beginning and ending article numbers separated by a "–".

Business Forum

Here is where you will find business discussions, economic news, and a consultants' database. The databases also contain useful business software (mostly for PCs and compatibles). Forum often has discussions of interest to entrepreneurs.

For in-depth information about the various commands and services, please see Chapter 4 on Computing.

Business Wire — Press Releases

The Business Wire is your source for up-to-date corporate and financial news. You can search for press releases of public companies by company name or ticker symbol, or select the newest release coming in off the wire.

You will be presented with a simple one-line prompt:

```
Enter Company Name, Ticker Symbol or ALL>
```

Type a stock ticker symbol to display a list of the press releases for the company. You may also enter the name of the company. If you want to see the most recent releases coming in on the wire, enter **ALL**.

Commodity Quotes

Continuous quotations from major world commodities exchanges are provided on a fifteen-minute delayed basis by this service. You can look at quotes for traded commodities on a selective basis, specifying the appropriate commodity symbols and month. Symbols and other aids are listed online.

When you select "Commodity Quotes" at the Business & Finance menu, you'll see this message and prompt:

```
Futures DD-MMM at HH:MM (Date and Time) Eastern Time.
Prices are aged at least 15 minutes from trade.
Symbol, HELP, or EXIT:
```

To obtain a quote, enter the ticker symbol and press «RETURN». For instance, to see the quote for treasury bills, you would type:

TB

The quote would then be displayed.

Listing Available Symbols. If you need to find the symbol for a commodity you wish, type in all or part of its name in English (for example, "GOLD," "ORANGE JUICE," or "FRENCH FRANC"). Its ticker symbol(s) will be displayed (with More? prompts, if necessary). You can then enter the selected symbol at the prompt when requested.

Dow Jones Averages

Half-hourly reports from the New York Stock Exchange are displayed here, covering the Dow Jones average of 30 industrials and the transportation, utilities and stock indexes.

When you select "Dow Jones Averages" at the Business & Finance Menu, the current averages are automatically displayed, after which you will be returned to the Business & Finance menu.

Financial and Commodity News

Provided by News-a-tron Market Reports, this service offers commodity prices from domestic and international markets and furnishes analyses of trading. It also carries commodities quotations (delayed 15 minutes), analyses of Wall Street activity, a look at Standard and Poors and Value Line indexes, and more.

Several News-a-tron services carry surcharges. Select the HELP and Rates selection on the News-a-tron menu for more information.

The News-a-tron Market Reports menu (Figure 3.2) offers access to continuously updated market reports in the categories listed on the menu, as well as a "gateway" to the Commodity Quotes service.

Using News-a-tron Services Read specialized market reports by selecting any of the categories on the News-a-tron Market Reports menu.

To select a category, simply type its name. For example, if you wished to read the current report on Federal Mortgage Rates, you would type **FED**. When you select a category, the current report is displayed automatically, after which you are returned to the News-a-tron menu. To redisplay the menu at any time, type **MENU**.

The Commodity Quotes selection on the News-a-tron menu provides access to the Commodity Quotes service. See the "Commodity Quotes" section earlier in this chapter for information on how to use the Commodity Quotes service.

Futures Focus

Futures Focus is a source of trading recommendations for commodity futures contracts in various markets. Provided and updated by News-a-tron Corporation weekly, Futures Focus carries a per-session surcharge.

MarketPulse

MarketPulse provides a continuously updated "snapshot" of the New York Stock Exchange, including the most active stocks and the biggest movers. You'll also find the Dow Jones Industrial average as well as market composite indexes (NYSE, AMEX and NASDAQ). MarketPulse carries a small surcharge for access.

Select MarketPulse, and the report will be displayed, after which you will be returned to DELPHI's Business & Finance menu.

Money Fund Report from Donoghue

The Money Fund Report from Donoghue contains updates on the top 50 Money Funds in abridged form from News-a-tron. Three reports are available: Government Only Money Funds, Tax-Free Money Funds, and General Purpose Money Fund. Reports are surcharged, with a combined rate for reading all three.

Select Money Fund Report from Donoghue at the DELPHI Business & Finance Menu and the menu will be displayed. Most Donoghue reports carry a surcharge — see "About Donoghue" for more details.

Mortgage Calculator

The Mortgage Calculator calculates the life (term), interest rate, principal (amount borrowed) or payments of a mortgage, loan, or lease. These calculations help you determine whether or not you can afford that house you have your eye on, or what difference a percentage point makes in the overall cost of a home.

Default entries are shown in brackets like [this]. You can press Control-Z at any time to exit. You must supply all of the other variables. For example, if you wish to determine the payments of a loan, you enter the principal, interest rate and term.

PR Newswire — Press Releases

PR Newswire, the world's largest press release wire service, provides news releases from thousands of companies, along with releases from the entertainment world — within minutes of their release to the media.

Releases from publicly traded companies can be searched by ticker symbol or company name. Over 100,000 releases are distributed by PR Newswire each year.

Rategram CD Reports

Select Rategram for information on Liquid Money Market accounts, certificates of deposit, Jumbo CD's, Mutual Funds, Rate Almanac, Top CD's of the week, and more.

Register of Public Corporations

The Executive Desk Register of Publicly Held Corporations is a continuously updated directory of approximately 5,000 domestic corporations and financial institutions that are currently trading on the New York Stock Exchange, the American Stock Exchange, and the NASDAQ National Market System. The directory is updated several times per month.

Information provided for each company includes its address, telephone number, ticker symbol, exchange affiliation, and the names of each company's Chief Executive Officer and Chief Financial Officer.

Listings are searchable by either stock ticker symbol or company name.

SOS - Stock & Options Advisors

Security Objective Services provides buy and sell recommendations via two newsletters, as well as options alerts.

Wall Street S.O.S. is a daily newsletter oriented to the technical analysis of the stock market and to the selection of stocks whose technical trading patterns indicate the maximum potential short-term profit. Each day's edition includes a summary of current market conditions.

S.O.S. also carries Current Recommendations, divided into two parts — New Recommendations and Active Recommendations. New Recommendations includes information on trade-reversal offers and on new trade orders; Active Recommendations contains information on all trade orders issued within the last 20 trading days.

Also accessible on the S.O.S. menu is the daily Options Alert, which presents trend analysis and specific recommendations for selected contracts of the four most widely traded Index Options.

The two publications of Security Objective Services are Premium Services and carry a surcharge, listed online.

Stock Quotes

The Stock Quotes service presents the last, closing, opening, high, and low prices for specified stocks, options, and mutual funds. The day's cumulative volume is also displayed. All you have to do is enter the appropriate ticker symbol(s). If you don't know the symbol for the stock or option, a symbol guide is available.

Over 9000 stocks traded on the New York and American exchanges and Over-the-Counter are available. Prices are aged at least fifteen minutes from trade. There is a small surcharge for each quote. This charge is displayed when you select Stock Quotes at the Business & Finance menu.

Obtaining Stock Quotes To obtain stock quotes, enter the ticker symbols of the stocks whose 15-minute delayed prices you wish to retrieve. If you want quotes on several stocks, enter their symbols separated by blanks.

If you don't know the stock ticker symbol for a company, enter the company name followed by a **?**:

```
Symbol(s), ?, or EXIT> Apple?
```

If you don't know which company a particular stock ticker symbol represents, enter a # followed by the symbol:

```
Symbol(s), ?, or EXIT> #AAPL
```

Translation Services

Use DELPHI's translation services to have your documents or messages translated into over 100 languages. All exchanges can be made immediately via E-Mail. The rates and languages available for translation services are specified online.

Sending Text for Translation. Text submitted for translation may be in one of several different formats, including PC and Macintosh, and a number of word processors, such as WordPerfect and Microsoft Word. In many cases, the material needs to be put in the Workspace area on DELPHI first, as a binary file, and cannot come through as just a mail message. To submit text for translation, select "Submit" on the menu, and follow the prompts.

Trendvest Ratings and Portfolio Analysis

Trendvest provides a wide range of services, including an investment management system, client portfolio analysis, and a complete issue of Trendvest Ratings for all issues.

You may access all Trendvest reports on the menu for a single-session surcharge. There is no surcharge for accessing the INFO menu, which carries explanations of each of the Trendvest menu items, and information on Trendvest services in general.

Chapter 4
Computing

Primary Menu Selections and Commands

```
COMPUTING GROUPS Menu:

Amiga SIG                      Midrange Systems
Apple ] [ Group                OS9 On-Line
Atari Advantage                PC Compatibles/IBM
BBS SIG                        Portable Place
Color Computer                 Tandy PC SIG
Commodore SIG                  TI Intl Users Net
Desktop Publishing SIG         HELP
Graphics SIG                   EXIT
Macintosh ICONTact


COMPUTING> What do you want to do?
```

Figure 4.1 Computing Groups Menu

Computing and Groups and Clubs, both of which are Main menu offerings, are among the most popular areas on DELPHI. They serve as a meeting place and a host of resources for members with common interests.

A group or club is designed to accommodate the sharing of information, ideas, creativity, and, in Computing groups, software of special interest.

Most groups cater to a particular type of computer, while others focus on hobbies or personal interests. This chapter details how to get the most out of DELPHI's groups and clubs. All of the information in this chapter pertains to both the Computing groups and Groups and Clubs (see Chapter 8).

Each group is managed by one or more DELPHI members who are responsible for the content. Managers maintain databases, schedule conferences, post announcements, and all other aspects of the operation. If you have specific questions, contact the manager via Electronic Mail, or leave a note in the Forum.

The group banner identifies the group, and may contain information about the group's area of interest, as well as the names of the group managers.

Log-on announcements follow the group banner. These are brief messages that each member sees only once. Group managers post these messages to inform members of newsworthy matters, or to call attention to new features or other changes.

After the banner and any logon announcements are displayed, you'll see the primary menu.

Joining a Group

The Non-Member menu is shown when you enter a group for the first time:

```
NON-MEMBER Menu:

Membership Agreement and Features
Join this Group
Enter as a Nonmember
Exit

NONMEMBER>(Member, Join, Enter, Exit)
```

Membership Agreement and Features

This selection describes the group's purpose, charter, and its rules. When you select the JOIN option, you are asked to provide your name and to agree to the group's rules. There are no extra charges for membership or participating in group activities. The membership agreement in each case basically commits you to such things as agreeing that you will not engage in illegal activities and that you will conduct yourself with courtesy and consideration in your dealings with others. (See each group's Membership Agreement for specifics.)

Most groups ask that a member supply and use his or her real name rather than the DELPHI membername when participating in group functions.

Member Status

If you agree to the membership provisions and join a group, you will have full access to all that group's services and features.

Enter as a Non-Member

You may enter a group as a Non-Member, but be aware that you will not be able to see everything the group has to offer. You will be restricted to seeing perhaps one database and Forum topic, and little else. So, it is to your advantage to join a group that seems to be of interest. Joining does not commit you to participation or any extra costs.

Primary Menu Commands

The first menu you see when you enter a group as a Member is the Primary Menu. Several of the selections are commands that you can use at the primary prompt. We'll review those first.

These commands operate at a group's Primary Menu:

ENTRY LOG

The Entry Log is a selection that is actually a command. Use it to see when a member last entered the group area. Type **ENTRY** (or simply **EN**), followed by the name of the member, to see when the member was last in the group area. For example, if you type **EN KZIN** at a Primary menu prompt, you'll see this:

```
Michael Banks (KZIN) was last on at 29-JUL-1992 22:29:36.43
```

Typing **ENTRY** followed by a star (**EN ***) displays the membernames and access times for the last ten members to enter the group.

EXIT

EXIT normally takes you to the previous menu, the Computing selection menu. However, if you wish to leave one group and immediately enter another, you can take a "shortcut" around the Computing menu by typing **EXIT** followed by the name of the group you wish to enter.

For example, if you are at the Tandy group's Primary Menu and wish to enter the CoCo group, type **EX CO**. The next menu you see will be the Color Computer group's Primary Menu.

SEND and /Send

SEND is a handy command that allows you to send a one-line message to another member in the group area. Type **SEND**, and you'll be prompted for a membername and message, like this:

```
WRITERS> SEND
To whom: AUTHOR
Message: Hello! Want to meet me in conference?
```

Or, you may type the command, membername, and message all at once:

```
WRITERS> SEND AUTHOR Hello! Want to meet me in conference?
```

The result is the same either way; the member to whom you send a message will see what you typed, preceded by your membername:

```
YOURNAME>> Hello! Want to meet me in conference?
```

If the member to whom you are sending has used the /BUSY command, you will be advised that he or she is busy. /SEND must be preceded by a slash at the Conference menu, within a Conference group, at Database and Database Action prompts, and at the Workspace prompt.

WHO and /WHO

Before you use SEND, you'll want to see who is in the group that you might send a message to. To do this, type **WHO**. WHO lists all the members currently in the group or club.

The membernames of those in conference are enclosed in parentheses. Use /WHO at the Conference menu, within a Conference group, at Database and Database Action prompts, and at the Workspace prompt, as well as at the Primary Menu and in forum.

Announcements

Select ANNOUNCEMENTS to read messages posted by the group manager under various categories. Type **ANNOUNCEMENTS**, and you'll see the *Category Selection* Menu. When you have reached a particular announcements category, you can see the table of contents by typing **SCAN**, and read messages by typing **READ**. To see a complete list of commands, type **?**.

Conference

Type **CONFERENCE** to enter a group's conference area. The conference area in most groups are separate from all other groups' conferences and the Main Conference. However, you may see the names of conferences in specific groups published in the Main Conference area. (See Chapter 5 for complete details on Conference commands.)

Databases

Each group's Databases are loaded with programs, articles, shareware, and other valuable and informative files. You can download any program or text file in a Database; a variety of download options are available. You can also read text files online, if you wish.

Each group's Database area is divided into *topics*, established by the group manager. For instance, a group may have separate Database topics for programming languages, telecommunications, business, utilities, peripherals, and hardware.

Each topic, then, is a separate Database. Thus, when you first enter a group's Database area, you must select a topic (enter it) before you can access Database files. Once you've selected a Database topic, you'll find that each Database contains *entries* that consist of one or more files. These are commonly referred to as file *groups*, even if they have only one item. Database entry names are listed in the Database directory.

Each entry has a *description*, which tells you the kind of material the entry contains (text, program, etc.), its size, and provides some explanation about the file(s) it contains. You read a Database entry's description by typing **READ** followed by the name of the entry as it is listed in the Database directory.

Now, let's take a look at the commands available in a Database. Type the name of the topic you wish to enter, and you'll see the *Selected Topic* menu. This is the menu through which you actually access the files grouped in a particular Database topic. If you wish, you may bypass the Topic Selection menu by typing **DA** and the first two or three letters of the topic you wish to see. (For example, typing **DA GEN** will take you to the group's General Database's Selected Topic menu.) Once you are at the Selected Topic menu, use the commands described in the next section.

Database Commands

The Selected Topic menu and its options are available when you first enter a database topic. Use its commands to scan the database directory, search the database, and read descriptions of files or groups.

DIRECTORY

The DIRECTORY (DIR) command displays a summary listing of all the Group Names for the current topic in date order (newest to oldest). You do not have to type **DIR**, however—simply press «RETURN» at the Selected Topic menu, and a directory of files will be displayed automatically.

The first column in a directory provides the file's name. The second column indicates the file's type—program, newsletter, article, transcript, documentation, data, or text. The third column lists the date the file was posted, and the final column identifies the provider by membername. Here is an example of a partial database directory:

```
SYNNERS       TEXT    28-JUL-1992   PKC
RASTERFILE    PROG    16-JUN-1992   LOISLANE
```

If you prefer to list the files alphabetically by name, type the command **DIR ALPHA** instead of **DIR.**

READ

READ displays the file's name and a description of its contents *only*. To actually read the contents of a text file or download a program file, you must

```
Name: 27> COMMO20.ZIP (MS-DOS)
Type: PROGRAM
Date: 12-MAY-1992 23:16 by ROCKGORDO
Size: 42522


Beautiful, small MS-DOS comm pgm. Similar to Procomm or Qmodem
interface, uses external programs for transfer protocol; this is
perfect for use on limited storage laptops like my NEC ULTRALITE.


Keywords: MS-DOS, COMM, MODEM, TELECOM, COMMUNICATIONS


ACTION> (Next, Down, Xm, List)
```

Figure 4.2 Database File Description

first issue the **READ** command and then issue the appropriate commands at the *ACTION>* prompt.

Typing **READ** displays the description of the first file in the directory (again, the order is newest to oldest). Or you can enter **READ** and the name of a specific file. Note that you may have to type several characters of a group's name. Otherwise you will be prompted to enter enough of the group's name to distinguish it from other entries that begin with similar letters, as in this example, in which **READ GOLF** is typed at the Selected Topic prompt:

```
DBASES:Hom>READ GOLF
 GOLF HANDICAPPER 1.0
GOLF SCORE DATABASE AND HANDICAP


More than one group matches that name, please be more specific.


DBASES:Hom> READ GOLF H
```

Database Entry Description. When you read a file description, you'll see text similar to that shown in Figure 4.2.

ACTION> Prompt Commands

The Action submenu and its options are available only after you read a database entry's description. You can view the menu at the ACTION> prompt by typing **?** or **MENU**. Use the commands described below to display or download a file, send a mail message to the owner of the file, to move on to another description, or to change database topics. In a multiple-file database entry you must specify the number of the file when you issue any download or display command (**LIST, DISPLAY, DOWNLOAD, KERMIT, XMODEM**).

«RETURN». Press «RETURN» to display the *next* database entry's description. Or, if used in a multiple-file group following a download or display command, «RETURN» will repeat the command with the next file in the group.

Next Group/File. If you have just listed or downloaded an item in a multiple-file group, and wish to move on to the next entry, type **N** (for **NEXT**). This command normally reads the next group in date sequence, but you can read alphabetically by group name by typing **NEXT ALPHA** (and switch back to date sequence by typing **NEXT DATE**). Using NEXT ALPHA is particularly handy if you found multiple groups starting with the same letters and want to check the descriptions of all of them. Enter the name of the first such group and then use **NEXT ALPHA** to show the remaining ones in alphabetic sequence.

Download. When you type **DOWNLOAD**, one of two things can happen. If you're a new DELPHI member, have never done a download from a database, or if you haven't set your preferred download method, you will automatically see the download menu and can specify the download method you prefer, as explained under *Download Commands.*

If you have already set your preferred download method, you will be prompted to begin the Receive File procedure on your computer, and DELPHI will send the file to you using the pre-selected protocol.

Download Commands

DELPHI offers a number of file download methods, so that you can download a database file with virtually any computer and communications software combination. See Chapter 18 for details on various file-transfer protocols.

You can specify a download method with a command at the ACTION> prompt, select your preferred download method from the Download menu, or set a permanent download technique (which will be implemented whenever you type **DOWNLOAD** at an action prompt).

DOWNLOAD initiates a download of the current or designated file using your default file-transfer protocol, as set in USING SETTINGS or at the *ACTION>* menu. (Type **/FX_METHOD** to see what your default download method is.)

MENU. If you wish to select from the available download methods, type **DOWNLOAD MENU** at the *ACTION>* prompt. There are seven download techniques. You can select a protocol from this menu to temporarily override your default download method. To make the selection your permanent default, type **/ SAVE** after the download.

XMODEM (128-byte blocks). Type either **XMODEM** or **XDOWNLOAD** to initiate an XMODEM download of the current or designated file to your computer. See Chapter 18 on Workspace for details, or type HELP.

Kermit. Type either **KERMIT** or **KDOWNLOAD** to initiate a download of the current or designated file using the Kermit protocol.

WXMODEM (Windowed XMODEM). Type **WXMODEM** or **WXDOWNLOAD** to initiate a download using Windowed XMODEM.

YMODEM (1024-byte blocks). Type **YMODEM** or **YDOWNLOAD** to initiate a YMODEM transfer (XMODEM with 1024-byte blocks rather than conventional 128-byte blocks). Some terminal programs call this XMODEM-1K.

ZMODEM. Type **ZMODEM** or **ZDOWNLOAD** to begin a ZMODEM transfer.

Buffer Capture. This selection tells DELPHI to type out the current or designated file to you with a delay, Control-Z, and a bell at the end (the Control-Z is required by many systems to mark the end of file). Downloading instructions are detailed in the Workspace chapter (Chapter 18) and are available online.

RT Buffer Capture. RT Buffer Capture is similar to Buffer Capture, with the exception of sending a Control-R at the beginning of a file and Control-T at the end of the file.

YB (YMODEM Batch). This protocol downloads files as a batch, automatically handling file-naming on your disk, in a manner similar to that of Kermit. Some terminal progreams call this YMODEM or "true YMODEM," to distinguish it from XMODEM-1K.

Buffer Capture and RT Buffer Capture should be used only with printable text files; files with 8-bit characters, such as programs and data files, should be downloaded using one of the binary file-transfer protocols (XMODEM, Kermit, WXMODEM, YMODEM, YMODEM Batch, or ZMODEM). If you have a lot of line noise it is a good idea to use one of the binary file-transfer protocols even with text files, since those protocols offer error-correction.

List (Unformatted). LIST displays the current or a designated file within a multiple-file group to your screen. The file is displayed non-stop and unformatted. (DELPHI doesn't reformat the lines to fit your profile specifications when you use this option.) This is a good way to capture a text file using your buffer capture; however, the file is displayed all the way to the ACTION> prompt, which you'll also capture.

Display (Word-wrapped). DISPLAY lists the current or designated file to your screen, formatted (using any special format commands included in the file, and reformatting the file to fit your screen as outlined in your profile). This is similar to LIST or DOWNLOAD, except you will be given the More? prompt (type **NO** at the More? prompt to terminate display of the file).

Downloading Multiple Files. If a group contains multiple files, you can download them all at once if you use a batch protocol (ZMODEM, YMODEM Batch, or Kermit). Type **DOWN ALL, ZD ALL, YB ALL,** or **KD ALL** at the ACTION> prompt. If you don't want all the files, you can type a list of file numbers or a range (DOW 1, 2, 6, 7 or DOW 2-5).

Description of Group. Typing **DESCRIPTION** (or just **DES**) redisplays the current entry's description.

Set Topic. Type **SET** followed by the name of a database topic to move to that topic without returning to the group's Primary Menu. This command moves you to another database topic, at which point you will be at the Selected Topic menu for that topic. Type **SET** at the DBASES> prompt to display the topic menu.

Changing/Setting Download Methods and /FX Commands. You can set your file transfer preference temporarily by typing it at the Download Menu. To make the selection permanent, type **/SAVE** before you exit the database.

If you prefer, you can type the command **/FX_METHOD** followed by the name of a file-transfer protocol you wish to set as your default file-transfer method. To clear a default selection, type **/FX_METHOD NONE.** If you do this, the Download Menu will be displayed the next time you type

DOWNLOAD at the ACTION> prompt or menu. Type **/FX_METHOD** to see your current default download method.

Reply

This command is not listed on the ACTION> menu, but it allows you to send an automatic mail message to the person who submitted the current file group (entry) to the database. The subject line will be entered for you automatically. Enter your message, then press **Control-Z** to send it.

Search (by Keyword)

SEARCH moves you to the SEARCH subsystem which you can use to search a database by keyword. This is a fast way to locate entries of interest in a large database. In effect, a search operation creates a small subset of the database, masking out items that do not meet search criteria; until you clear the search or widen or narrow it, only the selected items are available to you.

When you type **SEARCH** at a Selected Topic menu, you're prompted for:

```
Which keyword? (? for help):
```

At this prompt, you can type the name of a keyword, such as ARC. DELPHI will search for database entries containing the specified keyword, and tell you how many have been found. You may now use DIRECTORY or READ on the selected sub-group in the same manner as you would the entire database.

Using AND/OR Logic During Keyword Entry. If you know more than one keyword for which you want to search, you can type multiple keywords using boolean logic to link them. Type [**keyword**] **AND** [**keyword**] to find all files that contain *both* keywords, as in this example:

```
SEARCH CONF AND CAD-CAM
Starting a new search.
CONF: 35 found.
CAD-CAM: 2 found.
2 found so far.
DIRECTORY, READ, WIDEN, and NARROW will operate on selected items.
```

Type [**keyword**] **OR** [**keyword**] to find all files that contain either the first keyword OR the second keyword. This search creates a *larger* subset of files, as in this example:

```
SEARCH CONF OR CAD-CAM
Starting a new search.
CONF: 35 found.
CAD-CAM: 36 found.
36 found so far.
DIRECTORY, READ, WIDEN, and NARROW will operate on selected items.
```

Clearing a Search. To begin a new search on the full contents of the current topic, type **SEARCH**. To clear a search, cancel a currently selected subset, and regain access to the full contents of a topic, type **SET** [**topic**].

Narrow Search

Type **NARROW**, and you will be prompted for a new keyword, and the search will be narrowed to find only those entries with *both* keywords. (This is "AND logic," excluding all items that do not have both keywords. It creates a smaller subset.) You may narrow a search as many times as necessary. As with SEARCH, DELPHI will report the number of entries found, and you may use SELECT to access the entries. Your best bet is to search on the most specific keyword first and then narrow using more general keywords. If any narrow results in no matches, the previous selection will be retained so you can try narrowing on another keyword.

Widen Search

If a search returns what seems to be too few entries, or no entries at all, you can expand on your search criterion using the **WIDEN** command. Type **WIDEN** and you will be prompted for an additional keyword. The search will then be expanded to include the new keyword. You may expand a search as many times as necessary. As with SEARCH, DELPHI will report the number of entries found, and you may use SELECT to access the entries.

Set Topic

Type **SET** followed by the name of a database topic to move to that topic without returning to the primary group menu. This command moves you to another database topic, at which point you will be at the Selected Topic menu for that topic. Type **SET** alone at the *DBASES>* prompt to display the topic menu.

Submit

Typing SUBMIT initiates the process whereby you upload a text, data, or program file for inclusion in a group database. In many cases, your DELPHI billing is turned off during file submission. You should have the following information ready to enter:

• A brief description of the file's contents.

• The database topic in which you wish the file included.

• The type of file you are submitting (text, program, etc.).

• Keywords to use with the file (one of these must be one of the primary keywords already established for the database in question).

• Any special download filename that may be required.

• A name for the entry in the database.

To begin the submission process, type **SUBMIT** at a Selected Topic menu. DELPHI will guide you through the submission process with a series of questions. Type **?** at any prompt for help or a list of options. Once you are used to the way submit works, you can streamline the process by typing commands in the order you want. Type **?** at the *SUBMIT* menu for details.

When the submission is complete, the manager of the group to which you submit the file will receive the file and, after reviewing it, move it to the database you've specified during the submission process (usually within a day of submission).

You can submit multiple files for a single database entry by telling DELPHI that you'll be submitting more than one file at the appropriate prompt.

Workspace

Type **WORKSPACE** at a Selected Topic menu to move to your personal Workspace. (See Chapter 18 for full details on Workspace commands.)

FORUM

Forum is a conversational public message system, similar to a bulletin board but far more sophisticated in its message handling and tracking capabilities. Each group has its own Forum area, accessed by typing **FORUM** at the group's Primary Menu.

Forum Features

You can read public messages in a Forum, whether they are addressed to you or not. You can also add original messages, reply to existing messages, and edit or delete messages you've entered or received.

Forum messages are automatically organized into threads, which give the effect of a continuing conversation. A thread begins with an original message, and continues with each response to that message. You can read the messages in a conversational thread forward or backwards, beginning at any point.

A versatile directory system allows you to quickly locate messages by date, subject, to whom a message is addressed, who posted a message, by message number, and by searching for specified character strings in messages themselves. You can also use these criteria to read messages. You can exclude messages, or view only a set number of lines in each message, as well.

Additional commands allow you to reply to a Forum message by private E-Mail, forward copies of Forum messages via E-Mail, and to copy Forum messages to files in your personal Workspace.

You are notified when you enter a group if you have Forum messages waiting. DELPHI keeps track of whether you've read your messages, and will display them first if you press «RETURN» as soon as you enter the Forum area.

The Forum Menu

The Forum menu is not displayed when you enter a group Forum; instead, you'll see this prompt:

```
FORUM>(Read, Reply, Menu, Exit)
```

If you wish to see the menu (as shown in Figure 4.3), type **?** or **MENU**

Forum Messages

A group's Forum is divided into several topics—normally the same topics as are established for the group's databases. Each conversation thread is carried on under one of the topics.

You can select or de-select a topic using the SET command. You will not see messages in topics you have not selected. This is a timesaving feature if you like to follow all Forum threads except those under topics in which you have no interest.

Figure 4.4 shows a typical Forum message. As you can see, the message header shows the topic, as well as the message's subject, and the date and time of its posting. The header also shows who posted the message and to whom it is addressed.

The Forum Message Directory

DIRECTORY displays a summary list of the messages currently in a Forum. A directory listing includes the message number assigned each message, along with the date it was posted, the person to whom it was addressed, the person who posted it, the topic under which it was posted, and the subject (only

```
FORUM Menu:

ADD New Message (Thread)        FORWARD Message by Mail
REPLY To Current Message        DELETE Message
READ Message(s)                 EDIT a Posted Message
FOLLOW Thread                   NEXT Message
BACK to Previous Message        TOPICS (Set/Show)
DIRECTORY of Messages           HIGH Message (Set/Show)
MAIL                            HELP
TAG Interesting Message         EXIT
FILE Message into Workspace


FORUM>(Reply, Add, Read, "?" or Exit)
```

Figure 4.3 Forum Menu

```
17      28-APR 10:28 Music
        James Brown
        From: SORCERY   To: ALL


Hello everyone!
I heard through the grapevine that James Brown is coming out with
a new album.  Has anyone else heard this?  If so, any idea
when it's coming out?  I'm a big fan!


Thanks !


FORUM>  Read, Reply, Menu, Exit)
```

Figure 4.4 Forum Message

the first few letters of the subject are shown in a directory listing).

When you issue the DIRECTORY command, the summary is displayed one screen at a time. Press «RETURN» after each screen to see the next; DELPHI will tell you when you have reached the end of the summary list.

The DIRECTORY command can be used with a variety of qualifiers to provide summary lists of messages by topic, subject, or number. You can also specify new (unread) messages, waiting (unread, addressed to you) messages, or messages to or from certain members with DIRECTORY. The qualifiers may be combined, so that you can, for example, see a directory of all messages from a specified member on a particular subject.

Note that DIRECTORY shows only those messages under topics you have set as your default topics. (See the TOPICS section that follows in this chapter for more about default topics.)

The directory may not display each consecutive message for one of two possible reasons. Certain messages may have been deleted, or certain messages may be posted in topics not selected by you.

Using Qualifiers with DIR

As stated above, you can use qualifiers with DIRECTORY to define the messages you wish to see. Here are the qualifiers that you may use with DIRECTORY:

WAITING displays a directory of all unread messages addressed to you.

NEW lists all messages added to Forum since you last entered.

THREAD displays a directory of all messages in the thread of which the current message (a message you have just read) is a part. DIRECTORY THREAD followed by a message's number lists all messages in a thread based upon the message whose number you entered.

FROM followed by a membername displays a directory of all messages from the specified member.

TO followed by a membername displays a directory of all messages to the specified member.

xxx:xxx (Numeric Range). **DIRECTORY** followed by a numeric range displays a directory of all messages with numbers in the range specified. The range specification must be entered as **DIRECTORY 432:500**. This would give a directory of all messages between numbers 432 and 500. A partial range, such as DIR 27: is also acceptable.

SUBJECT. **DIRECTORY SUBJECT [subject string]** displays a directory of all messages with the specified string in the subject header.

TOPIC. Typing **DIRECTORY TOPIC [topic name]** displays a directory of all messages under the specified topic. For example, **DIR TOP GENERAL** would display a directory of all messages assigned to the GENERAL topic.

BEFORE/SINCE. You can specify messages posted before or after a certain date with the qualifiers BEFORE and SINCE, respectively. Follow the qualifier with a date in this format: MM/DD/YY. To see a directory of messages posted *before* a certain date, type **DIR BEFORE** followed by a date, like this: **DIR BEFORE 7/21/92.** To see a directory of messages posted *since* a certain date, type **DIR SINCE** followed by a date.

RECENT. Type **DIR RECENT** to see a directory of the last few messages you've read. This is useful if you see a reference to a previous message and are uncertain as to the message to which it referred.

FULLTEXT is a powerful qualifier that you can use to find a specific word or character string in a message's subject header or *in the text of the message itself.*

Type **DIR FULLTEXT** followed by a word or by a character string in double quotes, and DELPHI will show you the message header and the line from the message containing the specified word or string.

A FULLTEXT search can take some time. DELPHI recommends that you specify other attributes (topic, subject, since, from, to, etc.) at the same time, so the search will be much quicker.

ALL. Displays all messages and prints an asterisk beside any messages you haven't read in the current listing. This listing is useful if you've been following threads around and want to find a particular message.

NONSTOP (NS). You can also specify that the directory be displayed nonstop by adding **NONSTOP** (or its abbreviation, **NS**) after the DIRECTORY command and any qualifier, like this: **DIR NEW NS**. This would display a directory of all new messages without pausing.

LIMIT. Shows the first few lines of each message alone with the directory entry (helpful when you need to locate a message in a long thread where there are too many messages from the same people about the same subject).

Combining qualifiers. As previously mentioned, you may combine DIRECTORY qualifiers to obtain a precise listing of messages available. For example, you could type **DIRECTORY FROM KZIN TO ELLEN** to list only those Forum messages from member KZIN to member ELLEN. Similarly, typing **DIRECTORY FROM KZIN TO BUBBA SUBJECT HELP** would list only those messages from member KZIN to member BUBBA with "Help" in the Subject header.

Remember that you will see a directory of *all* messages that meet the specifications included with qualifiers. So, it is best, when searching for a message you've already read, to include as much as you can remember about the message if you wish to find it quickly. For example, you could get *really* detailed by using a set of qualifiers like this: **DIRECTORY FROM KZIN TO BUBBA TOPIC GENERAL SUBJECT HELP SINCE 07/21/92.**

For more information about directory, type **DIRECTORY ?**

Reading Messages

DELPHI offers a wide range of options in reading messages. You can pre-select and specify messages to read by almost any criteria, using the READ command with qualifiers or by pressing «RETURN» for default message display.

READ is used to display Forum messages on your screen one screen at a time. READ can be used with a variety of qualifiers to display messages by number, topic, or subject. You can also specify new (unread) messages, waiting (unread, addressed to you) messages, or messages to or from certain members with READ. The qualifiers may be combined so that you can, for example, read all messages from a specified member on a particular subject.

Note that you can read only those messages under topics you have set as your default topics. (See the TOPICS section later in this chapter for more about default topics.)

READ may or may not display consecutive messages, depending upon whether some have been deleted, and whether some are posted under topics which have not been selected by you.

The easiest way to read a message by number is to type the number by itself at the *FORUM>* prompt; it is not necessary to type READ.

Reading new messages. The first thing you'll want to do when you enter a Forum is read the new messages, and/or any messages addressed to you. In general, to READ new or waiting messages you need only press «RETURN» or type the message number, as in Electronic Mail.

Pressing «RETURN» when you enter Forum displays the first page of the first message posted since you last entered Forum— unless there are messages addressed to you, in which case those messages are displayed first. Each time you press «RETURN» you see the next page of the message, or, if there are no more pages, the next message. To skip additional pages of a long message, enter **N** at the More? prompt.

To read all new messages addressed to you, type **READ WAITING**. The default command to read messages waiting for you when you enter Forum is simply pressing «RETURN».

To read all new messages added to Forum since the last time you accessed Forum, type **READ NEW** and press «RETURN». If you have no messages waiting, this is the default command processed when you enter Forum.

NEXT. This command displays the message subsequent to the one on your screen. Pressing «RETURN» does the same thing. NEXT (or «RETURN») is interpreted as READ NEW; it skips any messages you have already read. «RETURN» also means READ NEW after an ADD command or after a DELETE, REPLY, or EDIT command with which a number has been used.

TAG. TAG "marks" a message, which can then be reread using the command READ TAG. This is a handy way to "set aside" a message or messages that you wish to refer to after you've finished reading and/or replying to other messages. To tag a message, type **TAG** after you read it, or type **TAG** followed by a message number. You may reread your tagged message(s) at any time before you leave Forum. Leaving Forum forgets your tags (DELPHI will remind you if you've tagged messages when you exit Forum, and give you the opportunity to read them). To reread tagged messages, type **READ TAG**. The qualifier **TAG** may be used with most of the qualifiers below.

Using qualifiers with READ. As stated above, you can use qualifiers with READ to define the messages you wish to read. Here are the qualifiers that you may use with READ:

- **READ WAITING** displays all unread messages addressed to you.
- **READ NEW** displays all messages added to Forum since you last entered.
- **READ THREAD** displays all messages in the thread of which the current message is a part. READ THREAD followed by a message's number displays all messages in a thread based upon the message whose number you entered.
- **READ FROM** followed by membername displays all messages from the specified member.
- **READ TO** followed by a membername displays all messages to the specified member.
- **RANGE**. READ followed by a numeric range displays all messages with numbers in the range specified. The range specification must be entered like this: **READ 432:500**.
- **READ SUBJECT** displays all messages with the specified string in the subject header.
- **READ CURRENT** or **READ** + (or, simply +) repeats the message on your screen.
- **#**. Each Forum message is referenced by number. Typing **READ** followed by the message number at the Forum> prompt displays that message. Or, you may type the number alone to achieve the same result. If the message you specify has been deleted or is not under one of your default topics, you will see the next available message.
- **- # and + #**. You also may refer to a message to read by its relative position. For instance, type **-5** to read the message with a number 5 less than the current one, or **+10** to read one 10 messages beyond.
- As explained above, **READ TAG** will redisplay messages you've marked by

typing **TAG** after reading them, and can be used with most of the qualifiers listed here.

- **BEFORE/SINCE.** You can read messages posted before or after a certain date with the qualifiers BEFORE and SINCE, respectively. Follow the qualifier with a date in this format: MM/DD/YY. To read messages posted *before* a certain date, type **READ BEFORE** followed by a date, like this: **READ BEFORE 7/21/92.** To read messages posted *after* a certain date, type **DIR SINCE** followed by a date.
- Type **READ RECENT** to redisplay the last few messages you've read. This is useful if you see a reference to a previous message and are uncertain as to the message to which it referred.
- **LIMIT #** displays only the specified number of lines of each message (used with or without other qualifiers). If you type **READ LIMIT 15,** you will see only the first 15 lines of each message (or the entire message, if it is 15 lines or less in length). If the message is longer than the number of lines you specify, DELPHI will add an ellipses (**...**) after the final line displayed to indicate that the message has more lines.   This is handy if you use READ NONSTOP to put messages in a file on your computer, because it prevents very long messages which you may not be interested in from filling up your buffer.
- **QUOTE #** displays a specified number of lines of the message to which the current message is a reply. For example, type **READ QUOTE 3** will read the current message and also show the first 3 lines of the message it replies to.
- **NONSTOP.** You can also specify that messages be displayed nonstop by adding **NONSTOP** (or its abbreviation, **NS**) after the READ command and any qualifier, like this: **READ NEW NS.** This would display all new messages without pausing.

Combining qualifiers. As with DIRECTORY qualifiers, you may combine READ qualifiers to view a very precise set of messages. For example, **READ FROM KZIN TO ELLEN** displays only those Forum messages from member KZIN to member ELLEN.

Thread Commands. You may follow a thread forward or backwards using these commands:
- FOLLOW displays the next reply to the current message. After you type **FOLLOW,** press «RETURN» to display subsequent replies in the thread. DELPHI will notify you when you've reached the end of the thread. After

you've reached the end of the thread, pressing «RETURN» will display the next new message.
• Type **BACK** to display the message to which the current message is a reply.

IGNORE

IGNORE is a command (not a qualifier) that allows you to temporarily exclude specified messages from a directory or prevent them from being displayed in response to a READ command. To use this command, type **IGNORE** followed by qualifier or qualifiers, just as you would with a DIRECTORY or READ command. For example, if you type **IGNORE SUBJ PROGRAMS**, you will see no messages that have the word "programs" in the subject header. The IGNORE settings you establish remain in effect until you leave the Forum, or until you type **IGNORE NONE**, which cancels IGNORE settings. To see what your current IGNORE settings are, type **IGNORE** alone. You can use the IGNORE command several times with the effect that any message that is ignored for any reason will be skipped. To see the options/qualifiers available for use with IGNORE, type **IGNORE ?** at the *Forum>* prompt.

Posting, Editing, and Deleting Messages

DELPHI's Forum allows you to enter messages "live" or upload and post prepared messages from your Workspace.

Adding a new message. To begin a new conversation (or thread of messages), you must ADD a new message to the Forum. You will have to provide the following information when you enter a message:
• To whom the message will be addressed.
• The subject of the message.
• The message topic.
• The message itself.

Here is an example of adding a new message:

```
FORUM> ADD
To:   TOPGUN
```

When responding to the *To:* prompt, you may direct your message to a particular member, in which case the member will be notified that there is a new message waiting when he or she enters the group and the Forum area. (In this example, the member is TOPGUN.)

If you wish to direct the message to all members of the group rather than to a particular person, type **ALL** at the *To:* prompt. No members are notified when a message addressed to ALL is entered.

The *Subject:* line informs others about the specific content of the message:

```
Subject: DIALUP OPTIONS
```

The *Topic:* line categorizes the message according to the broad categories established by the group's manager:

```
Topic: TELECOMMUNICATIONS
```

When designating the topic of the message, type its first few letters. If you wish to refer to the list of available topics, type **?**.

After setting up the header of the message, you see this prompt:

```
Please enter your message below.
Control-Z when complete. /HELP for Help.
```

Type your message as you would a DELPHI Electronic Mail message (see Chapter 11 for guidance). When finished, press **Control-Z**, or, if you change your mind and do not wish to post the message, press **Control-C**. You may also type **/EXIT** or **/QUIT** in place of these control keys. Using the commands is sometimes easier than control keys if you are preparing a script to post messages automatically at the speed of your modem. Be sure to type the commands at the left margin of a new line.

As your message is sent, it is assigned a number, and you see verification that it is stored. Verification looks like this:

```
Message 2413 Stored.
```

Adding a Workspace file as a new message. To ADD a message you have prepared as a file in your workspace, follow the ADD command with the name of the file. In this example, the file is called IDEAS.TXT.

```
FORUM> ADD IDEAS.TXT
```

After you enter the filename and press «RETURN», you will be prompted to enter the addressee's membername, the subject, and the topic.

Adding a message using an editor. If you wish, you may compose your message using an online editor, rather than entering it as you would a mail message. Type **ADD/EDIT** to use this feature. You can also invoke the editor while you are entering a message by typing **/EDIT** by itself on a line. See Chapter 19 for information about DELPHI's online text editors.

Editing a message. To edit a message you've posted, type **EDIT** after reading it, or type **EDIT** followed by the message number. (You cannot edit messages posted by others.) When you type **EDIT**, you will be prompted as to whether you wish to edit the current message's Subject, Topic, or Text. Follow the prompts and enter **Control-Z and then /EXIT** or another **Control-Z.** when you've completed your changes, or **Control-C** to cancel the edit.

Deleting a message. You may delete any message you have posted, or any message addressed to you, with DELETE. Type **DELETE** after reading a message to delete it, or type **DELETE** followed by a message number to delete the specified message. DELPHI will confirm that the message has been deleted.

Replying to Messages

REPLY allows you to add your comments to a conversation. Type **REPLY** to reply to a message you've just read (the message does not have to be addressed to you). You may enter a message at the prompt, use a text editor to compose a reply, post a Workspace file as a reply, or send a private reply via Electronic Mail.

Entering a reply. When you type **REPLY**, you will be prompted for an addressee; press «RETURN» to have the reply automatically addressed to the person who posted the message you just read, with the same subject header.

Composing a reply using an editor. You may compose a reply using your chosen editor by typing **REPLY/EDIT**.

Posting a Workspace file as a reply. To post a file from your Workspace file as a reply, type **REPLY [filename]**.

Sending a private reply via E-Mail. If you wish to send a private reply to the member who posted a message via private E-Mail, you can do so by typing **REPLY MAIL**. An E-Mail message header (with address and subject headers) will be created for you. Enter your message and enter **Control-Z** when finished.

Replying to a message by number. You may use any of the above commands with a message number, if you wish to reply to a message other than the one you have just read. For example, you can type **REPLY 27, REPLY 27 /EDIT, REPLY 27 [filename]**, or **REPLY 27 MAIL**.

Filing Messages

You can copy a Forum message to a file in your Workspace using the FILE command. Type **FILE** followed by a filename:

```
FORUM> File FORUM.MSG
```

In this example, DELPHI would copy the current Forum message to a file in your Workspace called FORUM.MSG. DELPHI will create the file, if it does not already exist, or will append the message to the end of a file that already exists.

Sending Copies of Messages via E-Mail

The command FORWARD sends a copy of a Forum message to another DELPHI member (or, if you wish, to your own electronic mailbox). Type **FORWARD**, and you'll be prompted for a membername and subject line.

You can also forward a Forum message by typing **MAIL [membername]** after you have read a message. You will be prompted for a subject line. (NOTE: You must include the membername with MAIL; if you do not, you will be issuing the MAIL command, and you'll find yourself in Electronic Mail.)

Setting/Showing Topics (TOPICS)

Each Forum message is assigned one of the available topics by its author. To read a message in any available topic, that topic must be listed as one of your defaults. Likewise, when you use the DIRECTORY command, only messages in the topics you have selected are displayed.

When you join a group, all topics are selected. To change or display your default topics, type **TOPICS** at the *Forum>* prompt.

You may bypass the Set & Show Default Topics menu by typing **SET**, **SHOW**, or **CLEAR** at the *Forum>* prompt. Each command will operate the same as if you had typed **Topics**—that is, as described below. Use these commands to set, clear, or show available topics:

SET. Use **SET** to add any topic to your topic default list. You can set one or all topics. Type **SET** followed by the topic name to set the specified topic. Here's an example in which "General" is made a default topic. First, the command **SET** is typed at the *DEFAULTS>* prompt. DELPHI then displays a list of available topics, along with the SET topic prompt:

```
General Interest          Science & Technology
Games  &  Entertainment   News & Reviews
Telecommunications        Current Issues
Utilities                 Home Use
Sound & Graphics          Music
Education


SET TOPIC>Which Topic to Set? GEN
```

Type * to select all topics or enter **Control-Z** or **/EXIT** to exit from this menu. In this case, **GEN** is typed at the *SET TOPIC>* prompt, and DELPHI responds:

```
"General Interest" is now one of your default topics.
```

SHOW. SHOW lists all available topics, and indicates which topics you have set as your defaults. If you type **SHOW**, you might see:

```
Topics Set:

General Interest          Science & Technology
Games & Entertainment     News & Reviews
Telecommunications        Current Issues

Topics Available:

Utilities                 Home Use
Sound & Graphics          Music
Education
```

CLEAR allows you to clear a topic from your list of defaults, which means you won't see messages that are under the cleared topic. Type **CLEAR** followed by the topic name to clear the specified topic. If you forget the available topics, type **CLEAR** alone to see a list of topics for the group you are in. Referring to our previous example, if you no longer want "General Interest" as one of your default topics, type **CLEAR** at the *DEFAULTS>* prompt. DELPHI responds with a list of topics and the *CLEAR TOPIC>* prompt:

```
CLEAR TOPIC> Which topic to clear? GEN
```

Type **GEN**, and "General Interest" will no longer be a defaulted topic. Or you may type * to clear all topics. Enter **Control-Z** or **/EXIT** to exit from this menu.

Showing/Resetting the High Message Number (HIGH)

The HIGH command has two purposes. First, it shows you the highest message you read when you last entered Forum and tells you your current high message. Second, it allows you to reset your high message for reference purposes. If you have read message number 6524 but would like to start at message 4326 the next time you enter Forum, you would do the following:

```
FORUM> HIGH
```

```
High Message on Entry: 4224
Current High Message : 6524
New Value (or «RETURN»): 4325
```

You would type **4325** after the *New Value (or «RETURN»):* prompt. Then, when you next enter Forum, message 4325 is the first message displayed. To leave the high message at its current value, you would simply press «RETURN» at that prompt. When you use the HIGH command, Forum no longer "remembers" which messages you have already read, and will regard all messages after the "new value" numbered message as "new" to you. If you are new to a group, you can type **HIGH NEW** to set your counter to read the 50 most recent messages.

Other Commands Available in a Forum Area

WHO. Type **WHO** to see a list of members currently in the group. This command operates the same as at a group's Primary Menu.

SEND. This command operates at the *Forum>* prompt in the same manner as at a group's Primary Menu. (Alternately, you can use /**SEND**.)

MAIL. Type **MAIL** to enter DELPHI's Electronic Mail system from the *Forum>* prompt. (Alternately, you can use /**MAIL**.)

QUIT. Type **QUIT** to exit Forum without resetting your high message counter. This is useful when you've followed a thread (thus updating your temporary high message pointer) and haven't gone back to read the intervening messages (or messages in other topics), and you want to come back to them another time.

HELP. Type **HELP** to receive detailed help with commands.

HELP

Typing **HELP** at a group's first-level menu enters a unique system of Helpful Hints files created just for that group. Use the commands listed for Announcements (discussed earlier in this chapter) to see the Table of Contents and read or download entries (i.e., DOWNLOAD, READ, READ #, READ #,#,#, and SCAN). To return to the menu, type **EXIT** or press **Control-Z**.

Mail

Typing **MAIL** at a group's Primary Menu takes you to DELPHI's Electronic Mail system. See Chapter 11 for complete details on using E-Mail.

Member Directory

Type **MEMBER** at a primary group menu to enter the group's Member Directory. Use the same commands you would use in (Chapter 12) to search the directory, read about other members, and enter information about yourself.

Poll

Here is where DELPHI group members survey opinions on matters of interest to them. You can create a poll, express your opinion by voting in a poll and adding comments, and see poll results.

Poll Commands

Use the following commands to read, vote, comment on, and create polls.

BROWSE. Type **BROWSE** alone to view the current voting results of all polls in sequence. Each poll's results will be displayed, followed by a prompt asking if you want to vote on the current poll, read the current poll's comments, or skip to the next poll. Using this feature, you can vote on every poll, in sequence. Or, you can type **BROWSE** followed by the first few letters of the name of a poll you wish to peruse, to see the results of that poll only. To see the names of the available polls, type **?** after you enter **BROWSE**. The option to read, vote, or skip will be presented after the voting results are displayed.

CREATE lets you create a poll to sample the opinions of your fellow DELPHI members. After typing **CREATE**, type the poll's name (up to 60 characters) and select a poll format from among the three available (YES-NO, Degree of agreement or disagreement, or Multiple choice). After this, enter text to present your issue to the voters, press **Control-Z**, and your poll is in place.

EDIT. Use **EDIT** to amend or add to your comments after you have voted on a poll. You'll be prompted to enter the text that will replace your current comments. Press **Control-Z** when you're finished or **Control-C** to cancel and leave your comment unchanged.

LIST. This command lists the names of all the polls available.

RESULTS. Use this command if you wish to see the *complete* results of a specific poll, including all comments. Type **RESULTS** followed by the name of a poll to see the results of that poll. (If you type **RESULTS** alone, you will be prompted for the name of a poll.)

VOTE. To vote on a specific poll, type **VOTE**. Voting is easy—just follow the online prompts. DELPHI will prompt you for the poll name, display the text presenting the issue, and prompt you for your vote and comments (up to four 80-character lines). Remember you can change your vote and your comments at any time after you've voted, using the EDIT command.

Set Preferences

The Set Preferences subsystem allows you to change your name (as entered when you joined the group), your default editor, and a variety of terminal characteristics and file transfer preferences. Type **SET** at a group menu, and you'll see the Preferences Menu. To bypass the Preferences menu, you can type **SET** followed by **NAME, EDITOR, TOPIC,** or **SETTINGS.** You will then be prompted for a choice. The following commands are available on the Preferences Menu:

Name Change. When you first join a group, you must enter a name for yourself (not your membername). If you entered it incorrectly or if you want to change it, Select Name Change on this menu to do that. Your name is visible to other members of this area when they use the Entry Log command.

Editor Preference. See Chapter 19 for information about DELPHI's online text editors.

Topic Selection. The Topic Selections menu is used to change the topics you wish to see when you access the Forum. The SHOW command shows you what your current selection is and the SET and CLEAR commands enable and disenable a topic for you.

Settings (Profile). The Settings menu allows you to change all sorts of terminal characteristics and file transfer preferences to match the computer you use. Select the appropriate item on the Settings menu, and DELPHI will guide you through the setting process.

Shopping Service

In some of the groups, there are vendors who offer products of specific interest to members of a group. If such a vendor is available in the group you are in, select SHOPPING SERVICE at the group menu. After you enter the shopping service, you can browse through product descriptions, get information on advertisers, specify how you wish to pay for products ordered, and order products online. The following options are available via a Shopping menu:

Locate Items. Use this selection to search by product name, a keyword, or date posted. After DELPHI finds all items meeting your search criteria, you will see a list of the items. At this point, you can narrow or widen your search, scan or read the list of items available, download descriptions, or place orders.

Directory of Vendors. Selecting this item lets you browse through information that online vendors have entered about themselves. Each entry contains information on the vendor's products, location, payment methods accepted, etc.

Set Billing Address. Use this option to enter information about yourself which is forwarded to a vendor when you place an order. The information you will enter includes your real name, company name, address, and telephone number.

Topics

The TOPICS selection lets you read descriptions of a group's database topics, as established by the group's manager. When you type **TOPICS**, you will see the Topics Available menu, where you must enter a topic name. To bypass the Topics Available menu, type **TOPICS** followed by the first two or three letters of a topic name. (Example: **TOPICS GEN**)

Usually, there will be only one description for each topic; if there is more than one description, use the commands listed under ANNOUNCEMENTS to read the descriptions (**DOWNLOAD, READ, READ #, READ #,#,#,** and **SCAN**). Return to the group menu with **EXIT** or **Control-Z**.

Chapter 5
Conference

Conferencing on DELPHI

CONFERENCE is DELPHI's "real-time," interactive conversation system. In Conference, you can converse with other members who will be able to read your comments, and vice-versa. Conference can be compared to a telephone "conference call" or a CB conversation — the main difference being that you type and read rather than speak and listen.

DELPHI's Conference offers far more than just talk. Need a record of a conference? You can log (save) any conference to a file in your Workspace for later editing or downloading. Want to have a private, uninterrupted chat with a friend or business associates? No problem—close your conference group to others with one easy command, or use another simple command to require a password for entrance to your group. If you're in conference with several people and want to make a private remark to just one or two others, you can do that, too. You can even participate in two or more conferences simultaneously!

And with Conference, you can:

- Change your name in conference—to your real name, or perhaps to a nick-name that suits your mood or personality.
- See who's online in your area, and who's in conference.
- See when a member was last in your current area.
- Read information about other members in conference
- Page members from anywhere on DELPHI.
- Enter DELPHI's Electronic Mail service without losing your place in a confer-ence, or send a quick one-line mail message to another member.
- Set special conference group attributes, such as the group name.
- "Customize" Conference to fit your style of communicating; you can have DELPHI echo your comments before you send them, after you send them, or both; display the membernames of members using conference nicknames; squelch members whose comments you don't want to read; and more.

Learning to Use Conference

Using Conference is as easy as typing what you want to say. The best way to learn about conferencing is to jump into one and try it out; you will find no shortage of people willing to assist you with "hands-on" training in conference. (DELPHI members really do enjoy sharing their knowledge with new people.) However, you will find it useful to go over the information that follows.

Conference Areas

You'll find a number of individual Conference areas on DELPHI—the Main Conference area, group and club Conference areas, Custom Forums, etc. The commands and options available in each are the same. The only difference between one Conference area and another will be the groups and members you see in each area. (NOTE: You will not be in a conference with other members when you first enter a Conference area; you must first create or join a conference group, as explained in the following pages.)

Conference Groups

You will not be able to talk with other DELPHI members immediately upon entering a Conference area—you must first join a conference *group*. A conference group consists of one or more members in a conference that they have created. A conference group may or may not have a title, but will always have an identifying number.

Type **WHO** at the Conference menu to see a listing of conference groups, which also displays the names of the members in each group and "available" members. (A sample of what you'll see when you type **WHO** at a Conference menu is shown in Figure 5.1, and explained in a few paragraphs, under "Seeing Who's Online.")

Conference Quick Start

While this Quick Start does not cover *every* Conference command, reading it will familiarize you with the basic commands and protocol of Conference. You'll learn how to find out who is in a conference area, how to join or create a conference, how to talk while in conference, how to invite others in, and how to leave a conference. (Later portions of this chapter elaborate on the uses of the commands discussed in this section, as well as the many additional commands available.)

We have included a sample conference, to give you a "feel" for using Conference and also some information on the conference environment and conference protocol (manners).

Seeing Who's Online

The first thing you'll want to do when you enter a conference area is use the WHO command to see who is online. Type **WHO** to display a report containing the following information:

• A GROUP LIST, which is a list of conference group names, accompanied by the membernames or nicknames of those in each group (you may join any of these that have not been made private).

• A list of members who are in the conference area but not in a conference group (listed as *idle*).

• An AVAILABLE LIST, which shows all members in the area, whether they are in Conference or not (note that the membernames of those in the conference area are enclosed in parentheses).

This report shows only those members who are in your current area—that is, the members who are in the Group, Club, Main Conference, or other area you

```
GROUP LIST: 19:40:19
2) SCRAMBLE Word Game
      GAME, PKC, ROSAB
3) GO BENGALS!
      RESNICK
5) The Big Time
      FREDSMITH, nancy, Bruce
13) 13
      Gayle, AUTHOR
 - idle
      ELLISCO, CHARLIE, DRL
AVAILABLE LIST: () = in conf
HITEST, (ROSAB), (FREDSMITH), (PKC), (ELLISCO), JIGHLAND, NJUNIPER,
BREADER, (GAME), VARIETY, (GAYLEC), (AUTHOR), CAJONES, (DRL),
(CHARLIE), CONFHEAD, MACMAN, BUCKETHEAD, MODELMIKE, KZIN, RESNICK,
PERRY, (ELLISCO), GUNGADIN, IOS, ALANGOULD
—— [26 in this area]
CONFERENCE>
```

Figure 5.1 Conference Group List

have moved to from the DELPHI Main Menu. (If one member is paging another, that information is also listed.)

Figure 5.1 is a sample WHO list. There are three conferences in the area. Two have titles: "GO BENGALS!" and "The Big Time." A third is not titled. Three members are idle (that is, not in a conference group, but in the conference area); they are probably preparing to join one of the conferences, or start one of their own.

Each group has a number, too. The group numbers may or may not be in sequence, depending on how many conferences are going on in other areas.

A total of 26 members are in the area, as indicated by the final line in the listing. The names of all members in the area are listed, with the names of those actually in the conference area (in a group or idle) enclosed in parentheses. (You may have noticed that several membernames, while enclosed in parentheses, do not appear in conference groups or as "idle." This is because those members have adopted nicknames; specifically, the names Gayle, nancy, and Bruce. A nickname is always displayed exactly as a member has entered it, while membernames are always in all-capital letters. Nicknames are also preceded by a period during a conversation.)

Joining an Existing Conference Group

To join a conference group, type **JOIN** *group name* or **JOIN** *group number*. If, for example, you wanted to join the **GO BENGALS!** conference shown in Figure 5.1, you would type **JOIN GO** (only the first few letters of a conference name are required). Or, you could type **JOIN 3**.

Creating a Conference Group

To create a group of your own which others may join, or into which you may invite others, type **JOIN**, optionally followed by a name that is not on the list displayed by the WHO command. (If you do select an existing name or number, you will be joined to that conference.)

Thus, to create a group named "CHAT", you would type **JOIN CHAT** (assuming no group with this name exists). A group with that name would be created, and a number automatically assigned to it. Then, other members could join you by typing **JOIN CHAT** or **JOIN <group number>**.

Talking in Conference

"Talking" in a conference group is simple—just enter what you want to say and press «RETURN». You will see your comment on your screen as you enter it, but nobody else can see your comment until you press «RETURN»; then it is displayed (sent) to all members in your conference group. Your comments are preceded by your membername or nickname and a "greater than" symbol. (NOTE: If you do not wish to see your comments repeated on your screen *after* you type them, type /**NOREPEAT**. If you do not wish to see your comments echoed to your screen *while* you are typing them—as when you are using communications software with a "chat window"— you can type /**NOECHO**. These commands can be reversed by typing /**ECHO** and also /**REPEAT**, respectively.)

Thus, if you type "Good evening! What's new?" you will see:

```
Good evening! What's new?


YOURNAME> Good evening! What's new?
```

If you are making a lengthy comment, it is best to press «RETURN» after entering one or two lines, then complete the comment. DELPHI "holds" the text you enter in a 255-character buffer. If you enter more than 255 characters (approximately three 80-column lines), your comment will be displayed automatically, just as if you had pressed «RETURN». You can let other members know that you have not completed your comment by typing ... before you press «RETURN».

Correcting comments. If you make a mistake or change your mind while you are entering a comment, you can correct it by backspacing (using your computer's backspace key, or **Control-H**) or pressing **Control-X** or **Control-U** to erase what you've entered. Backspacing allows you to write over and replace a character or characters, while Control-X or Control-U will erase an entire line.

Private comments. If you wish to send a private comment to someone in your conference group without others seeing it (the equivalent of a whisper) you can enter /**SEND** <membername> <comment> and press «RETURN». For example, if you are in a conference group and type:

```
/SEND HARRIMAN I don't think he knows what he's talking about!
```

member HARRIMAN will see this:

```
YOURNAME>> I don't think he knows what he's talking about!
```

Note that your membername is followed by *two* "greater than" symbols, rather than one; this lets HARRIMAN know that the line was a private remark. (Because a Control-G is sent with a private comment, some members' computers will "beep" when such a comment is received.)

You can also use **/SEND** to send a comment to another member in a different conference group, or not in conference at all— provided the member is in your current area. This is a fast way to say "Hello" or to exchange a few quick comments. (SEND <with no slash> operates at several prompts in Groups and Clubs, as well as at a Conference Menu, making it possible to "chat" without being in a conference group. See the Computing chapter for more information on using SEND in a group or club.)

Type **HELP** at the Conference menu, or **/HELP** within a Conference group, for more information on commands.

Using Commands Within a Conference Group

When you are in a conference group you see no menus or prompts, you type on a blank line, and anything you enter is displayed (sent) to other members in the group when you press «RETURN»—unless, that is, it is preceded by a slash (/). You may have noted that the /SEND command includes a slash; preceding a line with a slash tells DELPHI that the word or words that follow will constitute a command.

You can use the Conference Menu commands, most of the Immediate commands discussed in Chapter 2, and many special commands we'll discuss later, while you are in a conference group.

The most important command is /HELP; this displays a list of major commands, and can be used with a command name to provide full information on that command. (Figure 5.2 shows the Help screen you will see if you type **/HELP** while in a conference group.)

Be sure that you begin a command on a new line; if you do not (or if you forget to precede the command with a slash), you may embarrass yourself!

Inviting Others to Conference

If you wish to invite another DELPHI member to talk, you can do so by using /SEND. However, a more efficient way is to use the PAGE command. When you page a member, he or she will receive a polite invitation to chat with you, and can either accept or reject your page. (The invitation will appear in the form of: <MEMBERNAME> would like to talk with you in Conference.)

Paging Others. To page a member at the Conference Menu, simply type **PAGE <membername>**. If the member accepts the invitation to chat, a conference group will be created automatically and assigned a number (but no title). If the member rejects the invitation, you will be notified.

You can also page another member from within a conference group. Use the same command, but precede it with a slash (/). If the member accepts your page, he or she will join your group automatically.

Your Page will remain in effect until it is rejected or until you cancel it by typing **/CANCEL**.

```
   Immediate Commands:

 /JOIN [groupname or #]  /EXIT /BYE /NAME [name]
 /RNAME [name] /SHOWRN /SEND [name] [message]
 /BUSY /SQUELCH /WHO /MAIL /WHOIS [name]
 /ENTRY [name] /PAGE [name] /ANSWER /CANCEL /REJECT
 /GNAME [groupname] /TALK [gname or #] /GPRIVATE
 /GPASS /GLOCK /GROLL /GQUIET /PASS /PROLL /ROLL
 /[#] [message] /ECHO /REPEAT /WIDTH /TIME /KEYSUB
 /PROMPT /PAD /PORT /TERM /QUEUE /LOG /DIRECTORY
 /DISPLAY /WAIT /HELP


  for more help, example:
        /HELP /SQUELCH
 Some commands are reversed by including
  "NO" in the command, e.g., /NOECHO
 For other commands, type /HELP MORE
```

Figure 5.2 Conference Help Screen

```
DEBBIEJONES> Hello, Mike. Have a moment?
RESNICK> Yes. How've you been?
DEBBIEJONES> Fine. Still planning to fly in for the convention?
RESNICK> Yes. Should be in about noon—flight 321.

**AUTHOR just joined "CONVENTION" (3 members now)**

Hi-ho! What's new?
AUTHOR> Hi-ho! What's new?
RESNICK> Hi, Ralph. We're making plans for the convention in
Tucson. Do you know yet if you'll be there?

Still planning on it.  RESNICK> I'm flying in, and Debbie &
Charles are picking me up at the airport in Tucson.
How about if we all log on to DELPHI at 6 tomorrow night and see
if we can set up a time to meet for lunch, after registration?

AUTHOR> Still planning on it. How about if we all log on to DELPHI
at 6 tomorrow night and see if we can set up a time to meet for
lunch, after registration?

DEBBIEJONES> OK. I'll be here at 6. So long!

OK. See you then.
AUTHOR> OK. See you then.

RESNICK> — signed off —

DEBBIEJONES> — signed off —
```

Figure 5.3 Sample Conference

The /**PAGE** command is the only way to invite a member into a private group; no one can join a private group unless he is paged by someone already in the group.

Accepting or Rejecting a Page. If you are paged, you can accept the invitation by typing /**ACCEPT**, or reject it by typing /**REJECT**. (NOTE: You may receive a Page while you are not in a conference area; if this happens, the conference area in which the member paging you is located will be identified, and you must go to the conference area before /ACCEPTing.)

A Sample Conference

Figure 5.3 is an example of a DELPHI Conference conversation, which has been entitled CONVENTION, between member DEBBIEJONES and member RESNICK, and later joined by member AUTHOR.

After AUTHOR joins, the conversation is displayed as AUTHOR would see it, with his input echoed to him before it is sent to the other conference members. (This feature, which can be turned off, allows you to correct your lines before you send them.)

Notice that AUTHOR's comment beginning with "Still planning on it..." was interrupted by RESNICK's comment beginning with "I'm flying...." Nevertheless, when AUTHOR pressed «RETURN», his message was transmitted intact.

We included this to illustrate a situation that you may find confusing at first—someone else's comment appearing in the middle of yours as you type. As we've shown, this does not change your comment in any way; your comment appears in "clear" as soon as you press «RETURN». However, you may temporarily lose your train of thought when this happens. If so, press **Control- R**; your current comment will be redisplayed *to you only*, and you can continue typing or make corrections before it is sent. Alternatively, you may press **Control-X** or **Control-U** to erase the entire comment.

Group Attributes

We mentioned earlier that you can "customize" the conference environment to suit your needs and tastes. One way this is done is by setting what are known as "attributes" (or conditions) within a conference group.

A conference group may have one or more attributes, in any combination. An attribute must be set from within the group (with the exception of the "Private Group" attribute).

Private groups. If a group is created with the word "PRIVATE" in its name, other members will not be able to join unless invited (via a Page) by a member in the conference group. (This attribute may also be set after a group is created with the command **/GPRIVATE**, and canceled with **/NOGPRIVATE**.)

Password-protected groups. A group may be set up so that a password is required to join it. Members who wish to join a password group must type the correct password at the Conference menu, using the command **/PASS**

<password> *before* attempting to join the group in question. (This attribute is set with the command **/GPASS <password>**. It is turned off with the command **/NOGPASS**.)

Quiet groups. A "quiet" group is one where you are not disturbed by people coming and going. This means that members in the group will not see the usual "- <membername>> just joined -" or "- signed off -" messages. The command **/GQUIET** sets this attribute, and **/NOGQUIET** turns it off.

If you have set a group to quiet status, remember that you will not be notified when members enter or leave, and thus other members can join your group and see what you are saying without you knowing it.

Locked groups. The "group manager" (usually the person who created the group and who is displayed first in the group list) has the ability to "lock" the group. When a group is locked, no one other than the group manager may change the group's name nor any of its attributes. This attribute is set with **/GLOCK**, and turned off with **/NOGLOCK**.

Conference Protocol

Most members observe a simple protocol while in conference to avoid needless interruption and confusion. Based on old telex codes, this protocol provides signals to let others know when you have finished a thought, and when you are going to continue typing.

If you need to continue a comment over two or more lines, include an ellipsis (...) at the end of your current line. When you are finished with your comment, enter "ga" (the old telex code for "go ahead") before pressing «RETURN». Thus, a two-line comment in conference might look like this:

```
KZIN> My feeling is that it is not a very good idea. However...
KZIN> I'll wait until the final score is in to elaborate. ga
```

Additional protocol can include prefacing comments addressed to a specific member with the member's name, and making known a wish to ask a question or make a comment by typing **?** or **!** as appropriate.

And remember, common courtesy (an uncommon thing, at times!) goes a long way online.

Conference "Codes"

Once you've participated in a few real-time conferences on DELPHI, you'll probably notice some of the members using strange words and symbols from time to time. Things like "btw," for instance, or something like this: :-) .

While these may look like typographical errors, they do mean something in the special world of realtime conferences. They are a sort of "visual shorthand" that online service users have evolved to accommodate faster communication.

Most of the alphabetical terms are merely acronyms—"btw" stands for "by the way," and "ga" stands for "go ahead." (Some have been adapted from old telegraph or teletype communications conventions; "ga" is one.) The more alien character strings— those that look like the person typing lost everything but the punctuation marks on his or her computer—actually represent pictures and are known as "ASCII graphics."

Here's a quick glossary of some "conference codes" you may encounter:

- **BRB** - "Be right back." Used when someone leaves his or her computer for a moment, or exits the conference area. This lets others in the conference know that they should not expect responses from that person.
- **BTW** - "By the way." Used as you would use it in conversation.
- **GA** - "Go ahead." This is usually used after someone has typed several lines that continue a thought (using "..." as explained below) to indicate that he or she has finished the thought. Also used by one or more conference participants when several people type at once, to defer to one individual's comments.
- **IMHO** (or IMO) - "In my humble opinion." (Watch out— someone's dragging out a soapbox when IMHO prefaces a sentence!)
- **LOL** - "Lots of laughter." or "Laughing out loud."
- **TPTB** - "The powers that be."
- **<GRIN>** - Just what it says, but note that it is enclosed by greater than/less than symbols, a cue that you should visualize what the symbols enclose.
- **<g>** - Short for <GRIN>.

In addition to the abbreviations, you'll also see some cryptic "symbols" that aren't acronyms. These are "ASCII graphics," used to represent facial expressions and thoughts. Here are the basic ones:

:-) or **:->**- A smile (turn the book sideways if you don't see it).
;-) - A smile with a wink.

:-(- A frown or sad or disapproving face.

Finally, people in a conference with two or more will often use two dashes and a greater than (—>) symbol, or two greater than symbols (>>) followed by a name to indicate that the comment that follows is directed to a specific person. For example, if you were online and wanted to direct a comment to someone named RESNICK, you would type:

```
-> RESNICK You are so right.
```

And now you're an expert on the verbal shorthand used to make online communication easier. New codes pop up periodically. Some catch on, and some don't (but don't be afraid to ask if you don't understand). Conference "rules" and conventions are used or not used in informal conferences by mutual assent of the members present. Usually, no one makes the decision; members simply follow protocol as they see it (you can get a feel for how heavily a conference group is using protocol by observation).

Conference Menu Commands

WHO

Typing **WHO** (or /**WHO**) at a Conference menu displays a report that lists the Conference groups available for you to join, as well as the membernames of all the members in the current area. This report also indicates which members are in Conference.

If you follow **WHO** with a membername, that member's profile, as entered in People on DELPHI is displayed. Thus, **WHO MCAIDIN** is the same as **WHOIS MCAIDIN..**

Either will display the profile (if one has been entered) for MCAIDIN.

In some cases there may be so many people in Conference that the WHO listing is too big to fit on your screen. In that case you can use one of these special commands:

/WHO N   show only non-private groups
/WHO P   show only private groups
/WHO A   show who's available
/WHO I   show who's idle

JOIN

Use this command to create a Conference or join an existing Conference group selected from the conference listing. Typing **JOIN** by itself presents the question:

```
Which group? (/who for a list)? 1
  or
Which group? (/who for a list)? GO CINCINNATI REDS
```

Or, type **JOIN**, followed by a group number or group name, like this: **JOIN 1** or **JOIN GO CINCINNATI REDS**

Groups may be entered in upper- or lowercase. When you join a group, you and the other members in the group see a message like this:

```
** MCAIDIN just joined "GO CINCINNATI REDS" (3 members now) **
```

If you create a group (called "Attack of the Killer Tomatoes" in this example), you will see a message like this:

```
You have just created group "Attack of the Killer Tomatoes"
(Type Control-Z to exit back to menu)
```

NOTE: If you want to join a private group, you must be invited via a Page from a member who is in the private group. If you try to join a private group, you will be sent this message:

```
Sorry, you must be invited to join a PRIVATE group.
```

"Talking". Once you are in a group, enter a comment and press «RETURN» to "talk." When you press «RETURN», your comment is displayed (sent) to all members in the conference group, including yourself. (When you create a group alone, you are the only one in it until someone else joins, so you are the only one to see your comments.)

NAME

Use this command to adopt a pseudonym or "handle" to use while you are in conference. (DELPHI and this Handbook refer to your Conference pseudonym as your "nickname.") When DELPHI displays a nickname during a conference, it is preceded by a period to let others know they are communicating with someone using a nickname.

Here is how you change your name at the Conference menu (in this example, the assumed name will be "Mick Alan"):

```
CONFERENCE>NAME Mick Alan
```

When you join a Conference after assuming a nickname, others will see your comments preceded by your nickname, like this:

```
.Mick Alan> Hi, JR. How's business?
```

Your nickname will also appear in a WHO list. If you forget your nickname, type **NAME** alone, and DELPHI will display the nickname you are using and some other information about your status in Conference, as follows:

```
Name Mick Alan, In 0 groups
Nobody is squelched by you.
Not logging.
```

This tells you that you have assumed the name Mick Alan, that you have joined no conference groups, and that you aren't "squelching" anyone (more about squelching later in this chapter). Not logging means that you aren't recording the conversation in your personal Workspace (more about logging later in this chapter).

You may change your nickname as often as you like, but you may not assume the membername or nickname of anyone else who is using conference at the time. (You can change your name while you are in a conference group, too, as you'll learn in a few pages.) Your nickname disappears when you leave the Conference area.

PAGE

If you wish to solicit conversations with other DELPHI members—those already in a conference group or otherwise using DELPHI—you may page them. It's like paging someone at the airport: You can page them without knowing their exact location, as long as you see that they are online. (If you try to page someone who is not online or who has used the /BUSY command, you will be advised that the person is not available.)

If you do not include a name with PAGE, DELPHI will prompt you for it. You may use either upper- or lowercase letters, or any combination of both. Here are some examples. If you enter **PAGE ROSA**, DELPHI tells you:

```
ROSA being paged. Press RETURN to cancel pages.
```

If ROSA is not in Conference, but in another area of DELPHI, she receives the message:

```
YOURNAME would like to talk with you in Conference.
```

If you are paging from a group's Conference area, the message will include the name of the Conference area from which you are paging. If you enter **PAGE** at the Conference Menu, but don't specify the membername of the person with whom you wish to talk, DELPHI responds with:

```
Page whom?
```

Then you supply the membername by entering **ROSA**. If you are in a Conference area and are paged by another member (in this example, NANCY), you will see:

```
Would you like to talk with NANCY (Y/N)?
```

If you respond by typing **YES**, you will join a conference group with NANCY automatically. If NANCY is already involved in a Conference, you join NANCY's group. If NANCY is not yet in a group (which means NANCY used the Page command from the Conference menu), then you are both assigned to a group with a number but no name.

If you are not in Conference, but in another area of DELPHI when you are paged, you must exit the area you're in and move to the Conference menu. When you arrive there, you'll be asked if you'd like to talk to the person who sent the page.

If you respond by typing **NO** because you don't want to talk to NANCY, NANCY receives a message like this:

```
Sorry, YOURNAME cannot talk at the moment.
```

If your PAGE is declined, you are returned to the Conference menu. If you get tired of waiting for a response to a Page issued at the Conference menu, press «RETURN» to cancel the Page. Be patient, though—it sometimes takes a minute or so for a paged member to exit the area he or she may be in.

Commands to Use While in a Conference Group

Because Conference is set up so that everything you type is displayed (sent) to everyone in a conference group with you, you must let DELPHI know when you intend a word or words to be a command. This is done by preceding the command with a slash (/).

As indicated earlier, you can use all Conference menu commands and most Immediate commands—as well as a number of special commands—while you are in a conference group. Type **/HELP** for a summary of and/or help with these commands while in Conference. Many special Conference commands are disabled or reversed by preceding them with **NO**. For example, /BUSY disables sends, and /NOBUSY resumes them. Most commands affect only the member issuing them. Exceptions are commands beginning with the letter *G*, which are used to alter the attributes, or environment, of an entire Conference group. As with other DELPHI commands, you need only enter the first two or three characters of any command.

Joining/Creating/Exiting a Group

Use these commands to join or create a conference group, move from group to group, or leave a group.

/JOIN followed by a Conference group name—has the same function as the **JOIN** command in the main Conference menu. If you use this command while

you are within a group, it causes you to switch groups, exiting the one you're in and joining the new one.

/PAGE. This functions like the PAGE command at the Conference menu. It notifies the member whose name you supply that you wish to talk with him or her. You can supply either a membername or the nickname a member is using in Conference. For example, **/PAGE MODELMIKE.** The member being paged receives a message, starting with your membername, like this:

```
YOURNAME would like to talk with you in Conference.
```

If you are in a private or password-protected group, the member you are paging is granted an "admission ticket" into your group and may join it at any time until you cancel the page. You may cancel all your pages by typing **/CANCEL.**

/ACCEPT. You may accept another member's page without returning to the Conference menu. If you type **/ACCEPT**, you join the Conference group of the person who paged you. The advanced DELPHI member should note that /ACCEPT joins as /TALK does and not as /JOIN does. In this example, in which member MODELMIKE pages BETSYM, BETSYM sees:

```
MODELMIKE would like to talk with you in Conference.
```

By typing **/ACCEPT**, BETSYM indicates, "Yes, I'd like to talk with MODELMIKE."

/ANSWER is synonymous with /ACCEPT.

/REJECT means, "No, I don't want to talk to the person paging me." You may wish to use this if you are paged by a member while you are already talking in a group in which you wish to remain or you may be involved in reading your mail or another activity and don't wish to converse at that time. Typing **/REJECT** sends this message to the person paging you:

```
Sorry, YOURNAME cannot talk at the moment.
```

/CANCEL. Use this to cancel all your pages to other members. For example, KZIN is paged into Conference if you type **/PAGE KZIN**. That page is canceled if you type **/CANCEL.**

/PASS. This command sets your current password, which you must do before you can gain admission to a password-protected Conference group. Knowing and entering the right password lets you join a password-protected group (see **/GPASS**), which you can do by typing **/JOIN** or **/TALK** followed by the name or number of the group. /PASS also operates at the Conference menu, and you will probably use it more frequently there than from within a Conference group.

The Conference password scheme is like a lock and key. /GPASS sets the lock from within a Conference group, and /PASS is the key for a member to join the group. When you want to join a password-protected group, enter **/PASS** followed by the password as in this example, in which the password is **KNOCKKNOCK: /PASS KNOCKKNOCK.** Then, enter **/JOIN** followed by the group's name or number.

/EXIT removes you from your current Conference group and sends this message to others in your Conference group:

```
YOURNAME> — signed off —
```

If you are in more than one Conference group, you will be returned to the group you were in previous to the current group (see **/TALK**); if you are in only one Conference group, /EXIT will return you to the Conference menu.

/BYE. Typing **/BYE** logs you off DELPHI from within a Conference group, and sends the same message to others in your Conference as /EXIT.

Talking in a Conference Group

The following commands are used to talk with other members individually, "tune out" the comments of a specified member, address your comments to a different group, or to send a multiple-line comment to your group.

/SEND allows you to send a message to any member online, whether or not he or she is in Conference. You can send the same message to more than one member simultaneously by separating the membernames and/or nicknames with commas. But don't put spaces between the membernames. Here are two examples:

```
/SEND DRL,S.SHWARTZ Marketing talk at 9 tues.
/SEND DRL How was the convention in Paris?
```

If the person to whom you wish to /SEND has used /BUSY, you won't be able to /SEND to him or her. (See /**MAIL** in this chapter for some options in that case.) When used to send a message to someone in your Conference group, /SEND is like "whispering" a comment to that person, since nobody in the group can read a /SEND except you and the person to whom it is directed.

/SQUELCH. Using this command keeps you from seeing anything that the specified member types in a Conference group, even though others who haven't squelched him or her still see the specified member's comments. /SQUELCH also cuts off /SENDS from the specified member. Enter /**SQUELCH** followed by the membername of the person from whom you don't wish to hear. For example, /**SQUELCH NANCY.** Remember that if you /SEND to NANCY while she is squelched, you won't be able to see her answer! You can list your current squelches by typing /**SQUELCH** or /**NAME.** Type /**NOSQUELCH** to un-squelch a member, like this: /**NOSQUELCH NANCY.** To cancel all squelches you may have set, type /**NOSQUELCH.**

/TALK acts exactly like /JOIN with one important difference: /TALK does not remove you from your current Conference group. This means that you remain "in" the Conference group from which you issued the /TALK command and can see what others type, even though those in the first group won't be able to see what you type while you are in the second group. By using /TALK you can participate in several Conference groups simultaneously. You are listening to all the groups you are in, but talking to only one group at a time. You may switch the group to which you are addressing your comments by using the /TALK command again. (Comments by members from all groups in which you are participating appear on your screen only, preceded by the number of the group they are in.)

To direct your comments to a different group, type /**TALK** followed by the group's number or name, as in the example below, in which it is assumed you are in a group called "Attack of the Killer Tomatoes" (group #14) and want to /TALK in a group called "RAH CHICAGO BEARS" (group #1):

```
/TALK RAH CHICAGO BEARS
   or
/TALK 1
```

Typing a slash followed by the group number has the same effect. You can also direct a one-liner to a group like this:

```
/1 Hey, I heard that!
```

This does not affect the group you are talking in, except for the single mesage.

In each of the foregoing examples, your comments would be directed from your current group to the group named RAH CHICAGO BEARS. Again, you will be able to see the comments typed by members in the group you left, even though they won't be able to see your comments until you switch back to your original group with /TALK.

To leave a group that you joined with /TALK use **Control-Z**, **/EXIT**, or **/JOIN <group name>**. Any of these will cause you to exit the second group and remain in the first group.

/QUEUE is a feature used mainly in formal Conferences. It allows you to send a multiple-line message to the moderator of a moderated group (one with a "group manager"), which he or she may release all at once to the entire group. Type **/QUEUE**, and you will be prompted to enter your message, in a manner similar to that of entering an E-Mail message. (You do not have to know the name of the moderator to send a message in this manner.)

Press **Control-Z** when you've finished entering your message (or, if you change your mind, press **Control-C** to cancel) and you'll be prompted to enter a one-line subject for your message. After entering the subject, press «RETURN» again, and the moderator will be notified that your message is waiting. The subject of the message is not displayed to the Conference group at large. If there is no moderator, your /QUEUEd message is displayed as soon as you've entered the subject. This is useful if you are entering a message that won't fit on one line and you don't want to be interrupted by other people's comments while typing. To cancel a message sent with /QUEUE, type **/NOQUEUE**.

Getting Information

Use these commands to obtain information about the current group, the Conference area, other members in the group, or your own settings.

/ENTRY is a convenient way to find out when a member was last in your current area. Type **/ENTRY** (or **EN**) followed by a membername to see the date and time the specified member was last in the area.

If you type **/EN *** (* is a "wildcard" character), you will see the names of the last ten members to enter the area, along with the dates and times of their entry. (This command does not operate in the Main Conference area.)

/HELP enters DELPHI's Conference Help system. Type **/HELP** to see a quick-reference list of Conference commands. Type **/HELP** followed by the name of the particular command in which you are interested to see a detailed explanation of the command. (Example: **/HELP /SQUELCH**)

/NAME. If you type **/NAME** alone, DELPHI will display the nickname you are using and some other information about your status in conference, as follows:

```
Name Bob Tucker, In 1 group
Nobody is squelched by you.
Not logging.
```

This tells you that you have assumed the name Bob Tucker, that you have joined no Conference groups, and that you aren't "squelching" anyone (see **/SQUELCH**). "Not logging" means you aren't recording the conversation in your personal Workspace (see **/LOG**).

You may change your nickname as often as you like, but you may not assume the membername or nickname of anyone else who is using Conference at that time.

/RNAME. You may wish to know the membernames of those using Conference nicknames, perhaps for sending mail. Type **/RNAME** (think of this as **Real NAME**) followed by the nickname, as in this example where member KZIN has assumed the nickname "Bob Tucker":

/RNAME Bob Tucker

You are informed that "Bob Tucker" is really KZIN. You also can use /RNAME to discover the nickname of a particular member, if that member is currently in Conference. Type **/RNAME** followed by the membername.

/SHOWRN. If you are in a Conference where there are several members using (or frequently changing) nicknames, you may wish to see their membernames displayed along with their nicknames, to keep track of who's really saying what. The command /SHOWRN causes membernames to be displayed before nicknames with every comment, like this:

```
KZIN:Bob Tucker>
```

You can turn off the display of membernames with nicknames by typing **/NOSHOWRN**.

/SQUELCH. Type **/SQUELCH** to see the names of members you are squelching (if any).

/WHO tells you which members are currently in your area, who is in Conference, and the names of the Conference groups in your area. (This command displays the same report that you would see if you typed **WHO** at the Conference menu.)

Typing **/WHO** followed by a membername is the same as typing **/WHOIS**.

/WHOIS. followed by a membername, displays the Member Directory profile for the specified member. Enter it like this: **/WHOIS MRPEABODY**. If the member hasn't provided any information about herself or himself, you receive this response:

```
There is no information on file for MRPEABODY.
```

Customizing Conference

These commands change the way Conference operates for you only. You can, in effect, "customize" Conference to suit your tastes.

/BUSY. To disable /SENDs from people outside your group, type **/BUSY**. Those who are in your Conference group may still **/SEND** to you. **/BUSY** also disables Pages and new mail notification.

/ECHO turns on the display of your own Conference comments as you enter them (i.e., before you press «RETURN»). Type **/ECHO** to turn this feature on if it is off.

To turn the display of your Conference comments off (disable /ECHO) type **/NOECHO**. (The default is "on," which means you will see your comments as you enter them, unless you type **/NOECHO**.) /ECHO does not affect the status of /REPEAT. Use **/NOECHO** if your terminal program has a "keyboard buffer" or "chat window" feature that lets you type in a line and make changes before pressing «RETURN».

/NAME. Use **/NAME** to adopt a nickname while you are in a Conference group. Your nickname will also appear in a WHO list. Conference names (nicknames) are temporary; you lose your nickname once you leave Conference.

/PAD. Type **/PAD** to see or set your current pad parameters.

/REPEAT turns on the display of your own comments as they are displayed to others in a conversation (i.e., after you press «RETURN»). Type **/REPEAT** to turn this feature on if it is off. To turn the repeating of your Conference comments off, type **/NOREPEAT**. (The default is "on," which means you will see your comments repeated after you send them, unless you type **/NOREPEAT**.)

Some members are confused by seeing their own message twice; others like the repetition so they know when others in the group see their message. It assures you that the message was sent. If you use /LOG, you most likely will want your messages echoed back to you, or else they won't appear in the transcript. /REPEAT does not affect the status of /ECHO.

Changing Group Attributes

These commands are used to change the attributes of the entire Conference group, thus changing the environment in which a Conference is taking place.

/GLOCK or /NOGLOCK may be used by a Conference group's "manager" (usually the first person in the group). It acts to protect the group's attributes against changes by the members of the group. The manager of the Conference retains the ability to change attributes. A DELPHI Groups & Clubs manager can override a manager of a Conference in his or her own group or club. When

/GLOCK is in effect, these attributes are locked: the group's name, the group's password, and the group's privacy setting.

/GNAME. Use this command to assign a new name to the Conference in which you are communicating. Groups created without names (as when one member pages another at the Conference menu) are assigned a number for their names, but you may want to present a more descriptive name to let others know what the conversation is about.

For example, if you entered a group with another member via a Page from the Conference menu, and were assigned a group number of 2, you may want to change it to let other members know you are discussing politics. You would enter something like this: **/GNAME** Republicans vs. Democrats. You can change the name of a group at any time, even if it is already named. A group name can be up to 48 characters in length.

A group name that contains the word PRIVATE is automatically a private group, and can be joined "by invitation only," the same as if you had set the private group attribute with /GPRIVATE. Other DELPHI members cannot join your group unless someone in your group pages them and they accept. So, be careful not to use PRIVATE in a group name unless you really want the group to be private. /GNAME alone displays a list of a group's attributes (its name, whether it is private, etc.).

/GPASS. **/GPASS** sets a group's password. Once a password has been set, those seeking admittance to the Conference conversation must either be paged by one of the participants or know the password. With **/GPASS**, you place a lock on the Conference group "door," and only those who have the key in the form of the Password can get in.

To set a group's password, type **/GPASS <password>**. After you set a password, anyone wishing to join your Conference must first enter the appropriate password. (See the explanation of /PASS earlier in this chapter.) To "turn off" password protection, type **/GPASS** alone, or **/NOGPASS**.

A password-protected group and a private group are similar in that both keep out unwanted guests. If a group is both password protected and private, then only the password protection applies. (See also **/GPRIVATE**.) You can use /SEND to advise members who are not in the group of the password, or use a password previously agreed upon.

/GPRIVATE. Use **/GPRIVATE** or **/NOGPRIVATE** to change a group's private status. Normally, you use the word PRIVATE in the group name to establish the group as private. However, with these commands, you can have privacy or no privacy no matter what the group name indicates.

A private group is "by invitation only," and new participants may join in only by being paged.

/GQUIET or /NOGQUIET sets (or resets) the group's "quiet" attribute. When a group is "quiet," there are no notices given when people enter or leave the group.

Sending E-Mail

You can enter DELPHI's Electronic Mail system or send a one-line message to a member using these commands.

/MAIL. When you type **/MAIL**, you move to DELPHI's E-Mail system. (You will be at the MAIL> prompt.) Once you are in Mail, you can read and send mail, and perform all other mail operations. (See Chapter 11 for details on using Electronic Mail.) To return to your Conference group, press **Control-Z** or type **EXIT**. The first 1,000 characters typed by other members in your group while you are in Mail will be saved for you, and displayed when you return to the group.

/MAIL <membername> <message>. Alternately, following **/MAIL** with a membername or membernames and a one-line message causes **/MAIL** to function in a manner similar to that of **/SEND**. The advantage here is that you can **/MAIL** a message to a member who has used **/BUSY**, which would lock out a regular **/SEND**. The member receives the message when he reads his E-Mail, in the form of a one-line message in the *Subj:* header. Enter it as in this example:

```
/MAIL KZIN I have the figures you need. «RETURN»
```

File Directory and Display and Conference Logging

These commands allow you to see a directory of the files in your Workspace, to display the contents of a Workspace file to the members in your Conference group, or to save a transcript of a Conference to a file in your Workspace.

/DIRECTORY displays a directory of some or all of the files in your Workspace. You may use it with the "wildcard" character (*) either before a filename extension or after a filename (filename.* or *.ext). Typing **/DIRECTORY *.*** displays a complete directory of your personal Workspace. This command displays the directory to your screen only.

/DISPLAY. Use **/DISPLAY** to display the contents of a Workspace file to the members in your Conference group. Type **/DISPLAY** followed by the name of a file to display the contents of the file to your Conference group. The file is displayed one line at a time. To pause the file display, type **/NODISPLAY**. To resume the display from the point where it paused, type **/DISPLAY ***. (To delay the display of a line from the file for about one second, type / alone.) If you wish to halt a file display and do not expect to resume it, type **/NODISPLAY *** to stop the display and close the file.

/LOG. If you wish to have a transcript of a Conference for posting, reviewing, or downloading, use **/LOG**. The **/LOG** command captures your Conference session in a file in your Workspace. This is useful if you don't want to be bothered with saving your buffer in your personal computer while the Conference is ongoing, or if you are using a "dumb" terminal.

To log a Conference, type **/LOG**, followed by * or the name you wish to give the file, like this: **/LOG** MYFILE.DAT (Typing **/LOG *** assigns the log file the name CONF.LOG.)

If you type **/LOG** alone, you will see a status report telling you whether or not you are logging, and the filename (if any) of the file to which you are logging the Conference.

Typing **/NOLOG** ceases the file capture. You can restart the file capture, appending to the existing file, by typing **/LOG *** (provided you have not left Conference; once you leave Conference, the file to which you were logging is closed).

If you use the **/NOREPEAT** command, your remarks won't be recorded in the log file. In this case, use **/REPEAT** to see your own comments again and have them recorded in the log file.

Control-key Commands

Control-C. Pressing **Control-C** while in a Conference group will return you to the menu from which you originally selected Conference, bypassing the

Conference menu entirely.

Control-R. **To** redisplay a comment you have entered (on your screen only) press **Control-R**. (NOTE: Use this before you press «RETURN».)

Control-U or Control-X. **Press Control-U or Control-X** to erase a line you have entered but not sent. Use this before you press «RETURN».

Control-Z. **To** exit a Conference group and return to the Conference menu (or to your previous group if you are participating in more than one group), press **Control-Z**.

Chapter 6
DELPHI/Regional

What is DELPHI/Regional?

DELPHI has grown and established its reputation as a leader in international telecommunications. Now, DELPHI has taken several steps forward by combining the scope of an international service with services focused for specific cities. DELPHI/Regional is the result of DELPHI's movement in this direction. Probably the best analogy for DELPHI's regional services are local affiliates for a national television network. By having a regional service available, news and other specific information relevant to that specific region can be made available to members in that area.

Currently, there are four DELPHI/Regional affiliate services: DELPHI/Boston, DELPHI/Kansas City, DELPHI/Miami, and DELPHI/Argentina. The Boston and Kansas City networks are directly connected into the worldwide DELPHI network. Therefore, services like E-Mail and Conference will connect you with members who access through these two regional services. As a member of DELPHI, you can connect immediately to either of these local services and explore the local offerings.

DELPHI/Miami and DELPHI/Argentina are operated separately with Spanish menu names and prompts. At this writing, DELPHI/Miami and DELPHI/Argentina are not as tightly connected to the national DELPHI service, but you can request an account and then be able to "gateway" through into these networks. There is also a selection available for sending E-Mail to members of these networks, without having to apply for an account first.

Getting to and from DELPHI/Regional

Getting to DELPHI/Regional is easy. DELPHI/Regional is a selection on the DELPHI Main Menu, so all you have to do is type **DELPHI** (or **DEL**) at the Main Menu.

If you know which regional service you wish to use, you can bypass the DELPHI/Regional menu completely by typing **DEL** followed by the selection for the regional service you wish to access. For example, you could simply type **DEL KC** at the DELPHI Main Menu to go directly to DELPHI/Kansas City, or **DEL BOS** to go directly to DELPHI/Boston.

DELPHI/Boston

DELPHI/BOSTON is DELPHI with a Boston accent, the online service that serves the greater Boston area, including a large portion of New England.

As illustrated by the Main Menu in Figure 6.1, DELPHI/Boston is similar in structure to the worldwide DELPHI network, and offers many of the same services. You will, however, find some interesting original features as well as local and regional information that is not available elsewhere.

If you are planning on traveling to the Boston area for business or pleasure, you will find DELPHI/Boston particularly useful. You'll also find DELPHI/Boston an interesting way to take a trip without leaving your home. Try it!

DELPHI/Boston Features

DELPHI/Boston was the first of DELPHI's regional services, and as a result, has a large number of unique offerings. DELPHI/Boston also has a broad offering of information on Boston-area businesses, shopping, tourist spots, and more.

```
DELPHI/Boston Menu:


Arts-Entertainment          Merchants' Row

Business & Finance          News-Weather-Sports

Calendar                    Office Park

Communication-Mail          People Online

Conference                  Travel

DELPHI-Worldwide            Using DELPHI/Boston

Education                   Workspace

Fun & Games Online          Help

Groups and Associations     Exit

Guide to Boston


BOSTON>Which Service?
```

Figure 6.1 DELPHI/Boston Main Menu

Along with customized Boston regional services, DELPHI/Boston includes the best of DELPHI's services: E-Mail, Grolier's Encyclopedia, travel services, online shopping and information services, a real-time Conference system that is linked with the worldwide DELPHI network, and FAX and Telex services.

DELPHI/Boston Commands. DELPHI members can return to the worldwide network after accessing DELPHI/Boston by typing **DELPHI** at the DELPHI/Boston Main Menu. Otherwise, type **EXIT** or **BYE** to log off DELPHI entirely.

DELPHI/Kansas City

DELPHI/Kansas City is custom-tailored for professionals, businesses, and individuals in Kansas and Missouri. DELPHI/Kansas City services include local business news, interactive shopping from local merchants, forums for local clubs and associations, extensive information about local entertainment and events, and more. DELPHI/Kansas City members can also use real-time Conference (cross-linked to the worldwide Conference), E-Mail, Telex, and FAX services—just like DELPHI/Boston members.

DELPHI/Kansas City Commands. If you've accessed DELPHI/Kansas City via the worldwide DELPHI network and wish to return to DELPHI-Worldwide when you have completed a session on DELPHI/Kansas City, type **DELPHI** at the DELPHI/Kansas City Main Menu. Otherwise, type **BYE** or **EXIT** to log off DELPHI entirely.

DELPHI/Argentina

DELPHI/Argentina (Figure 6.2) is a Spanish-language network with services that focus on metropolitan Buenos Aires. It also includes a gateway to to a regional DELPHI service in Uruguay.

DELPHI/Argentina Features

If you speak Spanish, you might enjoy figuring out the menu selections and comparing them with menu selections on DELPHI's other services. For those who don't know Spanish, here's a breakdown of some of the more important selections:

```
Menu PRINCIPAL:

Anuncios Publicos          Gente en DELPHI
Area de Trabajo            Grupos y Clubes
Banco de Datos             Noticias
Biblioteca                 Shopping Center
Comunicaciones             Usando DELPHI
Conferencia                Viajes y Turismo
DELPHI/Internacional       AYUDA
Economia                   SALIR
Entretenimientos


PRINCIPAL>Que desea hacer?
```

Figure 6.2 DELPHI/Argentina Main Menu

Anuncios Publicas	Public Announcements
Area de Trabajo	Workspace
Banco de Datos	Database
Biblioteca	Library
Conferencia	Conference
Entretenimientos	Entertainment
Gente en DELPHI	People on DELPHI
Gurpos y Clubes	Groups and Clubs
Usando DELPHI	Using DELPHI
AYUDA	HELP
SALIR	EXIT

As you can see, DELPHI in Argentina and Uruguay offer the same services as DELPHI here in the United States and Canada. (The selection "Comunicaciones" leads to a sub-menu offering E-Mail and related services.)

DELPHI/Argentina Commands Control-key commands used on DELPHI/Argentina are the same as those used on the worldwide DELPHI network. Typed commands must be in Spanish, however.

Making the DELPHI/Argentina Connection

When you select DELPHI/Argentina by typing **ARG** at the DELPHI/Regional menu, you'll see a menu with three selections. One of the selections is Gateway to DELPHI/Argentina. In order to gateway into the Argentina network, you must have a separate username on that system. If you do have a username on DELPHI/Argentina, type **Gateway,** and you will be advised of the surcharges involved in accessing DELPHI/Argentina, which include a per-minute rate as well as a per-byte rate. You will then log on to DELPHI/Argentina and see the menu in Figure 6.3. (For voice telephone support *within Argentina*, call 541-331-6249.)

To connect with DELPHI/Uruguay from DELPHI/Argentina, select DELPHI/Internacional by typing **DEL.** You will see a menu from which you can select Miami, Uruguay, and DELPHI-Worldwide. (The DELPHI/Miami and DELPHI-Worldwide selections are intended for the use of those dialing in from South America, of course.)

DELPHI/Uruguay is a product of RAUL S.A., Montevideo, R.O.U. The telephone number is (5982)-90-6080.

DELPHI/Miami

DELPHI/Miami is DELPHI with a Latin flavor. A Spanish-language service, it offers menus, news, and information in Spanish, and supports all of DELPHI's communication services.

DELPHI/Miami Features

DELPHI/Miami offers many of the same services as DELPHI —*en Espanol.* Because of Miami's position as a commercial trade center, you'll find many Spanish-language services relating to business and trade with countries in Latin America. Many Miami-based business and groups have also developed custom services online.

DELPHI/Miami Commands Control-key commands used on DELPHI/Miami are the same as those used on the worldwide DELPHI network. Typed commands must be in Spanish, however. To log off DELPHI/Miami, type **CHAU.**

Making the DELPHI/Miami Connection

If you wish to establish a DELPHI/Miami membership, send E-Mail to MIA1A::OPERADOR, or call 800-327-6105, voice (if you're calling from Florida, call 305-674-1001).

Once your account is established on DELPHI/Miami, you can log in via the DELPHI/Regional menu by typing **Connect** or by direct-dial to the DELPHI/Miami modem access number, 305-534-4440. You can also access DELPHI Miami from anywhere in the U.S. by using SprintNet. Just follow the standard DELPHI log-on procedures and instead of typing **C DELPHI** at the "@" prompt, type **C ITI**.

Otros DELPHI (Other DELPHI's)

Besides connections to DELPHI/Argentina and the worldwide DELPHI network, DELPHI/Miami also includes gateways to DELPHI/Centroamerica (a product of Prodata, S.A., Guatemala, [5022] 51-9885] and DELPHI/Colombia (a product of Telecom, Bogota, Columbia, [571] 281-1678).

Chapter 7
Entertainment & Games

DELPHI's Entertainment & Games menu is where the fun is. You'll find DELPHI's popular TQ, FlipIt!, Poker and SCRAMBLE games, horoscopes, music, movie reviews, and more.

Some games pit you against an electronic foe; in others you face human opponents.

Game Instructions

With most games, you will be asked if you want instructions when you make the selection from the menu. It's a good idea to read all the instructions available; in fact, you may wish to download and print out the instructions for study offline and for reference during play.

Some games also guide you through play with prompts.

Saved Games

Some games allow you to stop a game and continue it later where you left off. Your progress in such a game is stored in a file in your Workspace with the extension .DAT. If you delete a .DAT file, you will lose the saved game.

Exiting/Quitting Games

Type **QUIT** to exit an adventure game. Enter either **Control-C** or **Control-Z** to discontinue most other games. After using QUIT or Control-C/Control-Z, you will be returned to the sub-menu from which you selected the game.

Adventure Games

These games pit you against electronic opponents as you try to annihilate an enemy, track a treasure, or make your way through a maze. Descriptions of your surroundings and what's going on around you are provided in the form of colorful text; you manipulate and examine objects, talk to and interact with characters you meet, by typing simple commands like **GET SWORD**, in the same manner as adventure games you've played on your personal computer in the past.

You'll find both adventure and role-playing games (RPGs) on this menu. The original adventure, "Colossal Cave," is here, along with a special adventure in French, called "Aventure - en Francais".

Instructions are available online, and you will find hints and advice in the GameSig (see Chapter 8).

Astro-Predictions

Astro-Predictions presents general information on astrology and relates it to compatibility and timing of activities. Weekly forecasts for each Zodiac sign provide generalized trends. You'll also find information on how to use astrology, and how sex and personality are related to the Zodiac.

As a special feature, you can order an extensive personalized natal chart from Phyllis, DELPHI's astrologer, for an extra fee which is listed online.

Board and Logic Games

This menu offers computer simulations of popular board games. You can play a fascinating game of "Aliens," in which you roam the solar system while blasting hostile aliens out of existence. Or, if human competition is more to your taste, you can take a shot at multi-player FlipIt! (discussed later in this chapter). The ancient classics, Othello and Reverse are here, along with the modern classic Lunar Lander.

To play a game, type the first few letters of its name. Complete instructions for each game are available online, when you select a game.

Critics's Choice

Critic's Choice offers entertainment news and reviews on movies, books, videos, and games. Information on coming atttractions in these areas is also available. Participatc in the Trivia contests and win movie, posters, tickets, and more.

If there is a feature you'd like to see, or an idea you would like to share, you may send a note to Critic's Choice simply by choosing "What Do You Think?" from the menu.

FlipIt!

FlipIt! is a version of a game sometimes called "Othello" or "Reversi." FlipIt! is played on an 8 by 8 or 10 by 10 board with two players, one represented by "X," and the other by "O." The players designate where they wish to place their playing pieces on the board in alternating turns by typing a grid designation corresponding to the desired "square" (such as 6D, in Figure 7.1).

The object of the game is to place your piece on the board in such a manner that one of your opponent's pieces is flanked by two of yours (has one of your pieces on either side of it). When a piece is flanked, it "flips," and belongs to the opposing

```
You'll be playing against MAX
the VAX.
You play X and move first.

   A B C D E F G H
1  . . . . . . . .
2  . . . . . . . .
3  . . . . . . . .
4  . . . X O . . .
5  . . . O X . . .
6  . . . . . . . .
7  . . . . . . . .
8  . . . . . . . .
Your move (X).
```

6d

```
KZIN (X) moves to D6.
   A B C D E F G H
1  . . . . . . . .
2  . . . . . . . .
3  . . . . . . . .
4  . . . X O . . .
5  . . . X X . . .
6  . . . X . . . .
7  . . . . . . . .
8  . . . . . . . .
```

```
MAX the VAX (O) moves to C4.

   A B C D E F G H
1  . . . . . . . .
2  . . . . . . . .
3  . . . . . . . .
4  . . O O O . . .
5  . . . X X . . .
6  . . . X . . . .
7  . . . . . . . .
8  . . . . . . . .
Your move (X).
```

Figure 7.1 FlipIt Game in Progress

player. The player with the most pieces at the end of the game wins. The game is over when the board is completely filled, or when neither player can move.

You can play against another player in the area when you enter FlipIt!, or you can play against the computer (as in the example here) by typing **PLAY SOLO** after you enter FlipIt!.

If you make a wrong move the computer will suggest a correct move. Full instructions are available (type **INSTRUCT**) within the game.

There are two groups of commands available in FlipIt! One group is available before a game starts, and the other during gameplay.

The commands available FlipIt! before a game starts are:

WHO	List all current games and players.
PLAY <membername>	Play against another person. (Get a name from the WHO list, or play the computer by typing **PLAY SOLO**.)
ENTRY	Display membernames of those recently in area.
RECORD <membername>	View the designated member's win/lose record.
CANCEL	Cancel an invitation to play.
PLAY10	Make the board 10 squares by 10 squares, rather than 8 by 8.
WATCH #	Watch another game (get the number from the WHO list).
INSTRUCT	View full playing instructions.
EXIT	Leave FlipIt!.

In addition to the above, these commands are available after a game starts:

BOARD	Redisplay the board (necessary when it scrolls off the screen).
PASS	Pass on current move if you see no available moves.
QUIT	Exit the game.
FORFEIT	Give up; your opponent wins by default.
SCORE	View the current score.

Modem-to-Modem Games

Modem-to-Modem (MTM) games are an exciting new service on DELPHI which allows to you compete head-to-head with anyone who has the same game on their computer. These games feature graphic screens, live action, and a "chat window," whilch lets you "talk" to your opponent during the game! Many MTM games are now commercially available, but there is also a growing list of shareware public domain games. The number of available modem games is increasing rapidly, and they include games of all descriptions — classic board and card games like chess, backgammon, and cribbage, as well as exciting new arcade and action games.

Until recently, playing a modem game required that you call your opponent's modem directly. This meant that you and your opponent had to set up a time to play, and one of you would have to keep the phone line open and wait for the call. Also, if your opponent lived far away, one of you would have to pick up the cost of the long distance call.

Now, through DELPHI, you can play a wide variety of modem games online. In the conference area, you can meet and chat with new opponents, and challenge available players to a match, any time at all. In the MTM Forum, you can participate in discussions about modem games, ask questions, or organize a tournament! In the Modem gaming area there are several shareware MTM games you can download and start playing immediately. The large pool of potential opponents, the ability to start a game on the spur of the moment, and DELPHI's low connect fees make modem gaming yet another great way to have fun with friends on DELPHI!

Movie Reviews by Cineman

Here you'll find brief reviews of new films from the Cineman Syndicate, as well as informative previews of coming attractions, and a searchable database of reviews of recent films.

To read and download new reviews and news of upcoming films, select "New Releases" or "Coming Attractions," respectively.

To search for a review of a specific film, select "Reviews - Search by Title" at the Movie News & Reviews sub-menu. You will be prompted to type the first word of the film title. Review(s) for the film(s) whose titles begin with that word will be selected from the database.

Poker Showdown!

Transport yourself into an online casino and join other players skilled at the art of online wagering. Introduce yourself and "talk" with your opponents before the game and between hands. Even if you don't find people playing, you can hone your skills against DELPHI's "robots" — some very cagey opponents who'll always give you a run for your money.

Seat yourself at one of several tables and play any of five types of poker including straight poker, five-card stud, five-card draw, seven-card stud, or "Texas Hold Em" Poker. For added fun and excitement, and prizes, join one of the regular tournaments. See the Poker menu for details and the current schedule.

Playing Poker Showdown

When you enter the Poker Showdown area, you purchase chips at $1.00 each (of course you don't use "real" money), with the limit based on how much "money" you have. Your winnings (and losses) and cumulative cash is recorded when you leave Poker Showdown, and the balance is available when you next enter the game.

After you buy chips, you are asked to select a table.

Starting a Hand

Type **GO** to start the game. You can type GO followed by a number, e.g. GO 4, to start a particular type of poker. The types available are:

1. Straight Poker
2. 5-card Stud
3. 5-card Draw
4. 7-card Stud
5. Texas Hold-em

If you don't specify a number, you'll play the same as the most recent hand at your table.

Getting Help

Type **HELP** if you need information on Poker hands and game play. Type **/HELP** for other information. It is recommended that you read the articles available in the "About Poker" selection on the POKER menu before playing.

Quest

QUEST is a fantasy game played in a medieval setting. Players can explore the kingdom, fight monsters for experience points in order to compete with other players, or find and return the Grail to the Wizard. For relaxation between quests, players can talk with other players, or gamble in the fully-equipped casino.

SCRAMBLE Word Game

SCRAMBLE Word Game is, as the name indicates, a challenge to make words from a scrambled set of letters. When the game begins, you are shown a block of 16 letters from which you type as many words as you can make from the letters in 90 seconds. You can play solo, or against others.

SCRAMBLE Scoring

The longer the word, the more points you score for it. To determine the points for a word, square the length or the word. (For example, a five-letter word is worth 25 points, a six-letter word is 36 points, etc.)

Playing SCRAMBLE

SCRAMBLE games are set up in conference areas, and you can talk with players between rounds. To begin a game, just type **GO**. The block of letters will be displayed and you can begin typing words. If you type a word containing a letter that is not on the list, you are notified that it is an invalid word; the same thing happens if you type a word that is not in the SCRAMBLE dictionary. SCRAMBLE knows many brand names and proper names.

You can redisplay the board with the letters re-scrambled in a new pattern, any time by pressing «RETURN». To stop a game in progress and start a new game, type **GO**. To exit SCRAMBLE, press **Control-Z**.

Scramble Commands

Type **/HELP** to see these special commands for use in Scramble:

/GO	Start a new game.
/SHOWWORDS	Lists all words that have been used.
/SCORE	Shows the score of the most recent game.
/SAY <comment>	Type a comment and display it during play.
/TOP	Lists current top 10 players and their scores.
/RECENT	Lists 10 recent players and their high scores.
/SWHO	Shows a list of who is in the game.
/VTWIDE 0,1, or 2	Set display to "VT100 high or wide" characters (requires a VT-100 terminal or emulation).
/WHO	See who is in the area.
/WORD<word>	Check to see if a word is in the SCRAMBLE dictionary.
/ADD<word>	Request that a word be added to SCRAMBLE's dictionary.

Stellar Conquest

Rule the galaxy as a captain of your very own starship! Search the galaxy and build up armies to fight other vessels that attempt to deter you. Do well and you may be accepted by one of the big–time interstellar teams with dozens of planets cheering you on.

For instructions on how to play Stellar Conquest, type INSTRUCTIONS at the game prompt.

TQ Trivia Tournament

Capitalize on your gift for trivial knowledge in a challenge with hundreds of online players. Questions run the gamut from movies to politics, sports, religion, and TV characters, with a few thrown in from out-of-the-blue. Stay on your toes as the contest progresses through several rounds. Early on, correct answers will help you accumulate points to wager in later rounds. Contestants converse freely. As the responses come in, a tally is displayed to compare how everyone answers each question. At the end of each round, contestants are given an in-progress ranking and score.

Several scheduled TQ games take place each week — check "About TQ" on the TQ Menu for schedules and prizes.

If you can't get enough of Trivia during the scheduled contents each week and if you want to hone your trivia skills, try "TQ Anytime." TQ Anytime is available 24 hours-a-day, seven days-a-week, except when the scheduled TQ Trivia contests are in progress. And you don't have to worry about missing scheduled contests because TQ Anytime is played right in the same room.

Like scheduled TQ contests, TQ Anytime is multi-player. The game proceeds automatically. There are several different types of questions, some require betting (Reverse Casino, for example, shows you the answers but not the question, and then asks you to bet).

Playing TQ

To play TQ Trivia, type **TQ** at the Entertainment & Games menu, then **ENTER** at the TQ Menu. You will be notified if other players are present, and whether a question is being asked.

The questions in TQ Trivia are multiple-choice, as shown in Figure 7.2.

As a question is displayed, type your answer; your answer is automatically evaluated, and scores and statistics calculated by DELPHI. Some rounds offer a set score per question, while others have more creative scoring options.

TQ Help and Commands

Type **/HELP** for a list of commands available at any time. Here's a partial list of commands:

/QUESTION	Redisplays the current question.
/SCORE	Displays your score.
/NEWS	Displays the latest TQ news.
/STANDINGS	Displays the standings of tournament players.
/RECORD <membername>	Displays TQ record of a specified member.
/TOP	Displays all-time record TQ scores.
/WHO	Show who's in the game.

A CASINO question is next. You will be presented with a category
and asked to bet between 25% and 100% of your current winnings.

The Category is "Around the World".
How much would you like to bet? (0 - 5)
CAT57 bets 22358 points.
5
KZIN bets 5 points.
All bets are in.

91973> The nuclear submarine that completed the first undersea
voyage around the world was the U.S.S.

a Triton
b Enterprise
c Nautilus
d Poseidon
a
Your answer "A" was recorded.

All answers are in.
Here is how all players have answered the question:

```
#-new-% old%  Answer
___ ___ ___   _____

 0   0   8  -  Did not answer
 2  100  30  a  Triton
 0   0   0  b  Enterprise
 0   0  52  c  Nautilus
 0   0   8  d  Poseidon
```

The correct response is:

a Triton
Launched in 1959 and propelled by two nuclear reactors, the sub
completed the 41,500-mile trip during 1960 in 84 days.

You got the answer correct and won 5 points.
So far, you have answered 1 question and have won 5 points.

Current TQ Anytime Standings:

```
Answers  Score Player
_____  _____ _____

   31    44716 CAT57
    1        5 KZIN
```

Figure 7.2 TQ Anytime Trivia Questions

Chapter 8

Groups and Clubs

The following is a listing of DELPHI's Groups and Clubs and a brief description of each. For in-depth information about the various commands and services, please see Chapter 4 on Computing.

Aviation

Information on learning to fly, flight safety, and the latest in avionics and gadgetry. Software of interest to pilots and enthusiasts is available for downloading, as is a collection of true-life aviation stories.

Business Forum

Business discussions, economics news, and a consultants' database. The databases also contain useful business software (mostly for PCs and compatibles). Forum often has discussions of interest to entrepreneurs.

Close Encounters

"The intimate side of computer telecommunications." Adult discussions of dating, sexuality, psychology and other issues relating to relationships.

Custom Forums

Custom Forum — a service for personal online networking — offers you the chance to exchange messages with specialized groups of DELPHI members. Some forums are set up for small, personal groups, others are open for anyone who wants to join in.

Specifically, this service includes a private "bulletin board" type message area, which on DELPHI is referred to as Forum. You'll also have immediate access to DELPHI's Conference system so you can participate in real-time discussions. Database and downloading are NOT included in the basic custom forum service.

There are no extra charges for using a custom forum. There are only charges to set up and operate a forum.

The person who initiates a Custom Forum becomes its "host." DELPHI members who have been granted access by the host may read and respond to messages posted in the forum and add their own messages. The conference feature allows groups of members to "talk" electronically by typing messages to one another.

To create your own forum, select "Starting Your Own Forum" (as shown in Figure 8.1) from the menu. You'll be given information on host privileges, pricing, and you will be asked for specifics on your forum topic.

To participate in an existing forum, review the directory listing to determine the number of the forum. Most forums can be accessed immediately. Some forums are "closed" which means you'll need to apply for access. Your

```
Custom Forums menu:


About Custom Forums
Access a Forum
Directory of Forums
Feedback
Starting Your Own Forum
Exit


Custom Forum> Enter Selection or Forum number:
```

Figure 8.1 Custom Forums menu

application will be send by electronic mail to the forum host. Access is usually granted within a day or two; simply enter in the number of the forum at the Custom Forum menu.

Some small-group forums may not be listed in the directory, because the Host has chosen not to make any information publicly available.

Environment SIG

Explore and discuss the many complex issues impacting on our global economy. Recycling energy generation and use, toxic chemicals and ecological philosophy are among the active discussion subjects; newsletters and other sources of data are available.

Foreign Languages SIG

An international meeting place and a venue for studying and practicing other languages, as well as a place to learn about other countries. The atmosphere is one of global communication.

GameSig

A club for game players everywhere. Members exchange advice, reviews, and product information — and, of course, play games! Some role-playing games are played in forum, special conferences, or via E-Mail.

Hobby Shop

Model builders, car buffs, model railroaders and rocketers, ham radio enthusiasts, and others come together to share ideas, product info, and software.

Internet SIG

DELPHI has created a special area devoted to the Internet. Within this Group are instructions for sending and receiving mail, and helpful hints for subscribing to mailing lists and contacting users of other services like CompuServe, America Online, and MCI Mail. The Internet SIG also has a database, with files related to the Internet.

For more on how to send mail via the Internet, see Chapter 9.

MensNet

An area where men can discuss the new Men's Movement organizations and philosophies, men's changing role in family and society, and responses to the Women's Liberation Movement.

Music City

For all who share interest and activity in music: by playing, listening to live or recorded music, or who have a general interest in the music business itself. An excellent resource for musicians involved in MIDI and other uses of computers in composition and performance.

New Age Network

For those interested in metaphysical topics such as astrology, meditation, alternative healing, and the like. The New Age Network also offers real-time classes and seminars, a forum (message base), and an online store from which you can order books, programs, and tapes.

Person to Person

As described by co-Sysop Jim Reed, "...the Person to Person Group is intended, above all, to be a meeting place, especially for young people, hence it is often call the Teen SIG. But, it is a place for anyone who wants to meet others and exchange correspondence and ideas."

Photography & Video

Provides the latest news and information photography for professionals and hobbyists. Many image files, programs and other resources are available.

Science Fiction SIG

Fans, readers, and writers join active forum discussions and lively weekly conferences. Award-winning authors offer advice and help to novices, and the databases contain information about upcoming conventions, movies, and other SF & Fantasy events.

Senior Forum

This is an area where computer-using seniors can communicate, socialize, and make new friends, using telecommunications technology to span generations and geographic distances.

Theological Network

The Network features discussions of a metaphysical, religious and theological nature. News of the religious world and software of interest to the clergy are also found here.

TV/Movie Group

Here is where members gather and discuss TV shows, movies, favorite actors, attend conferences with writers and directors or various TV shows, and more. A large collection of GIFs of actor and actresses and readable fiction based on TV shows shows are available.

WIDNet — Disability Network

Geared toward the disabled community, WIDNet provides comprehensive communications links between disabled individuals, communities, government and an extensive database of disability-oriented materials, ranging from Federal Register notices to ADA regulations.

World of Video Games

Information and discussions on video gaming. Talk with others about Nintendo, Genesis, TurboGrafx-16. Regular online conferences with industry experts and writers.

Writers Group

An active online group linking writers to editors and other writers. Writing and publishing tips for newcomers as well as an information resource for established writers; mutual support in conferences and Forum.

Chapter 9

Internet Services

ABOUT THE INTERNET

The Internet is a network linking millions of computer users worldwide. What people refer to as the "Internet" is actually a collection of thousands of smaller networks all interconnected using a common communication protocol or "language" for computers. This allows virtually all types of computer to participate in the exchange of data and information across the network. Some services operate on a simple PC and others run on supercomputers. The shared nature of the network allows for diverse information sources and the ability to connect to other computing centers to perform specialized tasks.

The Internet is growing and changing rapidly. The current Internet got its start as a national defense network called ARPAnet which later became the basis of the National Science Foundation Network, NFSNET. (NSFNET is still a large and active part of the Internet.) The original intent was to enhance research and education projects through open communication and exchange of data. Development of the telecommunications "backbone" was subsidized by the government. Until very recently use of the Internet has been restricted to people or organizations involved in research and education. The guidelines governing acceptable use were recently relaxed to allow commercial companies and online services like DELPHI to access the Internet. For this reason, the personality of the Internet still leans heavily toward education and research; many of the resources available through the Internet are provided by leading universities, government agencies, and high-tech companies.

Use of Internet services requires a willingness to learn and to explore. The network has generated a new vocabulary of terms that may sound foreign at first pass. The commands you need to know depend largely on where you want to go and what you want to accomplish. Your patience during the learning period will pay off; the wealth of information and contacts available through the Internet is unmatched.

The goal of this chapter is to introduce a few essential concepts and terms. More extensive help files are available directly off of the Internet menu. (Select *Internet* from DELPHI's main menu or type **GO INTERNET** at any prompt.) You can receive personal assistance by posting a message in the Internet message forum or participating in one of the regular conferences. There are also comprehensive Internet guidebooks available to purchase.

A few definitions will be required to understand the instructions in this chapter. The terms "host" and "domain" will be used to define a specific sub-network on the Internet. For example, DELPHI's host is identified as "delphi.com" to other people on the network. Harvard University's is "harvard.edu." The identifiers ".edu" and ".com" also convey something about what type of organization or network the host is. Here is a partial list of domestic domain identifiers and what they're used for:

com	commercial organizations
edu	educational organizations like universities and secondary schools.
gov	non-military government agencies
mil	military
org	other organizations
net	network providers

Foreign hosts usually use a two-letter domain identifier to signify the country in which the computer is located (e.g., the domain ".ca" is for Canadian host computers).

STORAGE CONSIDERATIONS

Because of the volume of information that can be sent and received via the Internet, it is critical that personal storage on DELPHI (files in mail and workspace) be managed properly. You should log in regularly to read new mail and delete messages immediately after reading them. If you use FTP to retrieve files to your workspace on DELPHI, be sure to download the files immediately and then delete them (downloading files from Workspace is covered in Chapter 18). Select *Using Internet Services* from the Internet menu for more helpful hints about managing mail and avoiding storage charges.

REGISTRATION

To use any Internet services on DELPHI, you must first register.* The registration process includes important rate information and use guidelines. By registering you are agreeing to abide by these terms.

To register for access to the Internet, simply select *Register/Cancel* from the Internet menu or type **GO INTERNET REGISTER** at any prompt. Once you register, you will immediately have access to all Internet features. You can also review the terms of use, check your registration status, or cancel at any time by choosing this same option.

* There is only one exception to this rule: if you already have access to the Internet and you just want to log into DELPHI from another network via Telnet, you don't need to register.

E-MAIL

Sending E-Mail:

As a member of DELPHI, you can exchange E-Mail with anyone who has access to the Internet. All you need to know is the person's user ID and the name of the host where they're located. Sending an Internet E-Mail message is just like sending DELPHI E-Mail, except you need to use a special format to route the message through the Internet. At the "To" prompt, type the word **Internet** and then immediately following — with no spaces — type the recipient's Internet address enclosed in quotes.

Here's what the commands would look like if you wanted to send a message to user JSMITH at Harvard:

```
MAIL>   send
To:     internet"jsmith@harvard.edu"
Subj:   DELPHI now offers full access to the Internet!
```

Then type in your text just like any other mail message on DELPHI.

You can send mail by first selecting *Mail* from the Internet services menu (or selecting mail from many other menus on DELPHI).

A special format is required when sending E-Mail to a member of the CompuServe online service; you must replace the comma which appears in every user ID with a period. Here's what the "To:" line of a typical message to a CompuServe user (user ID: 12345,6789) would look like:

```
To: internet"12345.6789@compuserve.com"
```

Here are examples for some other commercial services:

America Online —
```
To: internet"jsmith@aol.com"
```
MCI Mail —
```
To: internet"jsmith@mcimail.com"
```
AppleLink —
```
To:internet"jsmith@applelink.apple.com"
```

Receiving E-Mail:

To receive E-Mail through the Internet, you should have people at other networks send to YOURUSERNAME@delphi.com. For example, DELPHI's member service staff can be reached by sending mail to SERVICE@delphi.com. You may want to include this information on your business cards and other correspondence so you can be easily reached.

On a related subject, if you're looking to contact someone on the Internet, but you're not sure of their address, a suggested approach is to send mail to the "postmaster" account at a specific host asking for assistance. You can also try using *Whois* or *Finger* — utilities described in more detail after the next section, but these are far from comprehensive listings of users. Once again, the people providing assistance in the Internet message forum can offer some other recommendations.

If you receive a message through the Internet, you may notice that the message appears in your mail directory with a slightly different format. It will look something like this:

```
IN%"jsmith@harvard.edu"
```

There is no functional difference between this format and the format of internet"userid@hostname" described above; the word Internet has simply been set-up as a synonym to "IN%" since it's easier to remember. When you receive a message, you can send a reply by using the REPLY command. The "To:" and "Subject:" lines will be filled in automatically.

FTP

FTP, which stands for File Transfer Protocol, is a service which enables you to transfer files to and from other computers on the Internet. When you use FTP on DELPHI, a copy of every file you request is transferred to your personal workspace. From there you can download it for use on your own computer.

Many universities and other organizations make files available to the public. "Anonymous FTP" allows any Internet user, including DELPHI members, to access and download these files. You need only type the word "anonymous" at the login: prompt to gain access. At the password prompt you should enter your Internet address, i.e., JOHNSMITH@delphi.com.

To access the DELPHI FTP service, simply type FTP at the Internet menu. You will need the Internet address of the computer from which you want to retrieve files, and it is usually helpful to know the filenames and the directories where they are located. The Internet area on DELPHI contains the addresses of some popular FTP sites to get you started.

After typing in the Username and Password information for the remote host you'll have an active connection to the other computer. Typically there isn't much fanfare as the connection becomes active; you'll see a simple prompt that looks like this:

```
FTP>
```

At this point you can type **DIR** to see a listing of files and directories on the remote host. **LIST** and **LS** display a more abbreviated listing of filenames. The format of the display will depend on what type of computer you've connected to. You should be able to decipher filenames and directory names within the listing. (Don't be discouraged if you can't; just ask for little assistance from other members in the Internet forum.) If you want to change to another directory on the remote computer, you can type **CD <directoryname>**. Once you find a file you want to retrieve, use the **GET** command to move a file into your workspace.

For example, on a remote host you might type **GET "README"** to retrieve a file named README. Because other computers on the Internet have different file-naming conventions, you may need to put the file name in quotes in order to retrieve it (as in the "README" example above). You'll find this is necessary for any filenames that are in all capital letters or in mixed case. The FTP program assumes filenames are in all lowercase since this is the most common format.

Please keep in mind that you will incur storage charges for files left in your personal workspace if your monthly storage allowance is exceeded. Therefore, it is important that you download files that you want and immediately delete files that you don't want. Type **GO USING RATES STORAGE** for more information on storage and rates.

TELNET

You can use Telnet to actually log in to other computers on the Internet. For this reason, Telnet is often referred to as "remote log-in." The majority of hosts on the Internet require that you have an account to log into their computers (this is true of logging into DELPHI via Telnet). But many hosts allow for "anonymous" Telnet access. Some popular Internet search utilities like *Gopher* and *Archie* are available through Telnet. Several menu choices are set up to automatically connect to specific Telnet sites. If you choose one of them you'll wait for a few seconds as the connection is made and then you'll see the prompts of the other host. This is a good place to start experimenting with the features of Telnet. If you get stuck on any service and just want to return to DELPHI, you can use **Control** / (hold down the Control or CTRL key and press backslash). You'll see a reminder of this "escape" sequence as you log on to another host; it will say "use ^\ as an escape/attention character." The ^ symbol is used to represent the Control key.

If you are a DELPHI member and have direct access to the Internet through a university or another organization, you may use Telnet to access the DELPHI service. Using Telnet to access DELPHI carries no telecommunication surcharges, so you can Telnet to DELPHI around the clock at our regular rates, with no extra charges for daytime access.

To access the Telnet service, simply type TELNET at the Internet Services menu. When prompted, enter the Internet address of the computer you want to connect to. Many remote computers assume that your software is set to emulate a "VT-100" or "VT-102" terminal. You can usually specify VT-100 in the set-up or preferences menu of your communications software.

When connected to a remote computer via Telnet, the characters you type can be "echoed" to your screen display in a variety of ways. Depending on how this is done, you may see a small delay between when you type a character and when it appears on your screen, or your display may behave unexpectedly. The default method on DELPHI should work well for most users, but if you are having trouble, see the help files online or inquire in the Internet forum for alternatives.

UTILITIES

Because the Internet is so large, the task of finding a specific piece of information can seem formidable. Fortunately there are a series of ever-improving utilities that can help you in your search for the information you need.

Archie

Archie is a powerful utility used to search for specific files across the Internet. You can select a preassigned Archie site from the menu or use another site if you know the address — there are many Archie servers on the Internet.

Archie maintains a fairly current list of files available from a wide variety of Internet sites. If you know the name of a file, Archie will search the list and tell you where the file is located. You can then use FTP to retrieve it. You may also run a search on any string of characters that would likely be used in the name of a file or directory that you might be interested in. Since people tend to name directories and files so as to be descriptive of their contents, you will often find interesting files simply by searching for a word that relates to your field of interest. Filenames are often case sensitive in Archie. If a filename includes capital letters, enclose it in quotes.

If the Archie service is busy, there are alternate Archie systems that you can access by using any of these Internet addresses:

```
archie.sura.net
archie.unl.edu
archie.ans.net
```

Like other services on the Internet, these addresses are subject to change Check the Internet forum or database for an up-to-date listing.

Finger

Finger is a utility that can be used to "point" to other users on the Internet. In some cases you can find out information about the person and when they were last online. Other systems provide information files through Finger. For example, you might be able to learn more about NEARnet (a regional network provider in New England) by pointing to "nearnet-staff@nic.near.net". Many systems have disabled access via Finger. If Finger doesn't work for the address you've entered, you'll see an error message.

Gopher

Gopher is a menu-driven service which lets you browse resources on the Internet, read text files, and retrieve files of all kinds. The name "Gopher" was given by its creators at the University of Minnesota. It has a dual meaning: the service was designed to help users "go fer" things on the Internet and the University of Minnesota is known as home of the Golden Gophers.

Gopher uses FTP and Telnet to retrieve information for you, but hides the details behind a single menu system that's relatively easy to navigate. To use Gopher, select Utilities from the Internet menu, then select Gopher. At the login: prompt, enter GOPHER. Before entering the Gopher service, make sure your communication program is set for VT-100 or VT-102 terminal emulation. Check your program's documentation if you don't know how to set this.

Use your arrow keys to select an item from any Gopher menu. If you can't find what you're looking for on one Gopher server, you may select *Other Gopher Servers* from the top menu as well. Use "u" to go to the previous menu, and "q" to exit the Gopher service. Watch the bottom of the screen for special instructions.

WAIS: Wide Area Information System

WAIS (pronouced "wayz") is a powerful searching tool which allows you to search over 300 information sources by keyword. If you're looking for information on a particular topic, WAIS can help you find it. Although easy to get started with, WAIS is a complex system with many features too numerous to cover here.

To use WAIS, select Utilities from the Internet menu, then select WAIS. Before entering the WAIS service, make sure your communication program is set for VT-100 or VT-102 terminal emulation. Check your program's documentation if you don't know how to set this.

Upon entering the WAIS service, you will see a numbered list of sources, arranged alphabetically. Type a question mark (?) to see a list of available commands. You can search one source at a time, or any number of sources simultaneously. If you don't know which sources to search, start by searching the "directory of servers," which is itself a WAIS server, listed under the d's. To select servers for a search, use your arrow keys to highlight each source and press the spacebar. If you know the number of the source, you can go directly to it by typing in the number. WAIS marks each source you select with an asterisk. After you've selected all the sources you wish to search, type a "w" and type in your descriptive keyword(s). If you enter multiple keywords, separated by a space, WAIS will find documents containing all of your keywords. When the search is complete, WAIS will show you a list of documents found, with the documents containing the most "hits" at the top of the list. You may then display any of the documents found by highlighting the entry and pressing the spacebar.

Whois

Whois is both a directory of Internet users, and a utility for searching this directory. Started in the early days of ARPAnet as a directory of people running and researching the network, *Whois* now contains about 70,000 entries. This represents only a small fraction of the Internet community, so if the person you are looking for isn't involved in the operation or development of the Internet, you probabaly won't find them listed here. However, *Whois* can serve as a good starting point for user IDs and hostnames related to who you ultimately want to contact.

There are now literally millions of users of the Internet, and unfortunately, there is no single directory of users that you can search to find a particular person. If you know a person's name and the Internet address of the computer he or she uses, you can find them using the Finger utility discussed earlier in this chapter. At this time, better utilities for finding individuals are being developed, and we will be making these new services available to DELPHI members wherever possible.

World-Wide Web (WWW)

The World-Wide Web is one of the most exciting new tools available on the Internet. It is a "hypertext" service which connects widely scattered documents with "links," or references to other documents. You can jump to any linked document, which itself may contain links to even more documents. In this way you may move from one document to another, delving ever deeper into whatever subject interests you. The amount of information available through WWW is still fairly limited, but WWW provides a fascinating glimpse into the future of the Internet.

Chapter 10
Mail Services

FAX Service

Need to send a message to a Facsimile (FAX) machine, but don't have a FAX machine? You don't need one: DELPHI provides fast, efficient, and economical FAX delivery service to any FAX machine or network in the world. DELPHI's FAX service is an electronic gateway to the world.

All you need is a message in standard ASCII text (typed in online, or previously uploaded), and the area code and telephone number of the receiving FAX machine in the United States, Canada and the Caribbean. To send messages to FAX machines in other countries, you must supply the country code, city code and phone number.

Creating a FAX Message

There are three ways to create a FAX message.
1. For short messages, you can enter the message online after you have provided the telephone number(s) of the destination FAX machines.
2. If you think you'll need to edit a FAX message, you can create it in Workspace, and use DELPHI's text editors.
3. If you have a lengthy FAX message and wish to check the spelling and expect to do extensive editing, you can create the message on your computer, save it to disk as a text file. Then, upload it to your personal Workspace using your preferred file-transfer protocol or send it directly to the FAX system when it prompts for text. (See Chapter 18 for details on uploading.)

If you create your message on a word-processor to upload to workspace, it must be in *7-bit ASCII* text format. You will usually have to convert the file to 7-bit ASCII. This is normally done with a conversion utility or via a "print to file/disk" option. Consult your word processor's documentation for details.

FAX Message Format

Line length. No line in the message should be longer than 80 characters.

Page breaks. FAX machines normally print incoming messages without page breaks. If you wish to place page breaks in a message to force the receiving FAX machine to begin a new page at a specific point use the special command, **/PAGE**. First, type **/PAGE** at the beginning of a line by itself at the very beginning of your message (this lets DELPHI know that you will be specifying page breaks in the text). Thereafter, type **/PAGE** by itself at the beginning a line preceding the point where you wish a new page to begin.

Sending a FAX Message

To send a FAX message, first type **FAX** at the DELPHI Mail menu. You will be asked if you wish instructions on preparing and sending FAX messages and rate information.

Entering Destination Numbers and Receipt Notification. Whether you read the instructions or not, you will then be prompted to enter the area code for the destination FAX machine. Enter the area code (or, if the destination is to a country other than the United States, Canada, or the Caribbean, enter **I**, and you will be prompted for the country code and the rest of the phone number). When prompted, enter the phone number.

At the next prompt, you can enable receipt notification which requests an E-Mail message be sent to you, at a small extra charge, telling you the date and time the message was delivered.

You'll then be asked whether there are additional numbers to which you want the message to be sent. If you type **Y** at the prompt, you'll be prompted for the phone number and receipt notification again, and be asked if there are additional numbers. You can enter as many destination numbers as you wish.

Sending a Workspace File. When you have finished entering the destination number or numbers, type **N** at the prompt asking if there will be additional phone numbers. You will see this prompt:

```
Enter the name of the file that will be the body of the
message, or press RETURN to enter the message now. No line
should be longer than 90 characters.
Filename or RETURN? message.file«RETURN»
```

At this point, you enter the name of the file in your Workspace that you wish to send. Note that the file you send can be one that you uploaded, created online, or even a message you received via Telex or E-Mail.

Entering a Message Directly. To enter a message "live," press «RETURN» at the *Filename or RETURN?* prompt.

```
Filename or RETURN? «RETURN»
```

If you have a short message, type it in here. If you have a message file in your personal computer, send it here.

Press **Control-Z** when you are finished entering or sending text. (You can cancel message entry at any time by pressing **Control-C**.)

Final Verification

After you enter the filename and press «RETURN», DELPHI will tell you the number of characters in the file to be sent, to how many numbers it will be sent, and the approximate charge. Then you will be asked if it is okay to send the message; type **Y** and the message will be sent.

You can cancel the process at any time by pressing **Control-C**.

Notes on Message Delivery. While you may request a "return receipt" for a FAX message, DELPHI will notify you automatically if a FAX message could not be delivered.

FAX messages are usually sent within minutes of the time that you posted them. DELPHI automatically redials busy or "no-answer" numbers.

Rates and Charges

Rates are based on a FAX "page," which is 2500 characters, and a FAX half-page, which is 1250 characters. If a FAX message is less than a full page, you are charged for a full page; additional half pages (or portions thereof) are charged at a lower rate.

If you send a FAX message to multiple numbers, each message is billed at the same rate.

Current rates are listed online in the FAX help section. To get help and rates, type HELP FAX from the Mail menu, or enter the FAX area and specify that you would like help by typing "yes" when asked if you would like help.

If you wish to be notified of the date and time of delivery of a FAX message you've sent, there is a small fee per message. There is no charge for the automatic notification of non-delivery.

MAIL (Electronic)

Here you can send, read, forward, and reply to electronic mail messages. DELPHI's Electronic Mail system is fully described in Chapter 11.

Scan for New Messages

Prints a listing of new messages waiting to be read.

SetMail

Select SetMail at the DELPHI Mail menu to reset the counter that keeps track of the number of new (unread) mail messages waiting for you.

Telex

Telex is another gateway to the world outside DELPHI. You can send messages and documents to any of millions of Telex users around the world. There is a small, extra charge for sending—but not for receiving—Telex messages. That extra charge is stated online.

You can easily receive Telex messages at no extra charge, without having to open a Telex account. Or you can open your own Telex account through DELPHI at a minimal monthly charge and enjoy priority handling of your incoming messages. Either way, you can read, forward, file, and/or extract incoming Telex messages just as you would any E-Mail message.

Sending a Telex Message

Sending a Telex message via DELPHI is simple. All you need to do is select Send Telex and provide the Telex address number(s) and answer a few questions to let DELPHI know whether the message you are sending is domestic or international. You must have the country code if it is a foreign address other than Canada or Mexico. Then, type in your text message and press **Control-Z** when you're finished.

Message Format. When composing your Telex message, follow these guidelines:

- Easylink, Telex, and Worldwide Telex messages can be no longer than 50,000 characters.
- The line length of your message should be limited to 67 characters. A line of greater length will wrap to the next line.

Domestic Telex Service. Domestic Telex service includes the U.S.A., as well as Canada and Mexico. (The Mexico (00) or Canada (0) code that precedes an address is inserted by DELPHI if necessary.) Telex Numbers are up to 10 Digits. Do not include any spaces or hyphens (-) between the digits.

Telex Messages Via Specified Carriers. Domestic Telex messages can be sent via MCI, ITT, WUI, TRT, FTCC, and GRAPHNET anywhere in the U.S.A. You enter the numeric part of the address only (i.e., for RCA2967889 you enter 2967889). The Special Code (71) is inserted by DELPHI.

Foreign Telex Service. For all countries except the U.S., Canada, and Mexico, the network code is inserted by DELPHI. You must, however, provide the international code. Follow these procedures:
- Enter the 3-digit Country Code followed by the Telex address when requested.
- Do not include any spaces or hyphens (–) between the digits in the country code and Telex number.

A complete, searchable list of international codes is available at the USING-DELPHI menu.

Sending to Multiple Telex Addresses. You may include as many addresses as will fit within the 200-character address line limit. Multiple addresses should be separated by commas. If you intend to include foreign or Mexican addresses in your string then please enter them one at a time so DELPHI can prefix the correct country codes. You will save time by entering your domestic addresses first on the same line, separated by commas.

Receiving a Telex Message

If you wish to receive a Telex message on DELPHI, ask the person sending it to you to use the Telex ID 62918703. This is DELPHI's Easylink/Western Union Telex ID, and will route the message into the DELPHI system. A few international members may find that this Telex ID does not work. If so, they should use 5106017663 instead. This is DELPHI's worldwide TWX/Telex number.

In order for DELPHI to enter this message into your mailbox, your membername ALONE must appear as the first line of the message.

For example:

```
62918703
<YOUR MEMBERNAME>
Hi, Don. Sending you a Telex from Singapore.
Please clean the pool, be back on Friday.
Arlan
```

Obtaining a Private Telex Number. If you have a lot of incoming Telex traffic, you may wish to obtain your own private Telex number, in which case you will receive Telexes without delay, and the sender will not have to bother with your DELPHI membername. Messages can be sent to you just as they would be to anyone who has a Telex number.

In addition, delivery notices are sent automatically to you via E-Mail, advising you of the date and time your message is delivered. To register for your private telex number, select "Apply for Telex Number" on the MAIL TELEX menu.

There is a small monthly fee for maintaining a private Telex number via DELPHI. The fee is much less than that charged by Telex carriers for individual accounts.

Telex Codes and Rates

To see a list of Telex Codes online, type select "Rates and Telex Codes" on the MAIL TELEX menu. You will be prompted to enter a country name; enter a name and DELPHI will supply the international Telex code for that country, along with the charges per 200-character unit. If you wish to see a complete list for all the countries in the world, type * at the prompt.

Translation Services

Use DELPHI's translation services to have your documents or messages translated into over 100 languages. All exchanges can be made immediately via E-Mail. The rates and languages available for translation services are specified online.

Sending Text for Translation. Text submitted for translation may be in one of several different formats, including PC and Macintosh, and a number of word processors, such as WordPerfect and Microsoft Word. In many cases, the material needs to be put in the Workspace area on DELPHI first, as a binary file, and cannot come through as just a mail message. To submit text for translation, select "Submit" on the menu, and follow the prompts.

Workspace

This selection takes you to your personal Workspace, where you can create files, prepare files for sending, edit or download files extracted in E-Mail. See Chapter 18 (Workspace) for more information on using your personal Workspace.

Getting Help

Type **HELP** at the *DMAIL>* prompt for a summary of Mail and a list of topics on which detailed help is available. Type **HELP** within a service to obtain detailed help with that service, or type **HELP** followed by the name of a topic for help with that topic.

Chapter 11
Electronic Mail

Chapter 11

Advanced E-Mail Commands

E-Mail Overview

Electronic Mail (E-Mail) is a powerful private messaging system, and one of DELPHI's most useful features. Special commands provide for versatile file handling and you can personalize and customize E-Mail to suit your needs and preferences.

Like all DELPHI members, you have a personal electronic mailbox to which your E-Mail is delivered. DELPHI's sophisticated E-Mail software allows you to handle the messages you receive with ease. For example, a simple command sends a reply to any message. You can also send copies of your mail to other members, and file, copy, and delete E-Mail messages in several different ways.

Sending messages is easy and convenient, too. There are no addresses to remember—all you need to know is the membername of the person to whom you wish to send a message. Each message is automatically stamped with the time and date, and you can place a subject line on each message you send. Other features allow you to return a "carbon copy" of any message you send to your mailbox, and to place your full name, nickname, or company name in the message header.

This chapter presents DELPHI Electronic Mail in three segments. The first is an overview of E-Mail organization, structure, and commands. Next, you'll find a discussion of the most frequently used commands—commands you'll use to send, read, reply to, delete, and otherwise handle individual messages. The final section covers the advanced commands used to handle groups of messages and perform certain other tasks. These commands are primarily concerned with organizing a filing system for your messages.

Files

Your mailbox is organized first into files. These files are stored in your Workspace, and have the filename extension .MAI. However, you shouldn't attempt to read, delete, or edit these files in your Workspace.

Folders

To continue the file cabinet analogy, folders are like the paper folders often found within a file cabinet drawer. Folders can be created within an E-Mail file to store related messages (i.e., all messages on the same subject, from the same member, or whatever).

Messages can be moved or copied to and from folders, and extracted or deleted from folders. E-Mail automatically creates and deletes several folders as needed: WASTEBASKET, NEWMAIL, and MAIL. You can create other folders.

Messages

A DELPHI Electronic Mail message is composed of two parts: the Message Header and the Message Text.

The Message Header contains the following information:
• The number of the message within a folder or selection
• The date and time the message was received
• The folder name
• Whom the message is from (From:)
• To whom the message is addressed (To:)
• The subject of the message (Subj:)

```
#9                  25-JUL-1992 23:53:17                     NEWMAIL

From:   BOS1A::AUTHOR  "RALPH ROBERTS/ WRITERS GROUP MGR"
To:     KZIN, BUCKETHEAD
Subj:   Shareware


        Interesting how shareware is getting around... we should
look into writing some.
        Unlike most software publishers, shareware publishers
provide the documentation on the disk, so the special formatting
requirements for this type of doc (formatting for on-screen
display without inserting codes that word processors will reject,
etc.) will have to be taken into consideration on any such
project.


Ralph
```

Figure 11.1 DELPHI E-Mail Message

The remainder of the E-Mail message is the Message Text. This is usually textual information, however E-Mail can also be used to send binary files.

Figure 11.1 shows a typical DELPHI E-Mail message. The first line of the header shows the relative number of the message, the date and time it was received, and the folder name. The second line shows the membername of the person who sent the message. There may be a Personal Name, enclosed in quotes, after the sender's membername, "RALPH ROBERTS/WRITERS GROUP MGR." The third line of the header shows to whom the message is addressed. This line may show a single membername, or multiple member-names separated by commas, thus: KZIN, BUCKETHEAD. If the member has set his E-Mail parameters to have copies of messages he sends returned to his mailbox, you will see his name, as well. If the message was sent using a Distribution List, an "at sign" and a filename will appear on the To: line, like this: @CONF.DIS. A Distribution List is a file containing membernames which is used as an address file for sending the same message to a small group of members. The fourth line is the Subject line (Subj:). Here, you'll find a one-line description of the message's subject.

Getting To and From E-Mail

To get to E-Mail:
- From the DELPHI Main Menu, type MAIL MAIL
- From the top menu of one of DELPHI's Groups and Clubs, type MAIL
- From Conference, Workspace or a Groups Databases, type /MAIL (Note that when you are in Conference, you can send a one-line E-Mail message without entering E-Mail by simply typing /MAIL [membername] [message]).

To exit E-Mail, simply type **EXIT** or press **Control-Z**. At that time, all messages that have been put in the WASTEBASKET folder by the DELETE command will be purged and all new messages that you have read but not filed or deleted will be filed in the MAIL folder.

MAIN E-MAIL COMMANDS

Special Control-Key Commands

Control-C is used to cancel various E-Mail operations. Pressing **Control-C** at a *To:* or *Subj:* prompt, or while creating a message, will cancel an E-Mail message. Pressing **Control-C** interrupts directory and message displays.

Control-Z sends an E-Mail message or exits E-Mail. If you press **Control-Z** while you are creating a E-Mail message, the message will be sent. If you press **Control-Z** at the *MAIL>* prompt, you will return to the menu from which you entered E-Mail.

SEND

The easiest way to send E-Mail is to type **SEND** (or **MAIL**) at the *MAIL>* prompt. The prompt *To:* will appear. Type the membername(s) to which you want to send the message. You may send the same mail message to more than one person by entering membernames separated by commas.

The next prompt you'll see will be *Subj:*. Type the subject of the message and press «RETURN». You'll see a line telling you to enter your message.

When you've finished your message, press **Control-Z** to send it. See Figure 10.2 for a step-by-step "walk-through" of the basic SEND procedure. By the way, you can send a mail message to yourself as well as to other members.

```
MAIL> SEND
To:     MODELMIKE
Subj:   New scale rocket model.

Enter your message below. Press CTRL/Z when complete, or CTRL/C to
quit:

Mike,
Thought you'd be interested to know that Estes Industries is
coming out with a scale model of the Mercury Redstone! It's
a re-issue, actually, as they offered the same model back in
the mid-1960's.

Alan
^Z
```

Figure 11.2 How to send an E-Mail message.

All you have to do is type your membername at the *To:* prompt.

Cancel a Message at any time during the creation of the message or the header by pressing **Control-C**. You will return to the *MAIL>* prompt, and the message will not be sent.

Making Corrections. If you connected to DELPHI via SprintNet or Tymnet and need to back up and delete characters on a line, pressing your computer's back-space key (or **Control-H**) will move the cursor back one character. You may then type over the character, which may or may not have been deleted by the backspace). If you dialed DELPHI directly, press the DELETE key to delete.

Redisplay a Line by pressing **Control-R**. When you resume typing, the charac-ters will be placed where the cursor was previously located, no matter what you see on your screen.

Delete a Line by pressing **Control-U** or **Control-X** and resume typing. Although the line may not be erased from your screen, the version of the message that is sent will not contain the deleted line.

SEND Qualifiers

SEND /CC causes a prompt for carbon copy names, a list of additional people to receive the message. Enter the names just as you would at the *To:* prompt.

SEND /LAST is useful when you send a message and suddenly (before you exit from E-Mail) realize you have neglected to send the message to everyone who should receive it (and possibly to yourself as a file copy). Resend the most recent E-Mail message you've sent without retyping it by typing **SEND /LAST** at the *Mail>* prompt.

SEND /SELF sends a copy of the message you are sending to you.

Sending Files

You may send any file from your Workspace via E-Mail. Simply type **SEND [filename].[ext]**, after which you will be prompted for a membername and subject. After you enter the required information, a copy of the specified Workspace file will be sent. NOTE: You must type a period (.) after the filename even if there is no filename extension; otherwise DELPHI assumes a filename extension of .TXT, and if the file doesn't end in .TXT, DELPHI will tell you the file cannot be located. Thus, a file named MESSAGE must be entered as MESSAGE. , while a file name MESSAGE.NEW must be entered as MESSAGE.NEW

By preparing the message in Workspace, you can use DELPHI's online editors to make corrections or changes before sending (See Chapter 19).

Sending Internet Mail

DELPHI is connected to the Internet! With your personal membername and DELPHI's electronic mail, you can communicate with millions of people at colleges, universities, companies, and other online services. See also Chapter 9 for a complete listing of DELPHI's Internet Services.

All members are required to register if they wish to use Internet mail. To register, choose Internet from the Main menu . Once in this area, choose the "register" option to gain access to Internet mail.

Sending Internet Mail. Internet mail addresses are a combination of the name the person uses on the service, followed by an "@" and then the Internet domain name used to identify the service itself. For example, the Internet address for DELPHI Member Services is *service@delphi.com.*

All Internet domain names (hosts) consist of two parts: the first part is usually the name of the organization (or an abbreviation) and the suffix is the type or organization it is. Businesses use the suffix "com," educational institutions use "edu," military sites use "mil," and government offices use "gov." Therefore, a person's address at America Online might be johnsmith@aol.com and a person at Harvard University might be johnsmith@harvard.edu.

At the *MAIL>* prompt, type **SEND**. At the *To:* prompt, enter **internet"membername@hostname"**, where the membername is the person's account name on the other host and the hostname is the Internet address for the host. Note there is no space between the word Internet and the first quotation mark. You then write and send the message as you would an electronic mail message. Here's an example how you would send a message through the Internet to member JOHNSMITH on America Online:

```
MAIL> send
To:      internet"johnsmith@aol.com"
Subj:  test message
```

Internet Addresses and Other Networks. Here are some sample address formats for other commercial services.

To send to CompuServe members:

Domain name: compuserve.com
Example: 12345.6789@compuserve.com

Note: Compuserve's membernames usually consist of several numbers, a comma, and then a few more numbers. The comma within the user number needs to be replaced with a period when sending an Internet message.

To send to America Online members:

Domain name: aol.com
Example: johnsmith@aol.com

To send to MCI Mail users:

Domain name: mcimail.com or mci.com
Example: johnsmith@mcimail.com or mci.com

To send to AT&T mail users:

Domain name: attmail.com
Example: johnsmith@attmail.com

To send to AppleLink users:

Domain name: applelink.apple.com
Example: johnsmith@applelink.apple.com

Note that some commercial mail services have charges associated with receiving Internet mail. America Online has Internet mail file size and mailbox limits. Be sure to check with the user directly prior to sending messages.

Receiving Internet Mail. DELPHI's host address is "delphi.com". To receive mail, have the person sending the mail direct it to:

```
"<your membername>@delphi.com"
```

So, for example, if your DELPHI membername is JOHNSMITH, you tell them to send mail to **johnsmith@delphi.com**.

Each member is given a monthly Internet mail allocation. This is not a storage allocation; it is the total volume of incoming and outgoing mail messages. Further details are provided during the registration procedure.

Sending E-Mail Using Distribution Lists

Using a distribution list is a convenient way to send the same message to more than one member. With a distribution list, you only have to enter a message and message header one time, no matter how many people you send the message to. A distribution list is a Workspace file containing the member-names of the people you want on your mailing list. You must name the file with a .DIS suffix. Example: MARS.DIS

Each name in the file must be on a line by itself, as shown below. Do not enter extra words or extraneous characters; DELPHI will not recognize these as membernames. Check the spelling of each membername carefully, too.

```
AUTHOR
ROSAB
RICKWILBER
RESNICK
```

To send an E-Mail message to everyone listed in a .DIS file, type **@[file-name]** at E-Mail's *To:* prompt. Thus, if you wanted to send a message to everyone listed in the MARS.DIS file mentioned above, you would type **@MARS**.

Distribution lists should be kept small. You will be charged for storage if you send to a large group of members. The best way to get information to a large group is to use the Forum message system in an appropriate group or club (see Chapter 4).

DIRECTORY

DELPHI keeps track of the messages you send by date, sender, and subject. The messages are sorted by the date — oldest to newest. The order in which the mail is stored is called the Directory.

The **DIRECTORY** command presents a summary of all your messages. This listing includes the relative number of each message, the name of the sender, the date the message was received, and the subject of each message. If you have no messages in your mailbox, but want to try out the DIRECTORY command, SEND a message to yourself.

When you want to see a list of all the MAIL messages you have collected, enter **DIRECTORY** and you'll see a list similar to this:

```
# From          Date                Subject

1 ROSAB         12-MAY -1992        Thank you!
2 KZIN          21-JUN-1992         Science Fiction SIG
3 AUTHOR        4-JUL-1992          My new book
4 RESNICK       17-AUG-1992         Gossip
```

Optional DIRECTORY Qualifiers

DIRECTORY [folder name] lists all of the messages in the specified folder. This command also makes the specified folder the current folder, which means that READ and other commands will operate on the messages in that folder.

DIRECTORY /BEFORE (and DIRECTORY /SINCE) list all messages sent before (or since) the specified date. The proper format is : **DIRECTORY /BEFORE=DD-MMM-YYYY.** In this example, MMM represents the first three letters of the month; the other qualifiers are numbers for the date and year.

DIRECTORY /FULL will show the file size of all messages in the current folder, as well as noting messages to which you've sent a reply.

DIRECTORY /NEW displays a summary of new mail messages (messages in the NEWMAIL folder). This command also moves you to the folder NEWMAIL.

DIRECTORY /START=# lists a summary of messages in the current folder beginning with the specified message number. This is useful if it takes more than one screen page to display your Mail Directory.

DIRECTORY /FOLDERS displays a list of all folders in the current Mail file. Only the names of the folders are displayed; not their contents. /FOLDERS cannot be used with other DIRECTORY qualifiers.

READ

When you enter E-Mail, the current folder will be either the MAIL folder or the NEWMAIL folder. If you have no unread messages waiting, the current folder will be MAIL. Unread messages are waiting in NEWMAIL.

When you have E-Mail waiting, you'll be notified at logon:

```
You have 9 new Mail messages
```

The **READ** command is used to display a mail message. When used alone, READ always displays the next message. When used with a message number, READ displays the specified message.

«RETURN» functions the same as READ in displaying the first page of a message. If you are reading a message and press «RETURN» at the end of a page, you will see the next page of the message.

Optional READ Qualifiers

READ [message number]. The relative number of each message is listed in the mail Directory (obtained with the DIRECTORY command), and immediately preceding the message when you read your mail. For example, to read message 9 you can type **READ 9** or just **9**.

READ [folder name] displays the first message in the specified folder. This command makes the specified folder the current folder.

READ /BEFORE and READ /SINCE display messages sent before or since a specified date. (Example: **READ /BEFORE=12-JUL-1992**).

READ /NEW reads messages that arrive while you are in E-Mail.

Related Commands

BACK displays the message previous to the current message.

CURRENT redisplays current message from the beginning.

FIRST displays the first (or lowest-numbered) message in the directory.

LAST displays the last (or highest-numbered) message in the directory.

NEXT. If you encounter a long message and wish to skip reading all of the pages, type **NEXT**. NEXT moves to the next message.

REPLY

DELPHI Electronic Mail makes it easy to reply to a message. If you type **REPLY** during or after reading a message, DELPHI will create a message header for you. The *To:* and *Subj:* headers will contain the name of the person you are replying to and the subject used on the original message.

When you receive a message and want to respond to it, enter **REPLY** and the header will appear.

Optional REPLY Qualifiers

REPLY /CC allows you to direct your reply to additional people.

REPLY /SELF. If you wish to have a copy of a particular reply returned to you, type **REPLY /SELF**.

REPLY [filename.ext] sends a file from your Workspace as a reply to a message. As with other REPLY options, the addressee and subject will be entered for you. This is the easiet way to prepare a reply message with the DELPHI online editor.

FORWARD

You may often receive messages that you would like to share with another member or members. The **FORWARD** command allows you to do this. FORWARD creates a new message with your name and a subject you enter as the header. A copy of the message you are forwarding, with or without the original header, makes up the message itself.

Copies of a message may be forwarded to more than one member by entering multiple membernames at the *To:* prompt. Forwarded messages are not deleted from your E-Mail file.

FORWARD /NOHEADER sends the current message to the addressee, without the original header.

DELETE

As you accumulate E-Mail messages, you'll find that many are not important enough to keep. To simplify mail management and reduce the space taken up by your E-Mail file in your Workspace, you'll want to delete such messages as frequently as possible.

When you read a new message, unless you delete or file it, the message is automatically placed in your MAIL folder. So if you do not wish to save the message (and possibly pay storage charges for keeping it), it is a good idea to delete the message right after you read it by typing **DELETE**.

You can send binary information (such as spreadsheets or graphics) to another DELPHI member by uploading the file as binary (non-text) to Workspace and using the command *SEND [filename.ext]* at the MAIL prompt (where [filename.ext] is the name you chose when uploading). The recipient uses the EXTRACT command to make a file in his workspace which can be downloaded. It is important for both of you to DELETE the file from your workspaces. In addition, the recipient should DELETE the mail message right after extracting it from the NEWMAIL folder.

If you type **DIRECTORY** after you have deleted a message (or messages), the deleted message(s) will be displayed as such. In this sample Directory, message #2 has just been deleted:

```
# From          Date              Subject

1 ROSAB         12-MAY-1992       Thank you!
2 (Deleted)
3 AUTHOR        4-JUL-1992        My new book
4 RESNICK       17-AUG-1992       Gossip
```

DELETE alone deletes the current message.

Optional DELETE Qualifiers

DELETE [message number]. To delete a message by number, type **DELETE** followed by the number of the message you wish to delete. For example, if you wished to delete the second message in a group of messages, you would type **DELETE 2**.

DELETE /ALL deletes all messages in the current folder. If you have used **SELECT**, DELETE/ALL only deletes messages selected.

Recovering Deleted Messages

Deleted messages are automatically moved to a special temporary folder called WASTEBASKET. They are not permanently deleted until you exit E-Mail. If you set the current folder to WASTEBASKET, you will find all the messages you have deleted from NEWMAIL or other folders.

If you change your mind after deleting a message, type **SELECT WASTEBASKET** (see SELECT for more details). DIRECTORY will display a list of the messages in the WASTEBASKET. You'll be able to read them with READ.

To recover a deleted message, read it and type **FILE MAIL**; the message will be moved to your MAIL folder.

ADVANCED E-MAIL COMMANDS

SELECT

SELECT is used for two purposes. Its primary application is to change the current folder (from MAIL to WASTEBASKET, for example).

SELECT is also used to establish a temporary "folder" or group of messages within a folder, based on dates. You can then access or manipulate the group of messages. You can use other advanced E-Mail commands, including **EXTRACT, SEARCH,** and **FILE,** to handle a selected group as one unit. Or, you can READ and DELETE a selected group.

Manipulating several messages as a group can save quite a bit of time. You may, for example, wish to delete all messages sent before a certain date. If you use SELECT to create a group of messages sent before the date within a folder, you can then use DELETE /ALL to delete only those messages.

SELECT can be used with the qualifiers /**BEFORE** or /**SINCE**, and/or with a folder name, and with /TO=Name, /FROM=Name, or /SUBJ=Text to select messages based on who they are from or to or what is in the subject line.

NOTE: If you do not use a folder name with a SELECT command, the command defaults to the MAIL folder. Thus, if you wanted to select all messages sent before July 21, 1992, in the folder named PERSONAL, you would type **SELECT PERSONAL/BEFORE=21-JUL-1992**.

EXTRACT (filename)

If you receive a large document as a E-Mail message from another member and you wish to transfer it to your Workspace for editing, submission to a Group's database, or downloading, type **EXTRACT [filename]**. If you do not include a filename with the command, you will be prompted for one. If you do not specify an extension with the filename, the file will be saved with the extension .TXT in your Workspace.

EXTRACT does not delete mail messages from your E-Mail file. **EXTRACT TT** causes a message to be displayed nonstop (without the "Press RETURN to return to reading your mail" prompt), because TT is the filename of your screen. It can be used with the qualifier /ALL (**EXTRACT /ALL TT**) to display all messages in your folder nonstop (convenient if you want to capture your mail messages with your computer's buffer for later reading).

Optional EXTRACT Qualifiers:

EXTRACT /ALL copies all messages in the folder or group into the specified Workspace file. Each message in the file will be separated by a form feed.

Do not use EXTRACT/ALL if the folder contains binary files (EXTRACT/ALL produces a file which is only suitable to be downloaded as text). If you receive binary files they should be extracted and deleted individually before using EXTRACT/ALL to file the remaining messages into a text file.

EXTRACT /APPEND adds the message to an existing file in your Workspace.

EXTRACT /NOHEADER copies a message to the specified Workspace file without the mail header information. This is useful for large documents or program or data, with which the header would be inappropriate.

SEARCH

SEARCH [character string] scans every entry in your current folder or selected group for a match with the characters following the command. If the character string occurs anywhere in a message (including the *To:* or *Subject:* fields), the message is displayed. (Example: **SEARCH the matter of the contract**)

You need not retype a search string to continue searching for the next occurrence of that string once you've entered it. Simply type **SEARCH** to continue the search after a "found" message is displayed.

The SEARCH command operates on groups created with SELECT and on entire folders.

FILE

As explained at the beginning of this chapter, Mail allows you to move (file) messages from one folder to another. This feature is useful for organizing a large number of messages into related groups. You may, for instance, put all messages of a business nature into a folder named BUSINESS, and all personal messages into a folder named PERSONAL. Or, you might put all messages from a particular member into a folder with his or her name.

Type **FILE [foldername]** after reading a message to file that individual message. **Type FILE [foldername] /ALL** for entire folders or groups of messages created with the SELECT command.

A folder is created when you direct a message to a non-existent folder. If, for example, there is no folder named PERSONAL in your mail file, and you type **FILE PERSONAL** after reading a message, you will be asked if you want a folder created with that name. If you wish to have a folder created without prompting, type **/NOCONFIRM** after the FILE command and folder name. A folder is deleted when all of the messages it contains are deleted or moved and you exit from the folder.

SET

SET is used to set various attributes, as described below:

SET COPY_SELF SEND and SET COPY_SELF REPLY return copies of messages you SEND or REPLY to your mailbox. **SET COPY_SELF NOSEND** and **SET COPY_SELF NOREPLY** cancel this feature. You can temporarily override this command by typing **SEND /NOSELF** when you send a message.

SET FORWARD establishes a forwarding address for your mail. Type **SET FORWARD,** followed by the membername of the person you wish your mail forwarded to, to establish a forwarding address. **SET NOFORWARD** cancels a forwarding address. You will not receive copies of forwarded messages! This could be useful if you expect not to be online for a few weeks and want important messages to be read by a friend.

SET PERSONAL_NAME enables you to append a field following the *From:* field of mail messages you send. You can fill this field with your full name, business name, nickname, or any other information. You must type the quotation marks to use upper- and lowercase in your personal name; without them, whatever you type will be capitalized. (Example: **SET PERSONAL_NAME "John Smith".**)

Typing **SHOW ALL** displays the status of all options that can be set with the SET command.

COMPRESS

COMPRESS makes your MAIL.MAI file smaller. It is a good idea to use COMPRESS periodically if you accumulate and save very much mail. Otherwise, your MAIL.MAI file could take up a significant amount of storage in your Workspace.

To compress your Mail file, type **COMPRESS** at the *MAIL>* prompt. There will be a short delay while the compress takes place, and you will be blocked from receiving mail messages. After the procedure, you should go to your personal Workspace area and delete the file MAIL.OLD which is the old (now unused) version of your E-Mail file.

You will notice no difference when you use Mail after doing a Compression, but your Workspace will contain a much smaller MAIL.MAI file and it will be faster for other members to send you E-Mail.

Chapter 12
Member Directory

The Member Directory is where thousands of DELPHI members have entered information about themselves. You may inquire about other DELPHI members and post information about yourself and your interests in this area.

Member Directory Organization

The information a member enters about himself or herself is called a *profile*. Each profile consists of one or more information categories, called *keywords*, under which information has been entered.

You'll find common keywords such as NAME, OCCUPATION, and COMPUTER, or original keywords such as MOVIES or COMICS.

You can, if you wish, enter information about yourself so that others know who you are. Use existing keywords, or make your own. What you enter here is what is displayed when someone types **/WHOIS <YOURNAME>** command here or anywhere else on DELPHI.

You can search this database to find members who have entered certain information under a keyword. You can also display the profiles of others by membername, or browse the listings of profiles sequentially.

Member Directory Selections

I-Am. Use the I-AM function to enter new information about yourself, display and modify existing information, or delete all or part of your profile. The information you supply is up to you, and you may delete or change it at any time.

I-AM Menu Commands. The first time you enter the I-AM function, you are asked a set of standard questions to start your profile. After this initial sequence, you can ADD new keywords, or CHANGE or DELETE entries by keyword.

Answer each of the standard questions as you wish. Use the following commands to alter or expand your profile:

ADD. When you type **ADD**, you are prompted for the keyword you wish to add to your profile. After typing a keyword, you are prompted for the information. Enter **Control-Z** when you are finished entering text.

CHANGE. When you type **CHANGE**, you are prompted for the keyword whose information you wish to change. After typing a keyword, you are prompted for the new information. Enter **Control-Z** when you finish.

DELETE. Typing **DELETE** returns a prompt for a keyword. After you enter the keyword, all information under that keyword (and the keyword itself) is deleted from your profile.

If you wish to delete your entire profile in order to start over, or because you have decided you don't want the information available, type **DELETE *** (the * is a "wildcard" character — it means "any and all").

DISPLAY. Type **DISPLAY** to review your I-AM entry.

Who-Is. By selecting WHO-IS, you may ask DELPHI for information on file for a given member by supplying a DELPHI membername.

When you type **WHO-IS** (or, if you prefer, **WHOIS**), you are prompted for a membername. If there is information on file for that member, it is displayed. You may also type **WHOIS** followed by a membername, and avoid the prompt (example: **WHOIS KZIN**).

List-Keywords. LIST-KEYWORDS lists all keywords in use. The keyword provides an index to profiles and is used with SEARCH. The list of keywords also can help you fashion your own profile.

When you type **LIST**, you'll be asked if you want to see all keywords currently in use, or just the recommended keywords. The keywords are listed in alphabetical order, without definitions.

Use the recommended keywords when entering your own profile as well as when you are searching for members with specific interests.

Browse. The BROWSE command takes you through profiles of other members in alphabetical order, by membername. If you type **BROWSE SM**, for example, you start browsing profiles beginning with the first membername that starts with "SM," (such as "SMAUG"). If there is no match, DELPHI displays the first name it finds after that alphabetic point, perhaps a membername beginning with "SR," in this instance. Note that the database is organized in ascending (lowest to highest) order, starting with membernames that begin with numbers, and then going through the alphabet (A to Z).

Typing **BROWSE** alone starts you at the beginning, with the first member-name, whether it begins with numbers (most likely) or letters.

Search. Use SEARCH to scan for members with particular interests, occupations, or entries under any valid keyword category. You type the keyword, then type a string of characters — a partial word, a word or a phrase. DELPHI then searches all the profiles or you, and displays a list of members who have entered that word or phrase under the specified keyword.

Type **SEARCH** and you are prompted for a keyword under which DELPHI can search.

Or, you may type **SEARCH** followed by the keyword and word or phrase on which you'd like to search, on a single line, like this: **PEOPLE> SEARCH LOCATION CLYDE**.

This provides a list of all profiles that list "Clyde" as a location, be it "Clyde, North Carolina," or "Clyde Mountain."

When you are entering words or phrases under a keyword during a search, you can use spaces to narrow the list of matches; if you type **York** followed by a space, DELPHI will search only for "York," and ignore words such as "Yorktown" and "Yorkshire."

The use of parts of words can expand a search. For example, a search for "finan" under OCCUPATION will yield matches with "financial analyst," "finance specialist," "financier" and "VP of Financial Services," among others.

Guidelines for Creating an Effective Profile (I-AM Listing)

When you enter information about yourself, the idea is to make that information easy to find. Here are some guidelines for creating an effective listing:
• Use recommended keywords. You may create a keyword if the attribute you want to describe doesn't fall into any of the recommended keywords. Those

doing searches, however, won't know your unique keyword if they fail to ask for a complete list of keywords online. Also consider under which keyword(s) a member is likely to search for the information you are entering. You may enter information on what you do for a living under WORK, but it will never be found if a member is searching under OCCUPATION. This is why recommended keywords are listed.

• Use synonyms. If you list your occupation as attorney, and someone searches for lawyer, he or she won't find you.

Think, in general, what categories and words others would use to describe what you are trying to say as you create or edit your listing.

Chapter 13
News, Weather, and Sports

DELPHI's News, Weather, and Sports area features world and finance news from Reuters Information Services, articles on national and international events from United Press International, which also provides up–to–the–moment business, sports and entertainment coverage. You will also find weather forecasts for cities in the U.S. and abroad, show business reviews and gossip, and areas where you can voice your thoughts on the day's developments. Check in here to find out what's going on the same way TV stations and newspapers do.

Business News

UPI's continually updated coverage of Wall Street and other financial markets is supplemented by reports on companies and government actions that affect business.

Entertainment News

When something happens in Hollywood, on Broadway or elsewhere in the entertainment world, UPI is there.

Financial and Commodity News

This area includes general business news, government economic figures, Dow Jones and Standard & Poors information and analysis, and more.
There is a surcharge for each report.
See Chapter 3 for details on using this menu's selections.

Human Interest News

Stories that will surprise, shock and amuse you.

International News

In addition to articles about the U.S. and its overseas dealings, you will find stories about European, Asian and African matters often unavailable in local newspapers.

National News

When news breaks, you can count on finding it here immediately. Articles cover the federal government, regional, and local matters.

Newsbrief

Newsbrief is a capsule summary of the day's major news stories from United Press International (UPI).

Type **NEWSBRIEF** at the NEWS, WEATHER, AND SPORTS menu to see a summary of the latest news from the UPI.

Reuters Information Services

Reuters is the world renown, international news and financial information wire service network. Reuters has 118 bureaus in 74 countries with more than 1,300 journalists. With editing centers in New York, London, and Hong Kong, Reuters is bringing you timely, accurate, and objective reporting 24 hours a day.

Sports

More than just a scoreboard, this UPI service carries stories on major professional and college sports of all types, including baseball, football, basketball, hockey, soccer, tennis, and golf. If you prefer one of the less–publicized sports, such as bowling, cycling or gymnastics, you will find reports on your favorite athletes and events here. Fans with a penchant for statistics will find plenty to examine and analyze.

Views on News

Views on News is DELPHI's soapbox. You can respond to current events and issues by expressing your views, participating in debates with other members, and adding personal commentary on a wide range of topics.

Most Views on News activity takes place in the Forum, a topical message base. Archives contain interesting and humorous articles and essays to enlighten you on current events and lighten up your day. And the Views on News Conference (linked to the Main Conference area) provides a venue for lively realtime discussion.

Views on News is set up like a DELPHI group or club. See the Groups & Clubs chapter for complete information on using the Views on News Forum, the Archives (databases), and the other features.

Weather

DELPHI brings you up-to-the-minute forecasts and summaries from the world's leading private weather authority, Accu-Weather.

You can view city forecasts, capsule summaries of weather nationwide, a National Weather Summary, or weather around the world by selecting the appropriate item on the ACCU-WEATHER menu.

Using Accu-Weather Forecasts

CITY Forecasts — three-day forecasts for selected U.S. cities. When prompted, enter the name of the city for which you want a forecast. Type ? to list the names of cities for which forecasts are available.

CAPSULE Summaries (Nationwide) — one-line forecasts of three-day temperature and weather conditions for more than 100 U.S. cities. When prompted with **SEARCH ITEM**, enter the name of a city or type * for a list of cities.

NATIONAL Weather Summary — information on weather trends across the U.S.

INTERNATIONAL Accu-Weather — one-line forecasts of three-day temperature and weather conditions for more than 40 major cities worldwide. When prompted with **SEARCH ITEM**, enter the name of a city or type * for a list of cities.

Chapter 14

Reference and Education

The Reference and Education menu's collection of specialized information services provides information on a wide range of subjects. Some of these services carry an extra charge, which is stated online.

You'll find information on health, gourmet cooking, and personal topics, as well as Grolier's online encyclopedia and a gateway to the Dialog Information Service, which provides access to over 250 databases.

CAIN

CAIN (Computerized AIDS Information Network) is a service which carries general information and health agency recommendations related to the AIDS virus. It also contains lists of treatment centers, articles and abstracts from medical journals and information sources. Its Forum offers an exchange of information on AIDS, its treatment and ramifications. CAIN's services have been grouped into four general categories: Communication, Member Services, Database Services, and Using CAIN. These categories are denoted on the menu with asterisks (*).

The Communication Services, Members Services as well as the Using CAIN area operate using DELPHI's standard group structure, which is described in the Computing chapter (Chapter 4).

Database Services within CAIN

You'll find most of the timely news and information services grouped within the Database Services category.

Service Resources This is a listing of organizations providing services including hotlines, medical, psychological, dental, and financial. Select a topic and type **SCAN** to see the table of contents of available article titles; type **READ** with a number or numbers to read articles by number; type **SEARCH** to search by keyword. Type **?** to see the menu.

Organization Assistance This is a developmental assistance resource for new and existing organizations providing programmatic and funding information useful in forming AIDS-related projects and service organizations.

Research Library This is a database of Medical, Educational, Legal, Financial, and Psychosocial articles.

Informational/Educational Resources This section includes health care professional information, audio visual resources, book reference, newsletter, and brochure lists.

Dialog Research Library ($)

Through the Research Library selection, DELPHI provides gateway access to the Dialog Information Service, which provides access to more than 250 different databases.

Most Dialog databases consist of bibliographic citations and abstracts or summaries, but some full-text databases are available. The information pertains to scientific fields, educational work, professional associations and news-oriented general subjects. Each database can be searched for a specific word or words to help pinpoint the information in which you are interested. Rates for using Research Library, provided by Dialog Information Services Inc., are considerably higher than DELPHI's standard rates.

Because Dialog is a gateway service, it operates differently from most DELPHI services. And using Dialog is significantly more complicated than using the rest of DELPHI. Under the DIALOG menu, there is an introduction to using DIALOG. It is not intended to replace the training offered by DIALOG's staff and references, but to supplement the first-time user with accessing the databases offered by DIALOG with maximum success. DIALOG databases are expensive to use and the inexperienced user may find them more expensive if he or she is not conversant with the search terminology of DIALOG.

The menu selections are self-explanatory, and prompts will guide you through using each selection.

If you sign up to use Dialog, you may want to order a guidebook that explains the information-retrieval technique called "free-text" searching. It is recommended that you attend one of Dialog's training seminars, which are conducted periodically in various cities throughout North America. For information on dates and locations of Dialog seminars, call 800-334-2564.

Grolier Encyclopedia

Grolier's Online Encyclopedia contains the full text of the multi-volume Grolier's Academic American Encyclopedia. It contains more than 31,000 articles covering practically every topic imaginable. You'll find Grolier's Online

Encyclopedia useful for the same things as a printed encyclopedia — but easier, faster, and more effective to use. Entries are updated and new listings are added several times per year, making Grolier's one of the most up-to-date reference sources available.

Grolier's can be searched by keyword to find appropriate articles within seconds—far faster than you could locate material by a manual search through a book. And, once the articles are displayed, a single selection displays cross-referenced articles.

Using Grolier's Online Encyclopedia

When you select Grolier Encyclopedia from the Reference and Education menu, you will see the GROLIER Menu.

"Encyclopedia" is the primary selection; use it to "open" the encyclopedia and initiate a search.

Using the Encyclopedia To start a search, type **ENC**. A "Search for:" prompt will be displayed. Type a word that represents the topic for which you wish to search (a "keyword").

If there is one article for the topic, or the word you type exactly matches the keyword for one article, you will see the entire article.

More often, there will be several matching articles, and the encyclopedia will create a custom menu from which you can enter the number of the article you wish to read, as in this example, when the word **SPORTS** is entered:

```
Search for: SPORTS

11 items match BIRD.

    1   SPORTS MEDICINE
    2   SPORTS, HISTORY OF
```

At this point, you type the number for the article you wish to read. (You can also cause several articles to be displayed in sequence by entering the article numbers separated by commas.) In the above example, if you selected article 2, "SPORTS, HISTORY OF", you will be shown the following list:

```
3 topics for SPORTS, HISTORY OF
 1  ARTICLE
 2  BIBLIOGRAPHY
 3  REFERENCES


Enter Item Number, SEARCH, BACK, or EXIT:
```

At this point, you can select the item you wish to display. Or, you can type **SEARCH** to initiate a new search.

Other commands.. To view cross-references from a previous article, type **EXIT**. To keep track of what articles and cross-references you have accessed, type **TRAIL**.

HealthNet

HealthNet is the original, comprehensive, online home medical reference source for the personal computer user. It has been prepared and is updated continuously by a team of licensed, board-certified physicians.

Provided for education and enrichment, HealthNet information is not intended to be a substitute for your personal doctor. It shouldn't be relied upon to diagnose or treat any illness or condition. Should you believe that a HealthNet entry applies to you, please contact your personal physician.

Librarian

Librarian is an online research service. In this area you can ask questions on any topic, company, product, industry, technology, or person in the news. The subject(s) of your question(s) will be searched by the information specialists at Searchline Associates, Inc., of Brookline, Massachusetts.

Searchline Associates uses selected online information retrieval systems that list and summarize over 3,000 regional, national, and international trade journals and magazines, newspapers and directories. The results of literature searches will be delivered by the Librarian via E-mail on DELPHI.

Research costs are generally in the range of $275.00 to $475.00, depending upon the scope and depth of the assignment. These charges include all database costs and search service fees. Hard copy document delivery via U.S. Mail or Federal Express is also available, at an extra cost.

New Parents Network

The New Parents Network (NPNet) is a social and service information provider and has been created to serve as a central distribution point of information. All social services, support groups, and government agencies that assist parents and children are invited to have an article about their service on NPNet at no cost. State-by-state information is also available.

The New Parents Network is a non-profit 501(c)3 organization founded in 1988 and is fundeded by grants, contributions, and corporate sponsorship.

NRPA

The National Recreation and Park Association (NRPA) is a national non-profit service organization dedicated to promoting the importance of parks and recreation and to ensuring that all people have an opportunity to find the best and most satisfying use of their leisure time. NRPA works closely with national, state, and local recreation and park agencies, corporations and citizens's groups in carrying out its objectives.

NYNEX NortheastAccess

NYNEX NortheastAccess is an online classified Yellow Pages directory from NYNEX Information Resources Company.

NYNEX NortheastAccess contains all of the business telephone listings contained in the NYNEX Yellow Pages and Business-to-Business directories serving New York and New England Telephone. The listings cover Connecticut, Maine, Massachusetts, New Hampshire, New York, Rhode Island, and Vermont.

You can select information from among the 7,000 headings and 1.7 million listings culled from NYNEX's 300+ directories. The information is updated quarterly.

The database allows you to search a listing by company name (or partial company) and/or by product heading . You can narrow your search by limiting the search to a specific town, zip code, or area code.

Each listing contains the company name, address, zip code, phone number, and product heading.

To access the service, your terminal software must support VT-100 emulation.

Online Gourmet

The Online Gourmet serves up exciting menu ideas and tasty recipes that combine the best of American, Italian, and French cooking. Each week a new menu—complete with recipes—appears. New trends in food are covered in special articles.

Chapter 15
Shopping

Shopping Basics

The Shopping menu is the place to go to buy, sell, or swap merchandise and services. In Shopping you'll find online vendors offering a variety of computer merchandise, as well as coffee, gift items, flowers, and other items.

Most Shopping services provide three kinds of selections:

- Automatic text displays which display information on your screen, then return you the the service's menu.
- Online "catalogs," which offer a numbered sub-menu listing articles.
- Order or response forms, which prompt you through entering an order or a "Feedback" message, which is then sent to the service provider via E-Mail.

When you review products online, you will see that the menu prompt contains the option "Order." If you enter ORDER you'll be given the opportunity to then specify quantity. The shopping system will keep track of all the products you order and then ask for you to confirm the product type and order quantities as you exit from the merchant's service. If you've entered your address and billing information with the "Set Billing Address" option (described at the end of this chapter), this information will be automatically sent with your order. If your address isn't on file, you'll need to type in the information before your order will be submitted.

AutoVantage Online

AutoVantage Online is a gateway service for auto buyers, sellers, and owners. You can choose to join AutoVantage Online's separate membership plan for extended services. Or, you can browse through many of the options without becoming a member.

If you're buying or selling a new or used car, or own a car, AutoVantage online has a number of benefits for you, including:

- Summary guidelines to help you in new car shopping and selection.
- Used car price/value guides, to aid you in buying or selling a used car.
- Discounts on auto service at such nationwide chains as Goodyear, Firestone, Maaco, Amoco, K-mart and many others.
- Rebates on tune-ups, parts, accessories, oil changes and other maintenance if you do work yourself or use an auto service provider not on the discount list.
- An online discount service center locator service.

Boston Computer Exchange

The Boston Computer Exchange is an online brokerage of used computers and computer equipment, matching buyers and sellers at fair market prices. Disk drives, word processors, printers, and mainframe computers are just a few of the many items Boston Computer Exchange offers. Listings of computer equipment are searchable by maker, model, and price.

Car Quotes

Car Quotes, brought to you by Autoquot-R, provides reports on new cars. Use the SEARCH function to enter a make, model, or type of car.

Coffee Anyone ???

Coffee Anyone ??? has been selling the world's finest coffees and teas online for more than three years, as well as samplers, filters, grinders, cups, and other accessory items, and gourmet food items.

Comp-u-store OnLine

Comp-u-store OnLine is an online shopping service, offering thousands of computer and general merchandise products for direct delivery to your home. The Comp-u-store service is maintained and operated independently of the DELPHI network. So, you'll notice a short pause as your account is connected.

Computer Express

Computer Express is a service that lets you order software and accessories for your computer at great prices. Listings are categorized by computer or software type.

Long Distance Roses

Long Distance Roses offers nationwide overnight delivery of roses and other flowers and floral arrangements. All items are guaranteed, and all orders are shipped via Federal Express overnight air.

Parsons Technology

Parsons Technology offers the PC or PC-compatible home user with quality, functional software at raasonable prices. The software product line is designed for a variety of practical uses. Whether your needs are to manage finances, increase personal productivity, handle basic legal matters, study the Bible, of secure your computer hardware, Parsons Technology has the product for you.

Parsons Technology also offers free technical support and a 100% customer satisfaction guarantee.

Publications for Computers

Publications for Computers is the end-user's complete computer book store of the future. From beginner's guides to advanced programmer's manuals, over hundreds of titles are available at a discount. A selection of popular titles available for getting the most from your hardware and software.

UNICEF Online Greeting Cards & Gifts

UNICEF supports projects for children in the fields of health, nutrition, education, water supply and social services. It is funded entirely by voluntary contributions from governments and the public.

UNICEF Online Greeting Cards & Gifts is a seasonal service offering greeting cards and gifts, the proceeds of which go to benefit UNICEF directly.

Set Billing Address

Use this selection to set your billing address, which will be supplied to online vendors with whom you place orders.

When you select this item, you are presented with the options of adding your billing address (type **ADD**), deleting it (type **DELETE**, making changes in it (type **CHANGE**), or viewing your entry (type **LIST**).

The process of adding your billing address is simple and direct. Type **ADD**, and you will be prompted to enter your name, business name (if any), address, city, state, and zip code, one item at a time. You can cancel at any time by entering **Control-Z**.

Chapter 16
Travel and Leisure

DELPHI's Travel & Leisure area offers services to meet the needs of all travelers—from an individual on vacation to the international business traveler.

The Travel & Leisure service of DELPHI is operated by Interactive Office Services, Inc. of Cambridge, MA. (Username: TRAVEL).

Airlines

Bargain Finders International

Bargain Finders International is the first database of special international discount airfares. Search by Carrier, City, Country, or Region to locate listings. Read entries by number for complete details on the fare requirements — save as much as 50% off published fares confirmed in EAASY SABRE or TravelShopper. Submit requests using the Order command. You must be a VIP Club member to submit a request.

Commercial SABRE (sm)

Commercial SABRE is a service designed specifically for corporate users.

A full description of the service and its benefits is posted in this area for members who are not authorized to connect into the service.

Subscribing companies receive automatic rebates on all reservations placed through the system. Companies with a sufficient volume of travel may have tickets printed on site through the installation of satellite ticket printers.

EAASY SABRE (sm)

Through EAASY SABRE, you can "talk" directly to almost all airlines, as well as to hotels and rental car agencies to confirm flights, accommodations, and rental cars. There is no surcharge for this service.

Use EAASY SABRE to check airfares, schedules and seat availability, to compare car rental rates, and to check hotel rates and room availability. With EAASY SABRE, you can directly confirm itineraries for any date.

Before you are permitted to confirm reservations through EAASY SABRE you must complete a separate application. There is no charge.

The EAASY SABRE menu operates differently than other menus on DELPHI.

Official Airline Guide (OAG)

DELPHI provides access to the Official Airline Guide as another source of up-to-date flight and fare information for all domestic flights and most international flights. There is a surcharge for this service, which is listed online in Using DELPHI.

TravelShopper(sm)

TravelShopper (sm) is a service of the Travel Information Service and features direct computerized reservations for air service, hotels and car rentals.

The service is in most respects very similar to EAASY SABRE, except that it uses the host computer maintained by TWA, DELTA, and Northwest Airlines. For that reason you may find that the latest fares for those three carriers will be available sooner through TravelShopper. You will also occasionally see that seats for TWA, DELTA and Northwest which appear to be sold out on EAASY SABRE may be available through this channel. Members of the VIP Club receive the same discounts for reservations confirmed through Travelshopper as for reservations confirmed through EAASY SABRE.

Car Rentals

Information on Car Rental companies, including the latest news and promotions, is available through the Guide to Rental Companies menu. Just enter the name of the car company (or ? for a list of companies).

The Special Requests option permits VIP Club members to submit requests for assistance in reserving rental vehicles anywhere.

Both EAASY SABRE and TravelShopper (in the Airlines menu) offer access to rates, availability and confirmation of rental cars.

Communications

Instant Message to Travel

Use this selection to communicate with the agent servicing your requests.

Message Forum

The Travel & Leisure Message Forum is a place where you can share your travel tips with other members, or leave your travel questions for staff and other members to answer.

The Message Forum offers four topics: General Information, Private Mesages, Travel Tips, and EAASY SABRE & TravelShopper.

With the exception of the "Private" topic, the Message Forum operates the same as Forums in groups and clubs. See the chapter on Groups and Clubs for detailed information on using the Forum.

Use this selection to communicate with the agent servicing your account.

Cruises

CruiSEARCH

Locate the cruise of your choice. You may search by using any of the following criteria:
- Ship Name
- Cruise Line
- Areas and Ports
- Month
- Number of days

Discounts are offered on all cruises to members of the VIP Club, as well as special rates on selected sailings.

Hotels

DELPHI offers members several convenient databases for hotel information and discounted reservations.

Codes for Hotel Chains enables you to determine the chain name associated with codes found in EAASY SABRE and TravelShopper or to find the code for any chain name. simply enter a code or chain name.

The Guide to Hotel Chains offers information on hotel chains, as well as the latest promotions and news. Just enter the name of a hotel chain (or enter a ? for a complete list of hotels).

The Preferred Hotels database lists more than 500 properties offered to VIP Club members at rates averaging 18% off street or corporate rates. Search by City, Country or Chain affiliation. VIP Club members may request reservations using the "Request" command.

The Special Requests option permits VIP Club members to submit request for assistance in reserving hotels anywhere.

Note: hotel packages which may include airport transfers, city tours or airlines transportation are listed in the Tour Packages database (in the Tours menu).

News & Information Services

This section contains detailed travel information on a variety of topics.

Select the desired item and read individual articles and notices. Articles preceded by a "*" allow you to enter a request, using the Request command. (Available to VIP Club members only). Here are the kinds of information you'll find in each topic:

Corporate Travel News

News from the media, supplier communiques, and announcements of special offers negotiated on behalf of all corporate travel participants.

ESCAPE - Leisure Travel News

Check this area for complete details on the latest promotions offered by travel suppliers worldwide and for instructions on how to take advantage of these offers.

Guide to Codes

Find the codes used in the travel industry for airports, currencies, hotel chains, car rental companies or airlines. Enter a city name for the airport code, or enter a code to find the equivalent city name. For a list of all the airports in a country, enter the country name. Similarly, you may select the Currency Code or a country name of currency code.

International Events Calendar

National, regional and religious occasions are listed by event name, or country.

Sno Country Reports

This service provides daily updates of conditions for more than 500 ski areas throughout North America from November to April. Updates are posted at noon daily. There is a $1.25 access charge for each use of the service. The single charge allows you to view reports for an unlimited number of areas.

Tips for Travelers

Important notices such as closings of transportation facilities, currency changes, U.S. State Department Advisories, etc. The most recent postings are displayed first.

Trav-Alerts

Important notices such as closings of transportation facilities, currency changes, U.S. State Department Advisories, etc. The most recent postings are displayed first.

US Gov't Info (Dept. of State, CDC, DOT)

Search State Department Travel Advisories by country, view the latest Department of Transportation report on domestic airline ontime performance or check for health information from the Centers for Disease Control in Atlanta.

WorldLine Country Search

Here you'll find essential information for the foreign traveler.

When you see the prompt **Which Country?** type a country name (or type the first few letters of its name if you are unsure of the spelling). Or type **?** for a list of available countries.

Special Services

This menu offers a variety of travel-related service.

Insurance

Online purchase of various types of travel insurance.

Limousine Rental

Confirm limousine rentals in more than 200 cities worldwide.

Theater Tickets

Order tickets for Broadway and other entertainment in New York, and for events in Las Vegas, London and other cities.

Visa Application

You may request a visa application for countries requiring advance permission to visit. See the WorldLine entry for the country you intend to visit to determine if a visa is required.

Tours

DELPHI offers several services for selecting and reserving tours.

Tour Packages

This area lists hundreds of the most popular tour packages — everything from complete escorted tours to weekend hotel packages at destinations worldwide. Search by Area or City, Country, Features or Number of Days. The summary screen lists the package name, tour operator, price range, number of days and whether or not local tours are included in the package. For details and ordering select the entry number. VIP Club members may submit requests using the "Request" command. All published prices are discounted to members.

VIP Club

The VIP Club provides many benefits. Among them:
• Discounts on *all* airline tickets purchased online
• Help in finding lowest possible airfares
• Multiple options for tickets and delivery (including free Express delivery and prepayment for airport pick-up)
• Travel brochures by mail, and access to professional vacation planning services
• Savings on international itineraries as high as 55%
• Discounts on cruises, tours, and many travel-related products

There is an annual membership fee to join the VIP Club, and a special VIP User's Guide is available. To join, type JOIN at the VIP Club menu.

Chapter 17

Using DELPHI

Using DELPHI is the how-to and the what's new of DELPHI. Here you can read advice from the DELPHI staff, review DELPHI's credit policy and its rates and prices, determine your terminal settings, order Handbooks and find out what's new from DELPHI.

Also within this area you can send queries or suggestions to DELPHI's Member Service department, review your transactions and billing for up to a year in the past, customize the parameters that determine how DELPHI communicates with your computer, find out what's new on DELPHI, read DELPHI policies, gather information on rates and prices and how to access DELPHI.

Access Information

Information on accessing DELPHI via SprintNet, Tymnet, and Datapac is available here, as are lists of local-access phone numbers for the three networks.

To initiate a search, select an item from the ACCESS INFORMATION menu; you will be prompted to enter a search criterion. You may search the lists by city, state/province, or area code, or you may list all numbers by typing * at the search prompt.

Advantage Plan

DELPHI Advantage is the plan that helps you get the most from your DELPHI membership. With DELPHI Advantage, you are assured DELPHI's lowest access rates. You also receive updated editions of DELPHI Handbooks at a reduced rate and a monthly summary of all your charges.

You need only commit to using a small minimum of DELPHI services per month. And that use can be at any time — during either home time or office time.

You can apply online. The rates section of Using DELPHI shows a comparison of DELPHI Advantage rates to standard DELPHI rates.

Calendar of Events

A listing of regularly scheduled conferences, game tournaments, and other events taking place on DELPHI.

Guided Tour

The services on DELPHI are grouped into categories and formatted with a simple menu structure for ease of use. This section contains a brief description of the services available in each category.

Manuals and Documentation

Here you can order a command card or manuals to help you use DELPHI. Select the appropriate item on the menu displayed to see item descriptions and/or order items.

Member Services/Feedback

This section lets you request that changes be made to your account information, such as new addresses and updated credit card information. You may also read the Terms of DELPHI's Membership Agreement, send general comments and suggestions to the DELPHI Product Development Group, or check DELPHI's phone support hours.

News from DELPHI

Announcements of new services, enhancements, and other DELPHI-related developments.

Rates & Billing Policy

Here you find current DELPHI rates and prices for membership, connect time, premium services and additional storage. You also see a comparison of standard rates with DELPHI Advantage plan rates.

Review Bills/Invoices & Usage

Use this selection to review your online transactions. Select the desired month at the menu to see the information on your account for that month. You may also review your current and past DELPHI invoices. Invoices detail all charges applied to your account between the first and last billing day of the previous month.

Here is how to display a history of your transactions on DELPHI for a given date or period. The information displayed for each transaction is:
• the date and time of the transaction
• code of the transaction (for internal use)
• a description of the transaction. Members who have Associate Accounts may check transactions for those accounts as well as for their Principal Accounts.

Usage files generally go back three months. You are told the earliest date in the usage file when you first enter Usage. To exit the usage-history selection, press **Control-Z** at any of the prompts.

There are several options for entering dates for which you wish to review usage, as follows:

«RETURN» displays usage for the current month
7/15 displays usage for July 15 of the current year
7/15/92 displays usage for July 15, 1992
7/15, displays usage for July 15 and after
7/5/92,7/15/92 displays usage between July 5, 1992 and July 15, 1992

Service (Forum)

This is the feedback area of Using DELPHI where you may post a message in the public forum, or send us your requests and suggestions privately.

Settings (Profile)

Here you tailor DELPHI to the requirements of your personal computer. Set the level of prompting you want, change your password and set a default logon path. You may alter your settings at any time and as often as you wish.

Figure 17.1 shows the options available at the Settings menu.

Settings Menu Options:

BUSY-Mode Turn off or turn on pages from Conference or alerts to new Mail messages, as well as sends from outside your conference group.

DEFAULT-Menu Use this selection to bypass the Main Menu by choosing the menu you wish to greet you at sign-on. For example, selecting Conference as your default menu item puts you directly into Conference when you log on, bypassing the Main Menu. (When you leave your default menu with EXIT or Control-Z, you are returned to the Main Menu.) Most items on the Main Menu may be set as the default. Here is an example:

```
SETTINGS>MENU


Your current default menu is: MAIN
Do you want to change it? (y/n)
```

If you type **YES**, you may type any of the selections available at the DELPHI Main Menu at the next prompt:

```
Default Menu Item: CONFERENCE
```

```
SETTINGS Menu:

BUSY-Mode                      PROMPT-Mode
DEFAULT-Menu                   SET-High-bit
DOWNLOAD-Line-terminators      SLASH-Term-settings
ECHO-Mode                      TERMINAL-Type
EDITOR                         TIMEOUT
FILE-TRANSFERS                 UTILITIES
KERMIT-SETTINGS                WIDTH (Columns)
LENGTH (Lines/page)            XMODEM-SETTINGS
NETWORK-PARAMETERS             HELP
PASSWORD (Change)              EXIT

SETTINGS>What would you like to set?
```

Figure 17.1 SETTINGS Menu

You can also "chain" service menu commands. For example, if you wanted to make the Science Fiction group your default menu, you would enter it as **GROUPS SCIENCE**. This selects GROUPS as a default menu, and adds the selection SCIENCE FICTION from the next menu:

Default Menu Item: **GROUPS SCIENCE**

DOWNLOAD-Line-terminators Use this selection to adjust text-line termination to suit your computer type — such as carriage return, linefeed or carriage return+linefeed.

ECHO-Mode With this selection, you can control how characters are "echoed" to you as you type, by selecting no echo, pad echo or host echo.

EDITOR Select the editor — EDT or Oldie — for use in Workspace or E-Mail. (See Chapter 18).

FILE-TRANSFERS Specify your default file-transfer method here.

KERMIT-SETTINGS Here you can change options affecting the way you do Kermit file transfers. (See Chapter 18).

LENGTH (Lines/page) Set the length option to make DELPHI adapt its output to your computer screen's length. If you want DELPHI to stop sending information any time your screen is full, you may specify how many lines of text appear in your screen display. If you prefer continuous scrolling, you may set your length to 0 (zero) for an infinite screen length. Most personal computers have a length of 24 or 25 lines.

NETWORK-PARAMETERS Select settings here to suit your usual terminal and network configurations.

PASSWORD (Change) You should guard your password closely. Change it from time to time — especially if you feel that its confidentiality may have been compromised. (With the availability of Associate Accounts, there is no need for you to share a password.) In short, remember your password, and don't reveal it to anyone.

Passwords must contain at least six characters and/or numbers. To help ensure their confidentiality, passwords you enter won't appear on your screen.

When changing your password, you must verify the password you typed. If you type in a different password the second time, you again are asked for a new password. Here is an example of a password change, beginning with the selection of PASSWORD at the Settings menu:

```
SETTINGS>Password


Old Password: 123SCIENCE89
New Password: LANDOGOSHEN
Verification:LANDOGOSHEN
```

PROMPT-Mode Select the prompt level that suits you: BRIEF provides only a keyword, VERBOSE gives you a keyword and a prompt message, while MENU displays all your options at that level.

It is helpful to new members to see all DELPHI menus in order to get a better explanation of DELPHI services and how to access information. But as you become more accustomed to DELPHI, you can bypass most menus. You can always make a menu appear by responding to a prompt with **?**.

SET-High-bit This selection determines whether the high bit of each byte is changed during XMODEM or KERMIT text downloads. The default is that the high bit is not changed, so you probably do not need to change this. (See Chapter 17).

SLASH-Term-settings With this option, you can specify terminal settings to be maintained each time you log on to DELPHI.

TERMINAL-Type Here you indicate the type of terminal you operate. If your terminal software can emulate a VT100 or a VT52, you can take advantage of some graphics ability, mostly within the games section of DELPHI. Check the manual for your terminal or software to see if it is VT compatible. If you answer YES to the first prompt, you will be given the option of changing it to VT-52 or VT-100. If you are unsure of your terminal type, you may select UNKNOWN.

TIMEOUT At this selection, you indicate number of minutes DELPHI awaits your input before logging you off. This will help you avoid charges if you are called away from your terminal during a DELPHI session, but it is not guaranteed to work in all circumstances.

UTILITIES The UTILITIES selection offers advanced operations on your profile settings.

WIDTH (Columns) By setting WIDTH, you can make DELPHI adjust its output to accommodate the width of your computer screen, from 16 columns to 132 columns. DELPHI helps you determine your screen size if you do not know it. Most personal computers have a screen width of 80 columns.

XMODEM-SETTINGS Here you can alter the way DELPHI executes Xmodem file transfers. You may adjust such features as the error-checking mode, end-of-line handling for text files, timeout period, and retry count. (See Chapter 18).

Tips on Using DELPHI

A series of help files written to address frequently asked questions about using DELPHI.

Chapter 18
Workspace

Workspace Commands

DOWNLOAD and UPLOAD File (File Transfers)

Like all DELPHI members, you have a personal Workspace where your files—whether created by you online, uploaded, or copied from a group FORUM or elsewhere—are stored. DELPHI's advanced file-handling software allows you to do almost anything with a file that you might do on your computer system.

When in Workspace, you must type **?** to see the Workspace menu. (If you type **OTHER**, you'll see a list and explanation of additional commands having to do with file transfers).

Each file stored in your Workspace has a filename, an extension (usually three letters) and a version number (e.g., LETTER.TXT;7). In a directory of the files in your Workspace, these elements, plus the size of each file and the time and date it was created, are displayed.

APPEND to File

The APPEND command allows you to attach one file to the end of another. For example, typing **APPEND RULES.TXT AMEND.TXT** would copy the file RULES.TXT onto the end of AMEND.TXT, thereby changing AMEND.TXT but leaving RULES.TXT intact. RULES.TXT is unchanged, but AMEND.TXT now has the text from both files. Don't use the APPEND command with binary (non-text) files, because the appended file is only usable as a text file.

CATALOG (or DIRECTORY)

You can see a directory of the files in your Workspace by typing either **CATALOG** or **DIRECTORY** (or **CAT** or **DIR**)—whichever you are comfortable using. These commands display a directory listing that includes filenames, extensions, versions, sizes, and dates and times of creation as well as a summary total.

Figure 18.1 shows an what you might see when you type **CATALOG**. Reading across the first file, *ADDRESS* is the filename, *.DAT* is the extension, *;1* is the version number (the newest version of a file has the highest version number), *15* is the size in 512-character blocks, *12-FEB-1993* is the creation date, and *09:42* is the creation time.

If you have a large number of files in your Workspace, you may want to pick out those files with a certain extension, or to view only a portion of the

```
WS> CATALOG

ADDRESS.DAT;1   15      12-FEB-1993 09:42
BILLS;1          7      17-JAN-1993 18:11
NOTE.TXT;3       8      29-DEC-1992 10:53
NOTE.TXT;2       4       8-DEC-1992 22:16


Total of 4 files, 34 blocks.
```

Figure 18.1 Catalog of Workspace Files

directory. For instance, you might type **DIR B*.*** to see a directory of all files that begin with the letter B, or **DIR *.LET**, to see a directory of all files that have the extension .LET. Similarly, typing **DIR *.*;2** will display a list of all files for which there is a version 2. * is a wildcard character because it matches on any character.

COPY File

To create a duplicate of the file LETTERS.PAT named NOTES.PAT, you would type **COPY LETTERS.PAT NOTES.PAT**. If NOTES.PAT already existed before you typed COPY, a new version of NOTES.PAT (with the next higher version number) is created.

COUNT Words

COUNT gives you a brief report on a file. For example, if you want information on the file RESNICK.STR:

```
WS> COUNT RESNICK.STR
File RESNICK.STR: 13352 characters, 253 lines, 2447 words,
longest word "Schwarzenegger-type" (19), longest hyphenated word
"Schwarzenegger-type" (19).
```

CREATE File

The command CREATE lets you make a new text file by typing it in online. To create a file, type **CREATE** followed by the name of the file (if you do not enter a filename, you will be prompted for one). After you enter the filename, you'll see this message:

```
Ok, enter data, terminate with a CTRL/Z, or abort with a CTRL/C.
```

Type in the desired text, using your computer's backspace or "rubout" key (Control-H) to delete characters. Cancel the previous line by typing /**DELETE** at the beginning of the current line. List what you have entered so far by typing /**LIST** at the beginning of a line. If you want to edit what you have entered, type /**EDIT**. If you want to add a line that begins with slash (/), use two slashes and the first will be removed. If you only use one slash, the line will be interpreted as a command.

When you've finished typing the text, press **Control-Z** (or type /**EXIT**) to store the text. If you change your mind and decide to cancel the file, press **Control-C** (or type /**QUIT**) to cancel without saving the file.

DELETE File

DELETE deletes a file or group of files. You must either supply a version number or a wildcard. A protected file must have its protection removed before it is deleted. For example, to delete the most recent version of NOTE.TXT in Figure 18.1, you would type **DEL NOTE.TXT;**

To avoid accidental deletions, DELPHI asks you respond to the following question before each file is deleted , "DELETE [filename], YES OR NO?". If you are confident of what you are doing, you can complete your delete command with /**NOCONFIRM** and the file will be deleted without any verification (e.g. **DEL SAMPLE.TXT; /NOCONFIRM**).

If you see some files in your Workspace that do not make sense, or which you did not upload, be careful about deleting them, they may be mail files or files created when you played a game. Here are some samples: MAIL.MAI, MAIL$00040092508B2ABF.MAI, ADVENTURE.DAT. When you delete a message while in E-Mail, any special file that holds the message will automatically be deleted.

EDIT File

EDIT allows you to edit a specified file on a line by line basis. It must be a text file (you cannot edit a binary program file). For example, to edit NOTE.TXT, you would type **EDIT NOTE.TXT**.

LIST (or TYPE) File

LIST (or TYPE) prints a file to your terminal. Type **LIST** with a filename, like this: **LIST NOTE.TXT**. LIST only works with text files (you cannot list a binary program file).

PURGE Old Versions

The PURGE command automatically deletes all but the most recent versions of your files. Using PURGE is a convenient way to keep your Workspace manageable, without having to search for and delete files individually.

You can delete all old versions of a specified file by including its name with the PURGE command. If you type **PURGE** alone, all but the latest versions of *all* files in your Workspace will be deleted.

For example, if your Workspace contains the files shown in Figure 18.1 and you type **PURGE**, the only file deleted is NOTE.TXT;2, since it is not the most recent version of NOTE.TXT.

RENAME

To change the name of the file LETTERS.PAT to NOTES.PAT, you would type **RENAME LETTERS.PAT NOTES.PAT**.

SUBMIT (or PUBLISH)

In Workspace, SUBMIT or PUBLISH initiates the process whereby a file is submitted to a group or club database. The file is submitted to the group or club from whose menu you selected Workspace. See the "Databases" section in Chapter 4 for more information on using SUBMIT.

UNPROTECT (and PROTECT) File

The UNPROTECT command must be used if you wish to delete Mail files from Workspace. Normally, you delete messages while you are in the E-Mail area and the Mail files are automatically deleted.

You must type **UNPROTECT** followed by the filename, like this: **UNPROTECT MAIL.MAI**, after which you may delete the file in the normal manner by typing **DELETE MAIL.MAI**. Your Mail file will be re-created when you receive your next mail message. (NOTE: You may see some unusual errors if you try to read Mail while you do not have a Mail file. Of course, if you do not have a Mail file because you deleted it then certainly there will *be* no Mail to read anyway. DELPHI does not recommend that these files be deleted.)

KERMIT-Server

Typing **KERMIT** invokes the Kermit file transfer server. You are asked if you intend to send only text files. If you answer NO to this question, all files that you send will be stored as binary files. If you do not upload any files during this server session, your answer to this question has no effect.

Once you are informed that the server has started, you may use your terminal program's Kermit **GET** command to transfer files from your Workspace to your computer, or your program's Kermit **SEND** command to transfer files from you computer to your Workspace. The **RECEIVE** command will not work in server mode.

When you have finished transferring files, use your program's Kermit **FINISH**, **BYE** or **LOGOUT** command to stop the server. You may press three **Control-C** characters in a row to exit the file server at any time.

DOWNLOAD and UPLOAD File (File Transfers)

Introduction to File Transfers

Downloading is the process of transferring a file or files from DELPHI to your personal computer. Uploading is the opposite: transferring a file or files from your personal computer to DELPHI. The files you transfer may be programs, E-Mail messages, spreadsheets, graphics or even electronic music.

You can transfer files using a variety of techniques, including Buffer (buffer capture, a standard ASCII transfer; Buffer capture only works for standard text files), RT Buffer ("buffer capture" in which DELPHI sends Control-R and Control-T as signals to mark the beginning and end of a file, respectively), KERMIT, XMODEM (standard XMODEM using 128-byte blocks), Windowed XMODEM (transferring multiple blocks at a time), YMODEM (similar to XMODEM, but using 1024-byte blocks), YMODEM Batch (often called YMODEM, or true YMODEM, in distinction to XMODEM-1K, but the terminalogy varies from one terminal program to another) and ZMODEM. You can only use a transfer technique that is supported by your terminal software.

In Workspace, there are three ways to select a transfer technique:

1. Type DOWNLOAD or UPLOAD and Workspace will use your default file-transfer method. Type **/FX_METHOD** to view your default file-transfer method.

2. Type the appropriate command for a specific file-transfer method (this overrides any default file-transfer method you may have set):

Download Command	Upload Command	Transfer Method
XDOWNLOAD	XUPLOAD	XMODEM
WXDOWNLOAD	WXUPLOAD	Windowed XMODEM
KDOWNLOAD	KUPLOAD	Kermit
YDOWNLOAD	YUPLOAD	YMODEM
YBDOWNLOAD	YBUPLOAD	YMODEM Batch
ZDOWNLOAD	ZUPLOAD	ZMODEM

3. Select the desired method from the Download Method Menu or Upload Method Menu (this also overrides any default file-transfer method you may have set). To reach the Download Method Menu, type **DOW MENU** (the Upload Method Menu is similar and is reached by typing **UP MENU**).

Buffer Capture

Buffer Capture is the simplest file-transfer method. However, it is limited to text files and it does not correct for line noise (if the phone line you are using has any noise, the noise characters will be sent as part of the file transfer).

Buffer Capture Download types out the file to your terminal with as a standard ASCII file with a delay, Control-Z and a bell (Control-G) at the end. For example, to download file NOTE.TXT:

```
WS> DOWNLOAD NOTE.TXT
Ready ... Press «RETURN» to Begin:
```

After you press **«RETURN»** the file transfer procedure begins (you should begin the file receive or buffer capture procedures on your end before pressing «RETURN»). At the end of the transfer, you will hear a beep and see a message telling you how many lines were transferred and that the transfer is complete:

```
>>Download of 23 lines: complete
```

Buffer Capture Upload sends a file from your computer to DELPHI using ASCII file transfer. You can receive optional linefeed confirmation after each line you transmit. Your program should end transmitted lines of text with «RETURN» only (not return+linefeed) for best results.

RT Buffer Capture

RT Buffer Capture is identical to standard Buffer Capture, except that DELPHI sends Control-R and Control-T as signals to mark the beginning and end of a file, respectively. Like standard Buffer Capture, RT Buffer Capture should only be used with text files and only when line noise is not a problem.

XMODEM

XMODEM is among the most popular binary file-transfer protocols. It is supported by almost all communications software programs.

XMODEM Download any file from DELPHI to your microcomputer in an error-free way. To download file FOR.ME:

```
WS> XDOWNLOAD FOR.ME

Type three consecutive <Control-C>'s to abort.
Ok, receive! (130 bytes = 2 xmodem blocks, text)
```

At this point, you should instruct your terminal program to start an Xmodem receive of a file. You tell your program what name to give the new file (using the same name is helpful). Your program signals DELPHI to begin the transmission. When your program tells you that it is finished, you resume normal operation and continue with your DELPHI session by pressing «RETURN» to see the *WS>* prompt.

Some Xmodem programs won't instruct DELPHI to start file transfer until they have "timed out," which means you may have to wait 10 or 20 seconds for the transfer to begin. If at any time you wish to terminate the file transfer, press **Control-C** three times.

XMODEM Upload any file from your microcomputer to DELPHI in an error-free way. To upload file FOR.ME:

```
WS> XUPLOAD FOR.ME
Is this a text file (Type ? for help) YES
Type three consecutive <Control-C>'s to abort.
Ok, send! (text)
```

The question "Is this a text file?" determines how DELPHI interprets and stores information you upload. You respond by typing **YES** to indicate that it is a text file if you want the information to be used on DELPHI. Text files are normally "human readable" information, such as messages and letters.

When DELPHI prompts you "OK, send!", you should instruct your terminal program to start an Xmodem transmit of the file. You tell your program what file you want to send (using the same name is helpful). If necessary, DELPHI waits several minutes for your program to begin transmission. When your program tells you that it is done, you can resume normal operation and continue with your DELPHI session by pressing «RETURN» to see the *WS>* prompt again. If at any time you wish to cancel the file transfer, press **Control-C** three times.

Xmodem Options may be selected by using Settings from Workspace:
• In *Atari mode*, text files that are downloaded have the last block filled with a byte that represents the number of significant data bytes in the last block. If the last block has 120 data bytes, then the remaining 8 bytes will have 120 (78h or lower-case x) in them. If the last block is exactly full then an additional block of all nulls (0) will be appended.

- You can change the *Error Check Mode* to CRC, where all blocks have two error-checking bytes at the end instead of one. These two contain a 16-bit Cyclic Redundancy Check of the block's data. Using this mode helps reduce the (already small) odds that bad data might make it through. When you are downloading, Checksum or CRC is selected automatically based on DELPHI sees coming from your computer when it initiates the transfer. If DELPHI gets a NAK, it assumes the 1-byte checksum mode. If DELPHI gets a C, it assumes 2-byte CRC mode. For uploading, checksum is assumed unless you have selected CRC in the Settings area.

- *Set High Bit* for Apple][or other computers that require the high bit of data bytes be set to 1 to avoid blinking text. Carriage return also must have its high bit set. Selecting this mode will set the high bit (80 hex, 128 decimal) of all characters of text files you download. You may also wish to select no-linefeed mode if you need this.

- Download end-of-line terminator should be set according to the type of computer you are using. This affects text file downloads only. The terminator is normally carriage return + linefeed, but it can be changed to carriage return only or linefeed only. For example:

  ```
  IBM PC          CR+LF
  Apple ][        CR
  Macintosh       CR
  Amiga           LF
  UNIX            LF
  ```

- Normally, DELPHI assumes a file transfer is hopeless if there are too many errors on a particular block. Set the *Retry Count* to adjust the maximum number of successive errors on the same block that will be tolerated before an abort of the entire transfer. Normally, a count of 9 is satisfactory.

- When DELPHI is waiting for a block from you or waiting for an ACK or NAK from you, it will eventually time out and repeat the previous action. This Xmodem feature is to withstand the effects of lost data. You can adjust this *Timeout Period* from 1 to 99 seconds. Making it small allows faster response to errors, making it large allows for a slow connection to DELPHI. Normally, a delay time of 20 seconds is satisfactory.

Windowed XMODEM

Windowed XMODEM is a special version of XMODEM that can be faster than regular XMODEM (although it is slower than YMODEM). The commands and options are the same as those used with XMODEM.

Kermit

The popular Kermit protocol was developed at Columbia University in 1981. Kermit is the slowest file transfer protocol, but it sometimes works when all other methods fail. It may be useful if you connect to DELPHI using a local area network or by means of an international packet net that only allows 7-bit characters.

Kermit Download any file or files from DELPHI to your microcomputer in an error-free way. If you do not list filenames, you are prompted for them. You may use wildcards in filenames. When you see the *Ok, receive!* prompt, use your terminal program's Kermit **RECEIVE** command to receive the files.

Kermit Upload any file or files to DELPHI from your microcomputer in an error-free way. If you do not type a filename, you may use your terminal program's Kermit **SEND** command to upload a group of files. The files are given names that approximate the names they have on your system.

Kermit Options may be selected by using Settings from Workspace:
• Each packet transmitted in a Kermit file transfer contains error checking information. *Error Check Mode* may be a one-byte checksum, a two-byte checksum, or a three-byte Cyclic Redundancy Check (CRC). This value is computed by both the sender and sent with the packet. The receiver then computes a value again. If the value received in the packet is not the same as the receiver's computed value, then the packet must have been corrupted in transmission. In this case, the receiver ask the sender to re-transmit the packet.
• *Retry Count* is the number of times that Kermit will request re-transmission of a bad packet before it gives up and aborts the transfer.
• Use *Seven Bit Mode* to tell DELPHI to ignore the high bit of each byte. You may need this if you can not set your terminal software for no parity.
• *Timeout-Period* says how long Kermit will wait for a packet before deciding that it is lost and asking for another packet to be sent.
• For *Set High Bit*, see the description for XMODEM above.

YMODEM

YMODEM is similar to XMODEM, except that it transfers data in larger chunks. Therefore, for lines that are not too noisy, YMODEM is more efficient (faster) than XMODEM. The download and upload processes are the same as with XMODEM, and the XMODEM options can be used to improve YMODEM transfers. YMODEM is also known as XMODEM 1K.

YMODEM Batch

YMODEM Batch is a version of YMODEM that lets you transfer several files at the same time. When you select YMODEM batch, you will be prompted to each of the files you wish to transfer.

ZMODEM

ZMODEM is the newest and most powerful file transfer protocol available on DELPHI. If your communication program supports it, you should use it. ZMODEM is faster than other protocols, and it is better at recovering from transmission errors. It is a batch protocol, so you may download multiple files from databases, or any number of files from your workspace, as a single batch. Also, if your software supports ZMODEM, it will automatically start receiving data when you initiate a download on DELPHI, and it will assign the correct file names as well.

Type **ZMODEM** or **ZDOWNLOAD** to initiate a ZMODEM download.

Chapter 19
Using the Online Text Editors

There are several areas on DELPHI where you may use an editor to amend or compose text: Workspace and group Forums. DELPHI offers two online text editors: EDT, your initial default editor, and Oldie. You may select either one as your default editor in Using DELPHI's Settings selection. You may also set your editor of choice temporarily by typing /EDITOR = EDT or /EDITOR = OLDIE at most prompts (and your default will only be retained for the current session).

EDT

EDT allows you to edit the file you specify by moving through the text line by line. It uses the line as its point of reference.

To help you locate and edit text, each line is assigned a number. These numbers are not part of the text and are not retained when the editing session is over. Lines are assigned numbers in sequence and start with 1 and increment by 1 unless you insert lines, in which case lines are assigned fractional numbers, such as 1.5.

When you complete your editing by typing **EXIT** at the asterisk (*) prompt, your changes are saved and the numbers are removed.

Here are some general guidelines for editing:

- Type commands at the * prompt. If you don't have an * prompt, press Control-Z and it appears.
- To see the line numbers of an already existing file, type **TYPE WHOLE** at the * prompt.
- When you start editing, you will be placed at the beginning of your file.
- Press **«RETURN»** to read your file line by line. Each time you press «RETURN» you advance to the next line. Type a minus sign and press «RETURN» to go back to the previous line, like this: - **«RETURN»**
- When you finish editing, press Control-Z. Save your changes by typing EXIT at the * prompt. If you don't wish to save alterations you made on the file, type **QUIT** at the * prompt.
- The number of lines you may have in a file is virtually limitless. However, no line may contain more than 255 characters.
- Detailed help for editing is available by typing **HELP** at the * prompt. EDT was developed by Digital Equipment Corporation and they publish a comprehensive EDT manual.

Inserting Text

To insert text, type **INSERT** at the *. The cursor indents 12 spaces and waits for you to start typing. This 12-space indent is on the screen and does not become part of the edited text. You can insert as many lines as you need. Just press **«RETURN»** at the end of each line to move to the beginning of the next line. You leave insert mode by pressing Control-Z.

Lines are inserted above your current line. Inserted lines have decimal numbers. For instance, lines inserted before the original line 10 have numbers 9.1, 9.2, 9.3, etc.

Deleting Text

You delete individual lines or groups of lines by using the **DELETE** command. After a delete operation, you see the line following the last line you deleted; this line is the new current line.

Typing **DELETE** deletes the line you are on.

Following DELETE with a line number deletes the specified line. In this example, the fourth line of your text is deleted:

```
* DELETE 4
```

Following DELETE with a range of line numbers allows you to delete several lines at a time. In this example, the fourth through the sixth lines are deleted:

```
* DELETE 4 THRU 6
```

Substituting Text

When you want to substitute one string of characters for another, use the **SUBSTITUTE** command at the * prompt. This is the only line-editing command that can alter text within a line as opposed to changing an entire line. The substitute command operates on the current line or within a specified range. It also can make a global substitution; that is, you can replace every occurrence of one string with another by using only one command.

You substitute one word for another on the current line like this:

```
* SUB/Old-string/New-string/
```

Let's use this paragraph as an example:

```
I scream. You scream. We all scream for ice cream.
```

If you wanted to remove the word WE and replace it with the word THEY, you would do a substitution like this:

```
* SUB/We/They/
```

The paragraph would look like this:

```
I scream. You scream. They all scream for ice cream.
```

To substitute a word every place you used it throughout a file, follow the command with the word WHOLE, like this:

```
* SUB/Old-string/New-string/WHOLE
```

Using the previous example, to replace the word SCREAM with the world YELL, do a substitution like this:

```
* SUB/scream/yell/WHOLE
```

The paragraph would look like this:

```
I yell. You yell. We all yell for ice cream.
```

Moving Text

You may use the **MOVE** and **COPY** command to move one or more lines of text from one place to another. The effect of these commands is similar; the only difference is that the COPY command doesn't delete the text from its original location, but the MOVE command does.

When you use the MOVE command, the line or lines you indicate that you want to move are repositioned above the line you say to move them to. The original copy of the moved lines is deleted. For example, if you want to move lines 43 through 56 above line 13, you would type it like this:

```
* MOVE 43 THRU 56 TO 13
```

The moved lines are renumbered to be consistent with their new location.

Use the COPY command the same way to move text without deleting it from its original position. You would type it like this:

```
* COPY 43 THRU 56 TO 13
```

Replacing Text

The **REPLACE** command combines the DELETE and INSERT functions in one command. You use REPLACE when you need to delete a block of text and want to type new text in that same location. When you use REPLACE, the lines you specify are deleted and you receive a message telling you how many lines were removed.

If you supply no specifiers with the REPLACE command, the current line is deleted. As soon as the specified line is DELETED, you are automatically shifted to INSERT, and the cursor moves to the right, just as it does when you give the INSERT command.

Anything you type after pressing «RETURN» is inserted. When you finish typing your new text, press Control-Z to return to the * prompt.

Formatting Commands

In order to display text properly on different types of computers and screen widths, DELPHI has an automatic word-wrapping feature which may cause your Forum messages, Custom Forum banners, database file descriptions, and files created in your workspace, to display as you had not intended for it to appear.

There are special commands that you may insert into your text to control the display of the message. With these formatting commands, commonly referred to as "dot commands" since they all begin with a ".", you can specify page breaks, center text, modify right and left margins, indent paragraphs, and more.

These commands *must* be typed at the beginning of a line. They may be entered in either upper or lower case.

Blank lines (.BLANK and .B). When you insert a blank line in your text, that line is kept blank as output. A dot on a line by itself also signals DELPHI to start the next line on a new line. You can accomplish the same thing by inserting the formatting command **.BLANK** or **.B.**

.BLANK can be used with a value like **.B** 2, which inserts two blanks) or by itself will default to 1.

Beginning a new line. When you start a line with blank(s), the line is placed on a new output line. A leading space tells DELPHI that you want a new line started where the space or spaces appear.

Center text (.CENTER). This centers text on a line, no matter what the screen width. In the example that follows, inserting **.CENTER;FORMATTING COMMANDS** resulted the words FORMATTED COMMANDS being centered on the line:

```
                    FORMATTING COMMANDS
```

Literal display (.LT AND .EL). This makes your output appear on the screens of others exactly as you typed it. It would be used to structure poetry, addresses, lists, etc. Here is an example:

```
.LT

DELPHI
1030 Massachusetts Avenue
Cambridge, MA 02138


.EL
```

If you typed the same information without those commands, it would look like this when read:

```
DELPHI 1030 Massachusetts Avenue Cambridge, MA 02138
```

Note that our example ends with **.EL**. This causes the literal output to be turned off, and DELPHI's reformatting to be turned back on.

Margins (.LM, .RM, .WM, AND .I). **.LM** and **.RM** stand for left and margin, respectively, and must be followed by a number. Use it to temporarily reset the left and margins.

.WM stands for wrap margin, and must be followed by a number. This tells DELPHI that any lines that won't fit on the screen should be indented to column 4 when they appear on the next output line (normally 1). This is good for numbered lists.

.I can be used with a positive or negative value to move the line forward or backwards on the indentation. This will work only after a **.B** command.

Starting a new page (.P). **.P** stands for page. Enter **.P** when you want to end the display of text on page and start on the next page.

Oldie

Like EDT, Oldie is a line editor, and uses line numbers for reference. There are some major differences between Oldie and EDT, however. These include:
• Oldie does not automatically display text unless you enter the command **/VIEW**.

- When you enter text and press «RETURN» while editing a file with Oldie, the text is automatically inserted (you do not have to use an INSERT command).
- You can move to the beginning or end of a file with a single command while editing a file using Oldie.
- You can upload a text file from your computer directly into a file you are editing with Oldie.

Otherwise, Oldie offers many of the same features as EDT, but the commands have different names and must be preceded by a slash.

Inserting Text

Anything you type that is not preceded by a slash is automatically inserted as text. If you wish to insert a line that starts with a slash, enter two slashes (//) at the beginning and OLDIE will remove one of the slashes and insert the rest as text (any line that is entered with only one slash will be interpreted as a command).

Entering Commands

You remain in the Command mode while using Oldie. All commands start with a slash and can be abbreviated to just one letter (/A is the same as **/APPEND**). Here's a summary of most Oldie commands:

/APPEND/string/ appends the specified string to the end of the current line.

/BOTTOM moves the cursor to the bottom (end) of the file.

/CHANGE/string/new string/ changes specified string in the current line to the new string.

/DELETE DELETE the current line.

/DIRECTORY displays a directory of your Workspace files.

/EDT switches to the EDT editor without leaving the file.

/EXIT exits Oldie and saves the file (pressing Control-Z does the same).

/FETCH <filename> merges a file from your Workspace into the file you're editing.

/GLOBAL/string/new string/ is a global search and replace.

/INVISIBLE is a toggle for line number display. Line numbers are normally displayed; type **/INVISIBLE** to turn them off, and **/INVISIBLE** again to turn them on again.

/LOCATE/string/ finds the specified string.

/NEXT moves cursor to the next line forward.

/N# moves # lines forward in the file. If # is a negative number, the cursor moves that number of lines backward in the file.

/QUIT leaves the edit without saving the file (as does pressing Control-C).

/REPLACE/new text/ replaces entire current line with the specified new text.

/SAVE saves the file to Workspace.

/TOP moves to the top (beginning) of the file.

/HELP displays a complete list of commands.

Appendix A
Index to Services

Use these abbreviations to move quickly from the main menu prompt to the information you seek. Commands were kept at a length to help you remember them — but in many cases you can type even fewer letters — just enough to make your request unique. For instance, NEWS WEATHER can be reduced to NE WE.

A

US ACCESS — Access Information
US ADV — Advantage Plan
ENT ADV — Adventure Games
TRAV AIR — Airlines
COM AMIGA — Amiga SIG
COM APPLE — Apple][Group
ENT AST — Astro–Predictions
COM ATARI — Atari Advantage
SHOP AUTO — AutoVantage OnLine
GR AVI — Aviation SIG

B

COM BBS — BBS Forum
TRAV AIR — Bargain Finders Int'l
ENT BOA — Board & Logic Games
SHOP BOS — Boston Computer Exchange
GR BUS — Business Forum
NEW BUS — Business News
BUS BUS — Business Wire-Press Releases
BUS — Business and Finance

C

REF CAIN — CAIN – AIDS Info Network
TRAV CAR — Car Rentals
MAI CAT — Catalog (of mail files)
GR CLO — Close Encounters
SHOP COFF — Coffee Anyone ???
GR WR COLL — Collaborative Novel
COM COLOR — Color Computer
TRAV AIR — Commercial Sabre
BUS COM — Commodity Quotes
COM COM — Commodore SIG
SHOP COMP — Comp-u-store OnLine
SHOP COMPU — Computer Express
ENT CRIT — Critics' Choice
TRAV CRUIS — CruiSEARCH
GR CUST — Custom Forums

D

MEMBER — DELPHI Member Profiles
SHOP DEL — DELPHI Store
DEL ARG — DELPHI/Argentina
DEL BOS — DELPHI/Boston
DEL KC — DELPHI/Kansas City

DEL MIA — DELPHI/Miami
REF DIALOG — DIALOG's Research
  Library
COM DESK — Desktop Publishing SIG
BUS DOW — Dow Jones Averages

E

TRAV AIR — EAASY SABRE
US RATES — EasyPay Direct Debit Plan
MAI EASY — Easylink
MAI MAI — Electronic Mail
NEW ENT — Entertainment News (UPI)
GR ENV — Environment SIG

F

MAI FAX — FAX Service
REF DIALOG — File Numbers and Rates
BUS FIN — Financial & Commodity
  News
ENT FLIP — FlipIt!
INT FTP — Internet FTP files
BUS FUT — Futures Focus

G

GR GAME — GameGroup
BUS UPI — General Business News
COM GRAPH — Graphics SIG
REF GROL — Grolier Encyclopedia
US GUIDE — Guided Tour

H

REF HEALTH — HealthNet
GR HOBBY — Hobby Shop
ENT HOLL — Hollywood Hotline
TRAV HOTEL — Hotels
NEW HUM — Human Interest Stories

I

US ACCESS — International Access
GR FOR — Foreign Languages SIG
NEW INT — International News (UPI)

INT MAIL — Internet Mail (sending and
  receiving)
INT — Internet services

K

WORK KER — KERMIT File Transfer
REF KUSS — Kussmaul Encyclopedia

L

REF LIB — Librarian
SHOP LONG — Long Distance Roses

M

COM MAC — Macintosh ICONtact
MAI MAI — Mail (Electronic)
US MAN — Manuals & Documentation
BUS MARKET — MarketPulse ($0.50)
US MEMB — Member Services/Feedback
GR MEN — MensNet
COM MID — MidRange Systems
ENT MODEM — Modem-to-Modem
  Games
BUS MON — Money Fund Report by
  Donoghue
BUS MOR — Mortgage Calculator
ENT MOV — Movie Reviews by Cineman
GR MUS — Music City

N

NEW NAT — National News (UPI)
GR NEW — New Age Network
NEWS — News, Weather, and Sports
NEW NEWS — Newsbrief
REF NYNEX — NYNEX NortheastAccess

O

COM OS9 — OS9 On-Line
TRAV AIR — Official Airline Guide
REF ONLINE — Online Gourmet

P

SHOP PARS — Parsons Technology
COM PC — PC Compatibles/IBM
BUS PR — PR Newswire
GR PERS — Person to Person
GR PHOTO — Photography & Video
ENT POK — Poker Showdown
COM PORT — Portable Place
SHOP PUB — Publications for Computers

Q

ENT QUEST — Quest (for the Holy Grail)

R

BUS RATE — RateGram CD Reports
US RATE — Rates & Billing Policy
BUS REG — Register of Public
        Corporations
NEWS REUTER — Reuters Information
        Services
US REV — Review Bill/Invoices

S

ENT SCRAM — SCRAMBLE Word
        Game
BUS SOS — SOS - Stock & Option
        Advisors
GR SCI — Science Fiction
GR SEN — Senior Forum
US SER — Service Forum
US SET — Settings (Profile)
SHOP — Shopping
TRAV SPEC — Special Services (Travel)
NEW SPO — Sports (UPI)
ENT STELL — Stellar Conquest
BUS STO — Stock Quotes

T

COM TI — TI Intl Users Net
ENT TQ — TQ Trivia Tournament
GR TV — TV/Movie Group
COM TANDY — Tandy PC SIG

MAI TEL — Telex
INT TEL — Telnet
GR THEO — Theological Network
US TIP — Tips on Using DELPHI
TRAV AIR — Tips on Using OAG
TRAV TOUR — Tours (Travel)
MAI TRAN — Translation Services
TRAV NEWS — Travel News &
        Information
TRAV AIR — Travelshopper
BUS TRE — Trendvest Ratings &
        Portfolio

U

SHOP UNI — UNICEF Greeting Cards &
        Gifts
BUS UPI — UPI Business News

V

TRAV VIP — VIP Club (Travel)
NEW VIEW — Views on News

W

GR WID — WIDNet-Disability Network
NEW WEA — Weather
WORK — Workspace
GR WORLD — World of Video Games
TRAV NEWS — WorldLine Country
        Search
GR WRITER — Writers Group

X

WORK — Xmodem

Y

WORK — Ymodem

Z

WORK — Zmodem

DELPHI Membership Agreement

Terms of Membership Agreement Between
General Videotex Corporation (GVC)
1030 Massachusetts Avenue, Cambridge, MA 02138-5302
And "**Member**"

GVC agrees to provide and Member agrees to receive access to the DELPHI online information service according to the following terms and conditions:

GENERAL

1. All provisions of this Agreement apply to the Member's Principal Account and all Associate Accounts billed to the Principal Account.
2. The benefits of or rights conferred by this Agreement are non-transferable. Use of DELPHI accounts is expressly limited to the individual whose name appears on the account and dependents of the account holder living at the same address.
3. Member is responsible for all equipment and software necessary to connect to DELPHI.
4. Member agrees to use the service in a manner consistent with any and all applicable laws.
5. If Member is less than 18 years of age, Agreement must be signed by a parent or legal guardian, who is responsible for all charges related to use of Member's account(s).
6. Use of DELPHI for advertising or promotion of a commercial product or service without the express, written consent of GVC is prohibited.
7. Member is responsible for all use of Member's account(s) and confidentiality of password (s). GVC will suspend access or change access to Member's account(s) immediately upon notification by Member that his password has been lost, stolen or otherwise compromised.

BILLING

8. Member is responsible for all local or long-distance telephone charges for connecting directly to DELPHI or to a Tymnet, SprintNet or other network access node. Members outside the U.S. or Canada requiring access to an additional telecommunications network in order to connect to DELPHI are responsible for those charges.
9. Member agrees to pay GVC all charges relating to the use of Member's account(s) according to rates and prices published online at the time the service is used. Online rates and prices are incorporated into this agreement by reference. Member is also responsible for monthly storage charges as described online in USING DELPHI.
10. Access is subject to credit limits established by the issuer of Member's credit card and by GVC. A credit limit is applied to all accounts. GVC may suspend Member's access to the service if Member exceeds his/her credit limit unless prior arrangements have been made.
11. GVC reserves the right to charge a monthly billing charge to all members to whom an invoice must be sent.
12. Member is responsible for charges at the time the service is used and GVC may apply the amount due to Member's credit card at any time.
13. GVC reserves the right to change prices on 30 days' notice published online.
14. GVC reserves the right to suspend access to service for Member's account(s) upon an indication of credit problems including delinquent payments or rejection of any credit card charges.

OWNERSHIP/COPYRIGHT

15. Information available on DELPHI is the property of GVC or its Information Providers. Member shall not redistribute or commercially exploit such information without express written permission of its owner.

16. Information Providers shall have the right to assert and enforce such copyright provisions directly on their own behalf.

17. Member submitting information owned by Member for publication on DELPHI grants GVC non-exclusive permission to distribute the information product worldwide. Member retains all rights Member may have to such information.

LIMITATION OF LIABILITY

18. THE DELPHI SERVICE IS PROVIDED ON AN "AS IS, AS AVAILABLE" BASIS. NO WARRANTEES, EXPRESS OR IMPLIED, INCLUDING BUT NOT LIMITED TO THOSE OF MERCHANTABILITY OR FITNESS FOR A PARTICULAR PURPOSE, ARE MADE WITH RESPECT TO DELPHI OR ANY INFORMATION OR SOFTWARE THEREIN.

19. Neither GVC nor its Information Providers are responsible for any damages arising from Member's use of DELPHI or by his inability to use DELPHI.

20. GVC is not responsible for Member's personal files residing on DELPHI. Member is responsible for independent backup of his data stored on DELPHI.

OPERATION

21. GVC reserves the right to change without notice the DELPHI service, including, but not limited to, access procedures, hours of operation, menu structures, commands, documentation, and services offered.

22. GVC reserves the right to delete Member's personal files which have not been accessed for more than 1 month.

23. GVC reserves the right in its sole discretion to delete any information entered into DELPHI by Member. GVC and its authorized representatives shall have the right, but shall not be obligated, to edit publicly viewable information.

24. Member hereby agrees that any material submitted for publication on DELPHI through Member's account does not violate or infringe any copyright, trademark, patent, statutory, common law or proprietary rights of others, or contain anything obscene or libelous.

25. GVC, at its sole business judgment, may terminate this Membership Agreement immediately or suspend Member's access to the service upon any breach of this Membership Agreement by Member, including, but not limited to, refusal or failure to pay for services provided, or disruptive online behavior.

26. GVC reserves the right to terminate access to service for any Principal or Associate Account which has been inactive for 6 months.

27. Use of distribution lists in electronic mail or other mass electronic mailings is subject to approval of DELPHI Member Services. Any unauthorized use of distribution lists will be charged at the applicable per-message fee.

28. This Agreement shall be governed by the laws of the Commonwealth of Massachusetts. Any claims or causes of action related to DELPHI must be instituted within one year after the claim or cause of action has arisen or be barred.

29. GVC may modify these terms and conditions upon notice published online via DELPHI. Member's use of DELPHI after such notice shall constitute Member's acceptance of the modifications to this Agreement.

30. If any one or more paragraphs in this Agreement is found to be unenforceable or invalid, Member's and GVC's agreement on all other paragraphs is unaffected.

Appendix C
Local Access
Numbers

Signing on to DELPHI is simply a matter of using your communications software to dial your local access number, identifying yourself to the network, and then logging on to DELPHI by giving your membername and password.

If you do not live in the Boston or Kansas City area, and are not able to dial one of those local numbers, you may connect to DELPHI using either Sprintnet or Tymnet.

Sprintnet and Tymnet provide local connect number nationwide and throughout the world, and are specially designed to link computer users with services like DELPHI.

The following pages contain Sprintnet and Tymnet numbers in the United States. Tymnet also provides local access number in several provinces of Canada.

If you have any questions, or cannot find a local number in your area, please call Tymnet at 1-800-937-2862 or Sprintnet at 1-800-877-5045 (extension 5). You may also call DELPHI Member Services at 1-800-695-4005.

How to connect to DELPHI via Sprintnet:

1. Dial your local SprintNet access number.

2. Once connected, press @, then uppercase D, and «RETURN». (at 300 and 1200bps, press «RETURN» first, then D, «RETURN».)

3. When TERMINAL= appears, press «RETURN».

4. When @ appears, type C DELPHI and press «RETURN».

5. Answer the Username and Password prompts with your membername and password (remember to press «RETURN» after each entry).

ALABAMA

City	300-1200	300-2400
AL 205 ANNISTON	236-9711	
AL 205 BIRMINGHAM	328-2310	251-1885
AL 205 DECATUR	355-0206	
AL 205 DOTHAN	793-5034	
AL 205 FLORENCE	767-7960	767-0497
AL 205 HUNTSVILLE	539-2281	539-1631
AL 205 MOBILE	432-1680	438-6881
AL 205 MONTGOMERY	269-0090	832-4314
AL 205 TUSCALOOSA	752-1472	758-5799

ALASKA

City	300-1200	300-2400
AK 907 ANCHORAGE	276-0453	276-0453
AK 907 BARROW	852-2425	
AK 907 BETHEL	543-2411	
AK 907 COLD BAY	532-2371	
AK 907 CORDOVA	424-3744	
AK 907 DEADHORSE	659-2777	
AK 907 DELTA JUNCTION	895-5070	
AK 907 DILLINGHAM	842-2688	
AK 907 FAIRBANKS	456-3282	
AK 907 GLENNALLEN	822-5231	
AK 907 HOMER	235-5239	
AK 907 ILIAMNA	571-1364	
AK 907 JUNEAU	789-7009	
AK 907 KETCHIKAN	225-1871	
AK 907 KING SALMON	246-3049	
AK 907 KODIAK	486-4061	
AK 907 KOTZEBUE	442-2602	
AK 907 MCGRATH	524-3256	
AK 907 NOME	443-2256	
AK 907 NORTHWAY	778-2301	
AK 907 PALMER	745-0200	
AK 907 PRUDHOE BAY	659-2777	
AK 907 ST PAUL	546-2320	

City	300-1200	300-2400
AK 907 SEWARD	224-3126	
AK 907 SITKA	747-5887	
AK 907 SOLDOTNA	262-1990	
AK 907 TALKEETNA	733-2227	
AK 907 TANANA	366-7167	
AK 907 VALDEZ	835-4987	
AK 907 WHITTIER	472-2467	
AK 907 YAKUTAT	784-3453	

ARIZONA

City	300-1200	300-2400
AZ 602 PHOENIX	254-0244	256-6955
AZ 602 FLAGSTAFF	773-0588	773-0588
AZ 602 TUCSON	747-0107	747-9395

ARKANSAS

City	300-1200	300-2400
AR 501 FAYETTEVILLE	442-0212	442-0212
AR 501 FT SMITH	782-2852	
AR 501 HOT SPRINGS	623-3159	623-3159
AR 501 LITTLE ROCK	372-4616	374-2861
AR 501 TEXARKANA	772-6181	772-6181

CALIFORNIA

City	300-1200	300-2400
CA 805 BAKERSFIELD	327-8146	327-5321
CA 916 CHICO	894-6882	
CA 714 COLTON	824-9000	824-8976
CA 213 COMPTON	516-1007	
CA 510 CONCORD	827-3960	674-0127
CA 916 DAVIS	753-4387	753-4387
CA 619 ESCONDIDO	741-7756	741-9536
CA 707 EUREKA	444-3091	
CA 415 FREMONT	490-2050	490-2050
CA 209 FRESNO	233-0961	441-1861
CA 714 GARDEN GROVE	898-9820	895-1207
CA 818 GLENDALE	507-0909	246-3886
CA 510 HAYWARD	881-1382	727-1708
CA 805 LANCASTER	949-7396	949-7396
CA 213 LOS ANGELES	937-3580	622-1138
CA 213 MARINA DEL REY	306-2984	306-4922
CA 209 MERCED	383-2557	
CA 209 MODESTO	576-2852	
CA 408 MONTEREY	646-9092	646-5122
CA 213 NORWALK	404-2237	
CA 510 OAKLAND	836-4911	834-3194
CA 619 OCEANSIDE	430-0613	
CA 619 PALM SPRINGS	343-3470	343-3470
CA 415 PALO ALTO	856-9995	856-0484
CA 510 PINOLE	724-4200	724-2225
CA 714 POMONA	626-1284	
CA 916 REDDING	243-0690	243-0690
CA 916 SACRAMENTO	448-6262	443-7434
CA 714 SADDLE BROOK	458-0811	458-0811
CA 408 SALINAS	443-4940	443-8791
CA 415 SAN CARLOS	591-0726	595-8870
CA 619 SAN DIEGO	233-0233	231-1703
CA 415 SAN FRANCISCO	956-5777	788-0825
CA 408 SAN JOSE	294-9119	286-6340
CA 213 SAN PEDRO	548-6141	514-1590
CA 415 SAN RAFAEL	472-5360	472-2550
CA 510 SAN RAMON	829-6705	

City	300-1200	300-2400
CA 714 SANTA ANA	558-7078	550-4625
CA 805 SANTA BARBARA	682-5361	564-1158
CA 408 SANTA CRUZ	429-6937	429-9192
CA 805 SANTA MARIA	925-2969	925-2969
CA 707 SANTA ROSA	578-4447	578-1055
CA 209 STOCKTON	957-7610	957-7627
CA 805 THOUSAND OAKS	495-3588	
CA 805 VENTURA	656-6760	650-1070
CA 619 VICTORVILLE	951-2612	951-2612
CA 209 VISALIA	627-1201	
CA 818 WEST COVINA	915-5151	915-0349
CA 818 WOODLAND HILLS	887-3160	348-7141
COLORADO		
CO 719 COLORADO SPR	635-5361	635-2551
CO 303 DENVER	337-6060	696-0159
CO 303 FT COLLINS	493-9131	493-4014
CO 303 GRAND JUNCTION	241-3004	
CO 303 GREELEY	352-8563	
CO 719 PUEBLO	542-4053	
CONNECTICUT		
CT 203 BRIDGEPORT	335-5055	367-9130
CT 203 DANBURY	794-9075	792-5354
CT 203 HARTFORD	247-9479	724-9396
CT 203 MIDDLETOWN	344-8217	
CT 203 NEW BRITAIN	225-7027	
CT 203 NEW HAVEN	624-5954	773-3569
CT 203 NEW LONDON	447-8455	437-0909
CT 203 NORWALK	866-7404	
CT 203 STAMFORD	348-0787	359-9404
CT 203 WATERBURY	753-4512	756-0342
DELAWARE		
DE 302 DOVER	678-8328	
DE 302 NEWARK	454-7710	737-4340
WASHINGTON, DC		
DC 202 WASHINGTON	429-7896	429-0956
DC 202 WASHINGTON	429-7800	429-0956
FLORIDA		
FL 407 BOCA RATON	338-3701	338-3701
FL 813 CAPE CORAL	275-7924	275-4153
FL 407 COCOA BEACH	267-0800	
FL 904 DAYTONA BEACH	255-2629	
FL 305 FT LAUDERDALE	764-4505	524-5304
FL 407 FT PIERCE	466-4566	466-4566
FL 904 GAINESVILLE	338-0220	338-1700
FL 904 HOLLY HILL	257-4770	257-4770
FL 904 JACKSONVILLE	353-1818	791-9201
FL 813 LAKELAND	683-5461	687-0666
FL 904 LEESBURG	787-0799	787-0799
FL 407 MELBOURNE	242-8247	729-9156
FL 305 MIAMI	372-0230	372-1355
FL 813 NAPLES	263-3033	
FL 904 OCALA	351-3790	351-0263
FL 407 ORLANDO	422-4088	422-8858
FL 904 PANAMA CITY	763-8377	763-8377
FL 904 PENSACOLA	432-1335	434-2103

City	300-1200	300-2400
FL 305 POMPANO BEACH	941-5445	
FL 813 ST PETERSBURG	323-4026	327-1163
FL 813 SARASOTA	923-4563	925-1499
FL 904 TALLAHASSEE	681-1902	561-8830
FL 813 TAMPA	224-9920	223-5859
FL 904 VALPARAISO	897-3421	897-3421
FL 407 WEST PALM BCH	833-6691	655-2993
GEORGIA		
GA 912 ALBANY	888-3011	431-9384
GA 404 ATHENS	548-5590	548-9698
GA 404 ATLANTA	523-0834	584-0212
GA 404 AUGUSTA	724-2752	724-4494
GA 404 COLUMBUS	571-0556	323-8931
GA 404 GAINSVILLE	532-9880	532-9880
GA 912 MACON	743-8844	741-2108
GA 404 ROME	234-1428	
GA 912 SAVANNAH	236-2605	236-2875
HAWAII		
HI 808 OAHU	528-0200	528-0200 (2)
HI 800 OTHER ISLANDS	272-5299	272-5299 (2)
IDAHO		
ID 208 BOISE	343-0611	343-1272
ID 208 IDAHO FALLS	529-0406	529-0406
ID 208 LEWISTON	743-0099	743-5885
ID 208 POCATELLA	232-1764	232-1764
ILLINOIS		
IL 708 ARLINGTON HGTS	255-6465	255-6465
IL 708 AURORA	896-0620	896-3363
IL 618 BELLEVILLE	277-5483	-5483
IL 312 CHICAGO	938-0600	938-8725
IL 217 DECATUR	429-0235	429-6054
IL 815 DE KALB	758-2623	758-5046
IL 708 GLENCOE	835-8037	835-8037
IL 815 JOLIET	726-0070	726-8731
IL 708 LIBERTYVILLE	362-7838	362-7838
IL 708 NAPERVILLE	355-2910	355-2910
IL 309 PEORIA	637-8570	637-8582
IL 815 ROCKFORD	965-0400	965-0696
IL 217 SPRINGFIELD	753-1373	753-1391
IL 217 URBANA	384-6428	328-0317
INDIANA		
IN 812 BLOOMINGTON	332-1344	331-8890
IN 812 EVANSVILLE	424-7693	428-2522
IN 219 FT WAYNE	426-2268	422-3431
IN 219 GARY	882-8800	882-1835
IN 317 INDIANAPOLIS	299-0024	299-6766
IN 317 KOKOMO	455-2460	452-0073
IN 317 LAFAYETTE	742-6000	742-5488
IN 317 MUNCIE	282-6418	288-1113
IN 317 RICHMOND	935-7532	935-7532
IN 219 SOUTH BEND	233-7104	233-4031
IN 812 TERRE HAUTE	232-5329	234-4119
IOWA		
IA 515 AMES	233-6300	233-2603
IA 319 BURLINGTON	752-2516	752-2516

City	300-1200	300-2400	City	300-1200	300-2400
IA 319 CEDAR RAPIDS	364-0911	362-2764	**MICHIGAN**		
IA 319 DAVENPORT	324-2445	324-8902	MI 313 ANN ARBOR	996-5995	665-2900
IA 515 DES MOINES	288-4403	288-6206	MI 616 BATTLE CREEK	968-0929	968-9851
IA 319 DUBUQUE	556-0783		MI 616 BRIDGMAN	465-3248	465-3248
IA 319 IOWA CITY	351-1421	354-0676	MI 313 DETROIT	964-2988	963-2274
IA 712 SIOUX CITY	255-1545		MI 313 FLINT	235-8517	235-5477
IA 319 WATERLOO	232-5441	232-0195	MI 616 GRAND RAPIDS	774-0966	774-0131
KANSAS			MI 517 JACKSON	782-8111	
KS 913 LAWRENCE	843-8124		MI 616 KALAMAZOO	345-3088	345-3122
KS 913 LEAVENWORTH	651-0015	651-0015	MI 517 LANSING	484-0062	484-6301
KS 913 MANHATTAN	537-0948		MI 517 MIDLAND	832-7068	
KS 913 SALINA	825-7900		MI 616 MUSKEGON	726-5723	
KS 913 TOPEKA	233-9880	233-4660	MI 313 PONTIAC	332-5120	332-5979
KS 316 WICHITA	262-5669	262-7961	MI 313 PORT HURON	982-8364	
KENTUCKY			MI 517 SAGINAW	790-5166	799-3190
KY 502 BOWLING GREEN	782-7941	782-6380	MI 313 SOUTHFIELD	827-4710	
KY 502 FRANKFORT	875-4654	875-1942	MI 616 TRAVERSE CITY	946-2121	
KY 606 LEXINGTON	233-0312	233-7217	MI 313 WARREN	575-9152	558-8460
KY 502 LOUISVILLE	589-5580	583-1006	MI 313 WAYNE	326-4210	326-4210
KY 502 OWENSBORO	686-8107		**MINNESOTA**		
LOUISIANA			MN 218 DULUTH	722-1719	722-5032
LA 318 ALEXANDRIA	445-1053		MN 507 MANKATO	388-3780	
LA 504 BATON ROUGE	343-0753	343-0771	MN 612 MINNEAPOLIS	341-2459	338-1661
LA 318 LAFAYETTE	233-0002	234-8451	MN 507 ROCHESTER	282-5917	282-0253
LA 318 LAKE CHARLES	436-0518		MN 612 ST CLOUD	253-1264	
LA 318 MONROE	387-6330	322-9826	**MISSISSIPPI**		
LA 504 NEW ORLEANS	524-4094	522-3967	MS 601 HATTIESBURG	264-0815	264-0815
LA 318 SHREVEPORT	221-5833	424-2255	MS 601 GULFPORT	863-0024	
MAINE			MS 601 JACKSON	969-0036	969-0152
ME 207 AUGUSTA	622-3123	622-7364	MS 601 MERIDIAN	482-2210	
ME 207 BREWER	989-3081		MS 601 PORT GIBSON	437-8916	437-8916
ME 207 LEWISTON	784-0105		MS 601 STARKVILLE	324-2155	
ME 207 PORTLAND	761-4000	761-9029	**MISSOURI**		
MARYLAND			MO 314 COLUMBIA	449-4404	443-3432
MD 301 ANNAPOLIS	224-8550	224-0795	MO 314 JEFFERSON CITY	634-5178	634-8436
MD 301 BALTIMORE	727-6060	752-5555	MO 816 KANSAS CITY	221-9900	472-1430
MD 301 FREDERICK	293-9596		MO 314 ST CHARLES	723-5179	723-5179
MASSACHUSETTS			MO 816 ST JOSEPH	279-4797	
MA 617 BOSTON	292-0662	574-9244	MO 314 ST LOUIS	421-4990	421-0381
MA 508 BROCKTON	580-0721	588-3315	MO 417 SPRINGFIELD	864-4814	864-4945
MA 617 DEDHAM	326-4064	326-4064	**MONTANA**		
MA 508 FALL RIVER	677-4477		MT 406 BILLINGS	245-7649	248-6373
MA 508 FRAMINGHAM	879-6798	820-0480	MT 406 GREAT FALLS	771-0067	
MA 508 LAWRENCE	975-2273	683-0680	MT 406 HELENA	443-0000	443-0527
MA 617 LEXINGTON	863-1550	863-1745	MT 406 MISSOULA	721-5900	543-5575
MA 508 LOWELL	937-5214	453-8803	**NEBRASKA**		
MA 508 NEW BEDFORD	999-2915	999-9667	NE 308 GRAND ISLAND	381-2049	381-2049
MA 413 NORTHAMPTON	586-0510		NE 402 LINCOLN	475-4964	475-3839
MA 413 PITTSFIELD	499-7741		NE 402 OMAHA	341-7733	346-6419
MA 508 SALEM	744-1559		**NEVADA**		
MA 413 SPRINGFIELD	781-3811	737-9285	NV 702 LAS VEGAS	737-6861	737-5466
MA 508 WOODS HOLE	540-7500	457-9390	NV 702 RENO	827-6900	827-5290
MA 508 WORCESTER	755-4740	792-1785			

City	300-1200	300-2400	City	300-1200	300-2400
NEW HAMPSHIRE			NC 919 N. WILKESBORO	838-9034	838-1663
NH 603 CONCORD	224-1024	225-8710	NC 919 RALEIGH	834-8254	834-8254
NH 603 DURHAM	868-2924		NC 919 RES TRI PARK	549-8139	541-9096
NH 603 MANCHESTER	627-8725	625-8088	NC 919 TARBORO	823-0578	823-7459
NH 603 NASHUA	880-6241	880-3901	NC 919 WILMINGTON	763-8313	251-8900
NH 603 PORTSMOUTH	431-2302	431-7592	NC 919 WINSTON-SLM	725-2126	777-0312
NEW JERSEY			**NORTH DAKOTA**		
NJ 609 ATLANTIC CITY	348-0561	344-8571	ND 701 FARGO	235-7717	235-9069
NJ 908 FREEHOLD	780-5030	780-9122	ND 701 GRAND FORKS	775-7813	
NJ 201 HACKENSACK	488-6567	488-2063	ND 701 MANDAN	663-2256	663-6339
NJ 609 MARLTON	596-1500	596-8659	**OHIO**		
NJ 609 MERCHANTVILLE	663-9297	665-6860	OH 216 CANTON	452-0903	52-6642
NJ 201 MORRISTOWN	455-0275	644-4745	OH 513 CINCINNATI	579-0390	241-8008
NJ 908 NEW BRUNSWICK	745-2900	745-7010	OH 614 COLUMBUS	463-9340	461-9044
NJ 201 NEWARK	623-0469	623-7122	OH 513 DAYTON	461-5254	461-0755
NJ 201 PASSAIC	778-5600	773-3674	OH 216 ELYRIA	322-8712	322-8645
NJ 201 PATERSON	684-7560	742-4415	OH 419 FINDLAY	422-8188	422-8188
NJ 609 PRINCETON	799-5587	936-0231	OH 513 HAMILTON	863-4116	
NJ 908 RAHWAY	815-1885		OH 216 KENT	678-5115	678-5043
NJ 908 REDBANK	571-0003		OH 216 LORAIN	960-1771	
NJ 201 ROSELAND	227-5277	227-6722	OH 419 MANSFIELD	526-0686	
NJ 908 SAYREVILLE	525-9507		OH 419 SANDUSKY	627-0050	
NJ 908 SUMMIT	273-9619	273-9619	OH 513 SPRINGFIELD	324-1520	
NJ 609 TRENTON	989-8847	989-7127	OH 419 TOLEDO	255-7881	255-1906
NEW MEXICO			OH 216 WARREN	394-0041	
NM 505 ALBUQUERQUE	243-4479	242-1742	OH 216 WOOSTER	264-8920	
NM 505 LAS CRUCES	526-9191		OH 216 YOUNGSTOWN	743-1296	743-6843
NM 505 SANTA FE	473-3403		**OKLAHOMA**		
NEW YORK			OK 918 BARTLESVILLE	336-3675	
NY 518 ALBANY	465-8444	465-8632	OK 405 LAWTON	353-0333	353-0225
NY 607 BINGHAMTON	772-6642	772-9526	OK 405 OKLAHOMA CITY	232-4546	232-9513
NY 716 BUFFALO	847-1440	847-1825	OK 405 STILLWATER	624-1112	743-1447
NY 516 DEER PARK	667-5566	243-1105	OK 918 TULSA	584-3247	587-2774
NY 516 HEMPSTEAD	292-3800	485-3380	**OREGON**		
NY 607 ITHACA	277-2142	272-9980	OR 503 CORVALLIS	754-9273	754-0559
NY 212 NEW YORK CITY	741-8100	645-0560	OR 503 EUGENE	683-1460	342-6626
NY 212 NEW YORK CITY	741-4950	645-0560	OR 503 HOOD RIVER	386-4405	
NY 212 NEW YORK CITY	620-6000	645-0560	OR 503 KLAMATH FALLS	882-6282	882-6282
NY 716 NIAGARA FALLS	282-1462	282-3284	OR 503 MEDFORD	779-6343	773-7601
NY 518 PLATTSBURGH	562-1890		OR 503 PORTLAND	295-3028	241-0496
NY 914 POUGHKEEPSIE	473-2240	473-3200	OR 503 SALEM	378-7712	378-1660
NY 716 ROCHESTER	454-1020	454-5730	**PENNSYLVANIA**		
NY 315 SYRACUSE	472-5583	479-5445	PA 215 ALLENTOWN	435-3330	770-1405
NY 315 UTICA	797-0920	797-0228	PA 814 ALTOONA	949-0310	
NY 914 WHITE PLAINS	328-9199	682-3505	PA 717 CARLISLE	249-9311	
NORTH CAROLINA			PA 717 DAN	271-0102	
NC 704 ASHEVILLE	252-9134	252-0133	PA 814 ERIE	899-2241	453-3793
NC 919 BURLINGTON	229-0032	229-0032	PA 412 GREENSBURG	836-4771	836-4771
NC 704 CHARLOTTE	332-3131	333-6204	PA 717 HARRISBURG	236-6882	236-2007
NC 919 FAYETTEVILLE	323-8165	323-4148	PA 814 JOHNSTOWN	535-7576	536-3630
NC 704 GASTONIA	865-4708		PA 215 KING OF PRUSSI	337-4300	337-2850
NC 919 GREENSBORO	273-2851	275-1251	PA 717 LANCASTER	295-5405	295-7128
NC 704 HICKORY	326-9860		PA 215 LEVITTO	946-3469	946-3469
NC 919 HIGH POINT	889-7494		PA 412 MONROEVILLE	856-1330	856-1330

City	300-1200	300-2400	City	300-1200	300-2400
PA 215 PHILADELPHIA	574-9462	574-0990	TX 409 NEDERLAND	722-3720	727-4090
PA 412 PITTSBURGH	288-9950	471-6430	TX 915 SAN ANGELO	944-7621	949-1231
PA 412 PITTSBURGH	288-9974	471-6430	TX 512 SAN ANTONIO	225-8004	225-3444
PA 215 READING	376-8750	375-6945	TX 903 SHERMAN	893-4995	
PA 717 SCRANTON	961-5321	961-5480	TX 817 TEMPLE	773-9723	
PA 814 STATE COLLEGE	231-1510		TX 903 TYLER	597-8925	
PA 215 WARRINGTON	343-6010	343-6010	TX 512 VICTORIA	572-3197	572-3197
PA 215 WEST CHESTER	436-7406	436-7406	TX 817 WACO	752-9743	752-2681
PA 717 WILKES-BARRE	829-3108	824-8209	TX 817 WICHITA FALLS	322-3774	
PA 717 WILLIAMSPORT	494-1796		**UTAH**		
PA 717 YORK	846-6550	843-0039	UT 801 LOGAN	752-3421	752-3421
RHODE ISLAND			UT 801 OGDEN	627-1630	627-1640
RI 401 PROVIDENCE	751-7912	831-3990	UT 801 PROVO	373-0542	375-2084
RI 401 NORTH KINGSTON	295-7100	295-7100	UT 801 SALT LAKE CITY	359-0149	359-0578
RI 401 WOONSOCKET	765-0019	765-0019	**VERMONT**		
SOUTH CAROLINA			VT 802 BURLINGTON	864-0808	864-5485
SC 803 CHARLESTON	722-4303	577-4710	VT 802 MONTPELIER	229-4966	223-0758
SC 803 COLUMBIA	254-0695	252-0328	VT 802 RUTLAND	775-1676	
SC 803 FLORENCE	669-0042	669-0042	VT 802 WHITE RIVER JCT	295-7631	
SC 803 GREENVILLE	233-3486	271-0231	**VIRGINIA**		
SC 803 MYRTLE BEACH	626-9134	626-9134	VA 703 BLACKSBURG	552-9181	
SC 803 SPARTANBURG	585-1637	585-9197	VA 804 CHARLOTTESVILLE	977-5330	
SOUTH DAKOTA			VA 703 COVINGTON	962-2217	
SD 605 PIERRE	224-0481	224-2257	VA 703 FREDERICKSBURG	371-0188	
SD 605 RAPID CITY	348-2621	348-2048	VA 703 HARRISONBURG	434-7121	434-0374
SD 605 SIOUX FALLS	336-8593	336-6438	VA 703 HERNDON	435-1800	481-6807
TENNESSEE			VA 804 LYNCHBURG	845-0010	
TN 615 BRISTOL	968-1130	968-2480	VA 804 NEWPORT NEWS	596-6600	596-2710
TN 615 CHATTANOOGA	756-1161	265-7929	VA 804 NORFOLK	625-1186	625-2408
TN 615 CLARKSVILLE	552-0032		VA 703 OCCOQUAN	494-0836	494-0836
TN 615 JOHNSON CITY	282-6645		VA 804 RICHMOND	788-9902	343-4140
TN 615 KNOXVILLE	523-5500	521-5072	VA 703 ROANOKE	344-2036	344-2404
TN 901 MEMPHIS	521-0215	527-5175	**WASHINGTON**		
TN 615 NASHVILLE	244-3702	255-2608	WA 206 AUBURN	939-9982	
TN 615 OAK RIDGE	481-3590		WA 206 BELLINGHAM	733-2720	733-2873
TEXAS			WA 206 EVERETT	775-9929	774-7466
TX 915 ABILENE	676-9151	672-2280	WA 206 LONGVIEW	577-5835	577-3992
TX 806 AMARILLO	373-0458	373-1833	WA 206 LYNWOOD	774-7466	774-7466
TX 903 ATHENS	677-1712	677-1712	WA 206 OLYMPIA	754-0460	786-5066
TX 512 AUSTIN	928-1130	929-3622	WA 509 PULLMAN	332-0172	332-0172
TX 512 BROWNSVILLE	542-0367	544-7073	WA 509 RICHLAND	943-0649	946-2350
TX 409 BRYAN	822-0159	779-0713	WA 206 SEATTLE	625-9612	623-9951
TX 512 CORPUS CHRISTI	884-9030	884-6946	WA 509 SPOKANE	455-4071	838-9065
TX 214 DALLAS	748-6371	745-1359	WA 206 TACOMA	627-1791	383-2233
TX 817 DENTON	381-1897	381-1897	WA 206 VANCOUVER	693-6914	
TX 915 EL PASO	532-7907	541-1931	WA 509 WENATCHEE	663-6227	663-9180
TX 817 FT WORTH	332-4307	332-6794	WA 509 YAKIMA	575-1060	
TX 409 GALVESTON	762-4382	765-7298	**WEST VIRGINIA**		
TX 713 HOUSTON	227-1018	227-8208	WV 304 CHARLESTON	345-6471	345-7140
TX 512 LAREDO	724-1791		WV 304 CLARKSBURG	622-6827	622-6827
TX 903 LONGVIEW	236-4205	758-1161	WV 304 HUNTINGTON	523-2802	
TX 806 LUBBOCK	747-4121	765-9631	WV 304 MORGANTOWN	292-0104	292-0492
TX 512 MCALLEN	686-5360	686-2452	WV 304 WHEELING	233-7732	
TX 915 MIDLAND	561-9811	561-8597			

City	300-1200	300-2400
WISCONSIN		
WI 608 BELOIT	362-5287	
WI 715 EAU CLAIRE	836-9295	836-0097
WI 414 GREEN BAY	432-2815	432-0346
WI 414 KENOSHA	552-9242	
WI 608 LA CROSSE	784-0560	
WI 608 MADISON	257-5010	257-8472
WI 414 MILWAUKEE	271-3914	278-8007
WI 414 NEENAH	731-0620	731-1560
WI 414 RACINE	632-6166	632-2174
WI 414 SHEBOYGAN	452-3995	
WI 715 WAUSAU	845-9589	845-9589
WI 414 WEST BEND	334-2206	
WYOMING		
WY 307 CASPER	265-5167	265-8807
WY 307 CHEYENNE	638-4421	637-3958
WY 307 LARAMIE	721-5878	

How to connect to DELPHI via Tymnet:

1. Dial your local Tymnet access number.

2. For 2400 bps access, wait five seconds after connection, then type the letter O, but do NOT press «RETURN».

   For 1200 bps access, wait until a group of X's appears, then type the letter O, WITHOUT pressing «RETURN».

   For 300 bps access, wait until you see the prompt, "Please enter your terminal identifier," or a string of random characters. Then type the letter O. Do NOT press «RETURN».

3. When the prompt "Please Log In" appears, enter DELPHI and press «RETURN».

4. Answer the Username and Password prompts with your membername and password (remember to press «RETURN» after each entry).

ALBERTA		
CALGARY		403/232-6653
ALABAMA		
ANNISTON		205/236-3342
BIRMINGHAM	205/942-4141	205/942-7898
DOTHAN		205/794-7954
FLORENCE		205/760-0030
GADSDEN		205/543-3550
HUNTSVILLE	205/882-3003	205/880-8912
MOBILE	205/343-8414	205/460-2515
MONTGOMERY		205/265-4570
NORTHPORT		205/758-1116
OPELIKA		205/742-9040
TUSCALOOSA/NORTHPORT		205/758-1116
ALASKA		
ADAK		907/592-2557
ANCHORAGE	907/258-7222	907/258-6607
BARROW	907/852-2425	
BETHEL	907/543-2411	
CANTWELL		907/768-2700
CORDOVA	907/424-3744	
CRAIG		907/826-2948
DEAD HORSE	907/659-2777	
DELTA JUNCTION	907/895-5070	
DILLINGHAM	907/842-2688	
DUTCH HARBOR		907/581-1820
FAIRBANKS	907/456-3282	907/452-5848
GLENNALLEN	907/822-5231	
HAINES	907/766-2171	
HEALY		907/683-1350

City	300-1200	300-2400	City	300-1200	300-2400
HOMER	907/235-5239		BURBANK		818/841-4795
JUNEAU	907/789-7009	907/789-1976	BURLINGAME/SO. S.F.		415/588-3043
KENAI	907/262-1990		CANOGA PARK/SHRM OAK	818/789-9002	818/789-9557
KETCHIKAN	907/225-1871		CATHEDRAL CITY		619/324-0920
KING SALMON	907/246-3049		CHICO		916/343-4401
KODIAK	907/486-4061		COLTON	714/370-1200	714/422-0222
KOTZEBUE	907/442-2602		CONCORD/WALNUT CREEK		415/935-1507
MCGRATH	907/524-3256		CORONA		714/737-5510
MENANA	907/832-5214		COVINA/DIAMOND BAR		714/860-0057
NOME	907/443-2256		DAVIS		916/758-3551
NORTHWAY	907/778-2301		DIAMOND BAR		714/860-0057
PALMER/WASILLA	907/745-0200		EL MONTE/ALHAMBRA	818/308-1800	818/308-1994
PETERSBURG	907/772-3878		EL SEGUNDO	213/643-2907	213/643-4228
PRUDHOE BAY	907/659-2777		ESCONDIDO/VISTA		619/941-6700
SEWARD	907/224-3126		EUREKA		707/445-3021
SITKA	907/747-5887		FAIRFIELD		707/426-5900
SKAGWAY	907/983-2170		FREMONT		415/490-7366
SOLDOTNA/KENAI	907/262-1990		FRESNO		209/442-4328
ST. PAUL	907/546-2320		GLENDALE/BURBANK		818/841-4795
TANANA	907/366-7167		HAYWARD/OAKLAND	415/430-2900	415/633-1896
TOK	907/883-4747		INGLEWOOD/VERNON	213/587-0030	213/587-7514
UNALASKA/DUTCH HBR.		907/581-1820	IRVINE/NEWPORT BEACH	714/756-8341	714/852-8141
VALDEZ	907/835-4987		LANCASTER		805/945-4962
WASILLA	907/745-0200		LONG BEACH	213/436-6033	
WHITTIER	907/472-2467		LOS ALAMOS/ST. MARIA		805/922-3308
WRANGELL	907/874-2394		LOS ALTOS/SAN JOSE	408/432-8618	408/432-3430
YAKUTAT	907/784-3453		LOS ANGELES/VERNON	213/587-0030	213/587-7514
ARKANSAS			MAR VISTA/EL SEGUNDO		213/643-4228
FAYETTEVILLE		501/442-0234	MARINADELREY/EL SGND		213/643-4228
FT. SMITH		501/782-2486	MERCED		209/383-7593
HOT SPRINGS		501/623-3576	MODESTO		209/527-0150
JONESBORO		501/935-7957	MONTEREY		408/375-2644
LITTLE ROCK		501/666-6886	MOORPARK		805/523-0203
PINE BLUFF		501/535-2629	NAPA		707/257-6810
SPRINGDALE/FAYETTEVL		501/442-0234	NEWPORT BEACH	714/756-8341	714/852-8141
ARIZONA			NORWALK/LONG BEACH	213/435-0900	213/436-6033
FLAGSTAFF		602/774-3857	OAKLAND	415/430-2900	415/633-1896
MESA/PHOENIX	602/254-5811	602/258-0554	ONTARIO/DIAMOND BAR		714/860-0057
PHOENIX	602/254-3423		OXNARD/PORT HUENEME		805/985-7843
PHOENIX	602/258-0554		PACHECO/WALNUT CREEK		415/935-1507
PHOENIX	602/254-5811		PALM SPRNGS/CATH CTY		619/324-0920
TUCSON		602/297-2239	PALO ALTO/REDWD CITY	415/366-1092	415/361-8701
YUMA		602/343-9000	PASADENA/ALHAMBRA	818/308-1800	818/308-1994
BRITISH COLUMBIA			PLEASANTON	415/462-2101	
BURNABY/VANCOUVER		604/683-7620	PLEASNTHILL/WALNT CK		415/935-1507
VANCOUVER		604/683-7620	POMONA/DIAMOND BAR	714/860-0057	
CALIFORNIA			PORT HUENEME		805/985-7843
ALAMEDA/OAKLAND	415/430-2900	415/633-1896	POWAY		619/679-0200
ALHAMBRA	818/308-1800	818/308-1994	REDDING		916/241-4820
ANAHEIM/NEWPRT BEACH	714/756-8341	714/852-8141	REDWOOD CITY	415/361-8701	
ANTIOCH		415/754-8222	RIVERSIDE/COLTON	714/370-1200	714/422-0222
ARCADIA/ALHAMBRA	818/308-1800	818/308-1994	SACRAMENTO	916/448-4300	916/447-7434
BAKERSFIELD		805/325-0371	SALINAS	408/754-2206	
BELMONT/REDWOOD CITY	415/366-1092	415/361-8701	SAN BERNADINO/COLTON	714/370-1200	714/422-0222
BERKELEY/IOAKLAND	415/430-2900	415/633-1896	SAN CLEMENTE		714/240-9424
BEVERLY HILLS/SHR OK	818/789-9002	818/789-9557	SAN DIEGO	619/296-3370	619/296-8747
			SAN FERNANDO/SHM OAK	818/789-9002	818/789-9557

City	300-1200	300-2400	City	300-1200	300-2400
SAN FRANCISCO	415/974-1300	415/543-0691	**DELAWARE**		
SAN JOSE	408/432-3430	408/432-8618	DOVER		302/678-3569
SAN LUIS OBISPO		805/549-0770	GEORGETOWN		302/856-1788
SAN MATEO/SO. S.F.		415/588-3043	NEWARK/WILMINGTON	302/652-2060	302/652-2036
SAN PEDRO/LONG BEACH	213/435-0900	213/436-6033	WILMINGTON	302/652-2060	302/652-2036
SAN RAFAEL		415/453-2087	**WASHINGTON, DC**		
SANTA ANA/NEWPRT BCH	714/756-8341	714/852-8141	WASHINGTON	703/691-8200	703/352-3136
SANTA BARBARA	805/564-2354	805/965-1612	**FLORIDA**		
SANTA CLARA/SAN JOSE	408/432-3430	408/432-8618	BOCA RATON/DELRAY		407/272-7900
SANTA CRUZ		408/475-0981	BOYNTN BCH/WPALM BCH	407/471-9310	
SANTA MARIA		805/922-3308	CLEARWATER	813/441-9017	813/441-1621
SANTA MONICA/EL SGND	213/643-2907	213/643-4228	COCOA		407/639-3022
SANTA ROSA		707/527-6180	DELRAY		407/272-7900
SHERMAN OAKS	818/789-9002	818/789-9557	FORT MEYERS		813/337-0006
SO. SAN FRANCISCO		415/588-3043	FORT PIERCE		407/466-5661
STOCKTON	209/467-0601		FT. LAUDERDALE	305/463-0882	305/467-1870
SUNNYVALE/SAN JOSE	408/432-3430	408/432-8618	GAINESVILLE		904/335-0544
UPLAND		714/985-1153	HOLLYWD/FT. LAUDRDLE	305/463-0882	305/467-1870
VALLEJO		707/644-1192	JACKSONVILLE	904/721-8100	904/721-8559
VAN NUYS/SHERMAN OAK	818/789-9002	818/789-9557	KISSIMMEE		407/933-8425
VENTURA/PORT HUENEME		805/985-7843	LAKELAND		813/858-6970
VERNON	213/587-0030	213/587-7514	LONGWOOD/ORLANDO	407/841-0020	
VISALIA		209/625-4891	MELBOURNE/COCOA		407/639-3022
VISTA		619/941-6700	MERRIT ISLE/COCOA		407/639-3022
W.COVINA/DIAMOND BAR	714/860-0057		MIAMI	305/599-2900	305/599-2964
WALNUT CREEK		415/935-1507	NAPLES		813/434-8080
WEST L.A./SHRMN OAKS	818/789-9002	818/789-9557	OCALA		904/732-3707
WOODLAND/DAVIS	916/758-3551		ORLANDO	407/841-0020	407/841-0217
COLORADO			ORMOND BEACH		904/673-0034
AURORA/DENVER	303/830-9210	303/832-3447	PANAMA CITY		904/769-0709
BOULDER/DENVER	303/830-9210	303/832-3447	PENSACOLA		904/477-3344
COLORADO SPRINGS		719/590-1003	POMPNO BCH/FT. LDRDL	305/463-0882	305/467-1870
DENVER	303/830-9210	303/832-3447	PORT ST. LUCIE		407/337-1992
FORT COLLINS		303/224-9819	SARASOTA		813/952-9000
GRAND JUNCTION		303/241-1643	ST. PETERSBRG/CLRWTR	813/441-9017	813/441-1621
GREELEY		303/352-0960	TALLAHASSEE		904/422-0149
PUEBLO		719/543-9712	TAMPA	813/932-7070	813/933-6210
CONNECTICUT			VERO BEACH		407/569-8207
BLOOMFIELD	203/242-7140	203/242-1986	WEST PALM BEACH		407/471-9310
BRIDGEPORT	203/579-1479	203/332-7256	WINTERHAVEN/LAKELAND		813/858-6970
DANBURY	203/797-9539		**GEORGIA**		
FAIRFIELD/WESTPORT		203/454-2129	ALBANY		912/888-9282
HARTFORD/BLOOMFIELD	203/242-7140	203/242-1986	ATHENS		404/548-7006
MERIDEN	203/634-9249		ATLANTA/DORAVILLE	404/451-2208	404/451-3362
MIDDLETOWN/MERIDEN	203/634-9249		AUGUSTA/MARTINEZ		404/855-0442
NEW HAVEN/NO. HAVEN	203/773-0082	203/787-4674	COLUMBUS		404/327-0597
NEW LONDON		203/444-7030	DORAVILLE	404/451-2208	404/451-3362
NORTH HAVEN	203/773-0082	203/787-4674	MACON/WARNER ROBINS		912/923-7590
NORWALK/WESTPORT		203/454-2129	MARIETTA/DORAVILLE	404/451-2208	404/451-3362
NORWICH/NEW LONDON	203/444-7030		MARTINEZ		404/855-0442
SOMERS		203/763-3521	NORCROSS/DORAVILLE	404/451-2208	404/451-3362
STAMFORD	203/965-0000	203/327-2974	ROME		404/234-0102
STRATFORD/BRIDGEPRT	203/579-1479	203/332-7256	SAVANNAH		912/232-6751
WATERBURY		203/755-5994	WARNER ROBINS		912/923-7590
WESTPORT		203/454-2129			

City	300-1200	300-2400	City	300-1200	300-2400
HAWAII			SOUTH BEND	219/234-5005	219/234-6410
HILO	808/935-5717		TERRE HAUTE		812/232-0112
HONOLULU	808/545-7610	808/528-5300	**IOWA**		
MAUI		808/661-7688	AMES		515/232-0157
IDAHO			CEDAR FALLS/WATERLOO		319/236-9020
BOISE	208/343-0404	208/345-5951	CEDAR RAPIDS		319/363-7514
COEUR D'ALENE		208/765-1465	DAVENPORT/ROCK ISLAND		309/788-3713
IDAHO FALLS		208/522-3624	DES MOINES	515/277-7752	515/277-9684
POCATELLO		208/233-2501	DUBUQUE		319/582-3599
TWIN FALLS		208/734-0221	IOWA CITY		319/354-3633
ILLINOIS			MARSHALLTOWN		515/753-0670
AURORA		708/844-0700	SIOUX CITY		712/255-3834
BLOOMINGTON		309/827-2748	WATERLOO		319/236-9020
BRADLEY		815/935-2352	**KANSAS**		
CHAMPAIGN/URBANA		217/344-3400	KANSAS CITY/MISSION	913/384-1226	913/384-5012
CHICAGO	312/922-4601	312/922-6571	LAWRENCE		913/843-4870
CICERO/MAYWOOD		708/345-9100	LEAVENWORTH		913/651-8094
DANVILLE		217/442-1452	MANHATTAN		913/776-9803
DECATUR		217/425-8864	MISSION	913/384-1226	913/384-5012
DOWNRS GROVE/GLN ELN	708/790-4400	708/790-4955	SALINA		913/825-4845
E. ST. LOUIS		618/874-5702	SHAWNEE/MISSION	913/384-1226	913/384-5012
ELGIN	708/888-8113		TOPEKA		913/234-3070
FOREST PARK/MAYWOOD		708/345-9100	WICHITA	316/681-0832	316/681-2719
FREEPORT		815/232-7111	**KENTUCKY**		
GLEN ELLYN	708/790-4400	708/790-4955	BOWLING GREEN		502/781-5711
JOLIET	815/727-2169		FRANKFORT		502/223-0724
KANKAKEE/BRADLEY		815/935-2352	LEXINGTON	606/266-0019	606/266-7063
LAKE BLUFF		708/295-7075	LOUISVILLE	502/499-7110	502/499-9825
LAKE ZURICH/PALATINE		708/991-7171	OWENSBORO		502/685-0959
LANSING	708/474-1422		**LOUISIANA**		
LIBRTYVLE/LAKE BLUFF		708/295-7075	ALEXANDRIA		318/445-2694
MAYWOOD		708/345-9100	BATON ROUGE	504/924-5102	504/291-0967
NORTHFIELD		708/501-4536	LAFAYETTE		318/234-8255
O'FALLON		618/632-3993	LAKE CHARLES		318/494-1991
PALATINE		708/991-7171	MONROE		318/388-8810
PEORIA		309/637-5961	NEW ORLEANS	504/522-1370	504/525-2014
ROCK ISLAND		309/788-3713	SHREVEPORT		318/688-5840
ROCKFORD	815/654-1900	815/633-2080	SLIDELL		504/646-2900
SPRINGFIELD	217/525-8025	217/544-0312	**MASSACHUSETTS**		
ST. CHARLES/AURORA	708/844-0700		ATTLEBORO	508/226-6441	
URBANA		217/344-3400	BEDFORD		617/271-0420
WHEATON/GLEN ELLYN	708/790-4400		BOSTON	617/439-3400	617/439-3531
INDIANA			BROCKTON/RANDOLPH	617/986-0500	
BLOOMINGTON	812/332-0544		CAMBRIDGE/BOSTON	617/439-3400	617/439-3531
ELKHART	219/293-8860		FALL RIVER/SOMERSET	508/676-3087	
EVANSVILLE	812/464-8181		FITCHBURG/LEOMINSTER		508/537-6451
FT. WAYNE		219/422-2581	GROTON		508/448-9361
GARY		219/885-0002	HOLYOKE/SPRINGFIELD	413/787-0048	413/785-1762
HAMMOND/GARY		219/885-0002	KINGSTON		617/585-7616
HIGHLAND/GARY		219/885-0002	LAWRENCE		508/683-2680
INDIANAPOLIS	317/631-1002	317/632-6408	LEOMINSTER		508/537-6451
KOKOMO		317/453-7818	LOWELL		508/452-5112
LAFAYETTE		317/423-4616	LYNN	617/593-4051	
MARION		317/662-1928	MANCHESTER		508/526-1506
MISHAWAKA/SOUTH BEND	219/234-5005	219/234-6410	MARLBOROUGH		508/481-0026
MUNCIE		317/284-7821			

City	300-1200	300-2400
NEW BEDFORD		508/999-4521
PITTSFIELD	413/499-0971	
RANDOLPH	617/986-0500	
SOMERSET		508/676-3087
SPRINGFIELD	413/787-0048	413/785-1762
TAUNTON		508/824-6692
WOBURN/BEDFORD		617/271-0420
WORCESTER		508/791-9000
MARYLAND		
ABERDEEN		301/273-7100
ANNAPOLIS		301/224-0520
BALTIMORE	301/547-8100	301/528-9296
BETHESDA	703/691-8200	703/352-3136
CUMBERLAND		301/777-9320
FREDERICK/MYERSVILLE		301/293-9504
HAGERSTOWN/MYERSVLLE		301/293-9504
MYERSVILLE		301/293-9504
ROCKVILLE		301/294-4522
SALISBURY		301/860-0480
MAINE		
AUBURN		207/795-6013
AUGUSTA		207/622-3083
BANGOR		207/990-0529
LEWISTON/AUBURN		207/795-6013
PORTLAND		207/775-5971
MICHIGAN		
ANN ARBOR		313/973-7935
BATTLE CREEK		616/964-9303
BENTON HARBOR		616/925-3134
BURTON		313/743-8350
CADILLAC		616/775-9242
DETROIT	313/962-2870	313/963-3460
FLINT/BURTON		313/743-8350
FREELAND		517/695-6751
GRAND RAPIDS		616/459-2304
JACKSON		517/788-9191
KALAMAZOO		616/388-2130
LANSING	517/482-5721	517/484-5344
MARQUETTE		906/228-3780
MIDLAND/FREELAND		517/695-6751
MUSKEGON		616/739-3453
PLYMOUTH		313/451-2400
PONTIAC	313/338-8384	
PORT HURON		313/982-0301
ROSEVILLE	313/774-1000	
SAGINAW/FREELAND		517/695-6751
SOUTHFIELD		313/424-8024
ST. JOE/BENTON HRBR		616/925-3134
TRAVERSE CITY		616/947-0050
MINNESOTA		
DULUTH		218/722-0655
MANKATO		507/387-7313
MINNEAPOLIS	612/333-2799	612/332-4024
ROCHESTER		507/282-0830
ST. CLOUD		612/251-4942
ST. PAUL/MINNEAPOLIS	612/333-2799	

City	300-1200	300-2400
MISSOURI		
BRIDGETON/HAZELWOOD	314/731-8002	314/731-8283
CAPE GIRARDEAU		314/335-1518
COLUMBIA		314/874-2771
HAZELWOOD	314/731-8002	314/731-8283
INDEPENDENCE		913/384-5012
INDEPENDENCE/MISSION	913/384-1226	913/384-5012
JEFFERSON CITY		314/634-8296
JOPLIN		417/781-8718
KANSAS CITY		913/677-5002
KANSAS CITY/MISSION	913/384-1226	913/384-5012
ROLLA		314/364-2084
SPRINGFIELD		417/881-6225
ST. JOSEPH		816/232-1455
ST. LOUIS/HAZELWOOD	314/731-8002	314/731-4507
MISSISSIPPI		
GULFPORT		601/868-2331
HATTIESBURG		601/582-0286
JACKSON		601/355-9741
MERIDIAN		601/482-4335
PASCAGOULA		601/769-0121
TUPELO		601/841-0090
VICKSBURG		601/638-1551
MONTANA		
BILLINGS		406/252-4880
BOZEMAN		406/585-9719
BUTTE		406/494-6682
GREAT FALLS		406/727-9510
HELENA		406/443-0112
MISSOULA		406/721-8960
NORTH CAROLINA		
ASHEVILLE	704/253-8945	
CHAPEL HILL/DURHAM	919/549-8952	919/549-9025
CHARLOTTE	704/377-0521	704/374-0803
DURHAM	919/549-8952	919/549-9025
FAYETTEVILLE		919/424-9610
GASTONIA		704/867-2203
GREENSBORO		919/273-0332
GREENVILLE		919/758-0102
HIGH POINT		919/883-6121
KANNAPOLIS		704/932-4131
RALEIGH	919/829-0536	
ROCKY MOUNT		919/937-4828
WILMINGTON		919/762-1865
WINSTON-SALEM		919/765-1221
NORTH DAKOTA		
BISMARCK		701/255-0869
FARGO		701/280-0210
GRAND FORKS	701/746-0344	
MINOT		701/839-4210
NEBRASKA		
GRAND ISLAND		308/382-3176
LINCOLN		402/464-6235
OMAHA	402/393-0903	402/393-1305

City	300-1200	300-2400	City	300-1200	300-2400
NEW HAMPSHIRE			HUNTINGTON/MELVILLE	516/420-1221	516/420-4579
CONCORD	603/228-4732		ITHACA	607/257-6601	
DURHAM		603/868-1502	JAMESTOWN	716/488-0794	
HANOVER		603/643-4011	KINGSTON		914/336-2790
MANCHESTER		603/623-0409	LAKE GROVE		516/471-6080
NASHUA		603/882-0435	MELVILLE	516/420-1221	516/420-4579
NORTH HAMPTON		603/964-7779	MINEOLA/HEMPSTEAD	516/485-7422	
PETERBOROUGH		603/924-7090	NEW CITY		914/634-0388
SALEM/NASHUA		603/882-0435	NEW YORK	212/943-4700	212/809-9660
NEW JERSEY			NIAGARA FALLS	716/285-2561	
ATLANTIC CITY		609/345-4050	PERINTON/PITTSFORD	716/385-5817	716/385-5710
CAMDEN/PENNSAUKEN	609/665-5600	609/665-5902	PITTSFORD	716/385-5817	716/385-5710
CHERRY HILL/PENNSKN	609/665-5600	609/665-5902	POUGHKEEPSIE		914/473-0401
EATONTOWN/RED BANK		908/758-0337	ROCHESTER		716/586-0820
ELIZABETH/NEWARK	201/824-1212	201/824-3044	ROCHESTER/PITTSFORD	716/385-5817	716/385-5710
ENGLEWOOD CLIFFS	201/567-9841	201/567-8951	RONKONKOMA/LAKE GRVE	516/471-6080	
FAIR LAWN/ENGLWD CLF	201/567-9841		SCHENECTADY/ALBANY	518/458-8300	518/458-9724
JERSEY CITY/NEWARK	201/824-1212	201/824-3044	SYRACUSE	315/437-7111	315/433-1593
LONG BRANCH/RED BANK		908/758-0337	UTICA		315/797-7001
LYNDHURST/UNION CITY		201/864-8468	WHITE PLAINS	914/328-7730	914/761-9590
MORRISTOWN	201/539-1222		WINDSOR	914/561-9103	
NEWARK	201/824-1212	201/824-3044	**OHIO**		
PATERSON		201/742-0752	AKRON	216/376-6227	216/376-8330
PENNSAUKEN	609/665-5600	609/665-5902	CANTON		216/456-0840
PISCATAWAY	908/562-8550	908/562-8550	CINCINNATI	513/530-9019	513/530-9021
PRINCETON/SO. BRNSWK	609/452-1018		CLEVELAND	216/241-0024	216/861-6709
RAHWAY	908/396-8550		COLUMBUS	614/221-1862	614/221-1612
RED BANK		908/758-0337	DAYTON	513/898-0124	513/898-0696
RIDGEWOOD/PATERSON		201/742-0752	ELYRIA		216/324-7156
S. BRUNSWICK		609/452-8640	HAMILTON	513/874-1744	
SOUTH BRUNSWICK	609/452-1018	609/452-9529	LIMA		419/228-6343
TRENTON		609/394-1900	MANSFIELD		419/529-3303
UNION CITY	201/864-8468	201/617-9103	NEWARK		614/345-8953
UNION/NEWARK	201/824-1212	210/824-3044	SPRINGFIELD		513/325-0511
VINELAND		609/691-6446	STEUBENVILLE		614/266-2170
WAYNE/PATERSON		201/742-0752	TOLEDO	419/255-7790	419/255-7705
NEW MEXICO			WARREN		216/392-2542
ALBUQUERQUE	505/242-8344	505/242-8931	WINTERSVILLE		614/266-2170
LAS CRUCES		505/525-3401	YOUNGSTOWN		216/759-8892
SANTA FE		505/471-0606	**OKLAHOMA**		
NOVIA SCOTIA			ARDMORE		405/226-1260
HALIFAX		902/492-4901	ENID		405/242-0113
NEVADA			LAWTON		405/353-6987
BOULDER CITY	702/293-0300	702/294-0602	OKLAHOMA CITY	405/495-8201	405/495-9201
CARSON CITY		702/885-8411	TULSA	918/585-2010	918/585-2706
LAS VEGAS/BOULDER CTY	702/293-0300	702/294-0602	**ONTARIO**		
RENO/CARSON CITY		702/885-8411	DUNDAS		416/628-5908
NEW YORK			HULL/OTTAWA	613/563-2970	613/563-2910
ALBANY	518/458-8300	518/458-9724	KITCHENER		519/742-7613
BINGHAMPTON		607/724-4351	OTTAWA	613/563-2970	613/563-2910
BUFFALO	716/893-1306	716/893-1014	TORONTO		416/365-7630
CENTEREACH		516/471-6080	WINDSOR		519/977-7256
CORNING		607/962-4481	**OREGON**		
ELMIRA		607/737-9065	CORVALLIS		503/757-6341
HEMPSTEAD	516/485-7422	516/481-0150	EUGENE		503/343-0044

City	300-1200	300-2400
MEDFORD		503/772-0831
PORTLAND	503/222-0900	503/222-2151
SALEM		503/370-4314
SPRINGFIELD/EUGENE		503/343-0044
PENNSYLVANIA		
ALLENTOWN/BETHLEHEM		215/865-6978
ALTOONA		814/943-5848
BETHLEHEM		215/865-6978
BUTLER	412/283-2286	
COATESVILLE		215/383-0440
DOWNINGTON/COATSVLLE		215/383-0440
ERIE		814/456-8501
GREENSBURG		412/836-4470
HARRISBURG/LEMOYNE	717/763-6481	717/975-9881
JOHNSTOWN		814/539-5059
KING OF PRUSSIA/NORSTWN		215/666-9190
LANCASTER		717/569-1081
LATROBE/GREENSBURG		412/836-4470
LEMOYNE	717/763-6481	717/975-9881
LEVITTOWN		
MT. PENN	215/779-9580	
NEW CASTLE		412/658-5056
NORRISTOWN		215/666-9190
PHILADELPHIA	215/592-8309	215/592-8750
PITTSBURGH	412/642-6778	412/642-2015
READING/MT. PENN		215/779-9580
SCRANTON		717/348-0765
SECANE		215/543-3045
STATE COLLEGE		814/234-3853
VALLEY FORGE/NORSTWN		215/666-9190
WILKES BARRE		717/826-8991
WILLIAMSPORT		717/323-0386
YORK		717/852-8186
QUEBEC		
MONTREAL/ST. LAURENT	514/747-2996	
QUEBEC CITY		418/647-1116
ST. LAURENT		514/747-2996
RHODE ISLAND		
MIDDLETOWN		401/849-1660
NEWPORT/MIDDLETOWN		401/849-1660
PAWTUCKET/PROVIDENCE		401/273-0200
PROVIDENCE		401/273-0200
WARWICK/PROVIDENCE		401/273-0200
WOONSOCKET		401/765-5994
SOUTH CAROLINA		
CHARLESTON		803/553-0860
COLUMBIA	803/254-7563	803/252-7375
FLORENCE		803/664-0550
GREENVILLE	803/271-9213	
MYRTLE BEACH		803/448-5401
SPARTANBURG	803/585-0016	
SOUTH DAKOTA		
PIERRE		605/224-7700
RAPID CITY		605/341-4007
SIOUX FALLS		605/334-0085

City	300-1200	300-2400
TENNESSEE		
CHATTANOOGA		615/265-1020
CLARKESVILLE		615/645-8877
JACKSON		901/423-1244
JOHNSON CITY		615/928-9544
KINGSPORT		615/378-5746
KNOXVILLE	615/690-1543	615/693-0498
MEMPHIS	901/527-8006	901/527-8122
NASHVILLE	615/885-3530	615/889-5790
OAKRIDGE		615/482-1466
SEVIERVILLE		615/453-0401
TEXAS		
ABILENE		915/676-0091
AMARILLO		806/355-7088
ARLINGTON/FORT WORTH	817/877-3630	817/332-9397
AUSTIN	512/444-3280	512/448-1096
BAYTOWN		713/420-3389
BROWNSVILLE		512/548-1331
BRYAN		409/823-1090
COLLEGE STATN/BRYAN		409/823-1090
CORPUS CHRISTI	512/883-8050	512/887-9621
DALLAS	214/638-8888	214/630-5516
DENTON		817/565-0552
EL PASO		915/533-1453
FORT WORTH	817/877-3630	817/332-9397
GALVESTON	409/762-8053	
HOUSTON	713/556-6700	713/496-1332
KILLEEN		817/526-8118
LAREDO		512/727-8308
LONGVIEW		903/236-7475
LUBBOCK		806/797-0765
MCALLEN		512/631-6101
MIDLAND		915/683-5645
MIDLAND		915/561-8401
NEDERLAND		409/721-3400
ODESSA/MIDLAND	915/561-8401	915/683-5645
PORT ARTHUR		409/721-3400
SAN ANGELO		915/658-4590
SAN ANTONIO	512/225-8002	512/222-9877
SHERMAN		903/868-0089
TEMPLE		817/773-0982
TEXARKANA		903/792-4521
TEXAS CITY/GALVESTON	409/762-8053	
TYLER		903/581-8652
VICTORIA		512/576-9200
WACO		817/776-0880
WICHITA FALLS		817/723-2386
UTAH		
OGDEN	801/393-5280	
PROVO	801/373-2192	
SALT LAKE	801/364-0780	801/533-8152
VIRGINIA		
ALEXANDRIA/FAIRFAX	703/691-8200	703/352-3136
ARLINGTON/FAIRFAX	703/691-8200	703/352-3136
BETHESDA	703/691-8200	
CHARLOTTESVILLE		804/977-5661

City	300-1200	300-2400	City	300-1200	300-2400
FAIRFAX	703/691-8200	703/352-3136	PARKERSBURG		304/485-9470
HAMPTON		804/727-0572	WESTOVER/MORGANTOWN		304/292-3092
HARRISONBURG		703/433-6333	WHEELING		304/233-7676
LYNCHBURG		804/846-0213	CASPER		307/234-4211
MANASSAS		703/330-9070	CHEYENNE		307/638-0403
MIDLOTHIAN/RICHMOND	804/330-2465	804/330-2673	LARAMIE		307/742-9441
NEWPORT NEWS		804/596-0898			
NORFOLK	804/855-7751	804/857-0148			
PETERSBURG		804/861-1788			
PORTSMOUTH/NORFOLK	804/855-7751	804/857-0148			
RICHMOND	804/330-2465	804/330-2673			
ROANOKE		703/344-2762			
VIRGINIA BCH/NORFOLK	804/855-7751	804/857-0148			
WILLIAMSBURG		804/229-6786			

VERMONT

City	300-1200	300-2400
BARRE/MONTPELIER	802/229-4508	
BURLINGTON		802/862-1000
MONTPELIER	802/229-4508	

WASHINGTON

City	300-1200	300-2400
AUBURN		206/735-3975
BELLEVUE/SEATTLE	206/285-0109	206/281-7141
BELLINGHAM		206/671-5990
BREMERTON		206/377-2792
ENUMCLAW/AUBURN		206/735-3975
EVERETT	206/258-1018	
LONGVIEW		206/423-9072
OLYMPIA	206/943-9050	
PORT ANGELES		206/452-6800
PULLMAN		509/332-3760
RICHLAND		509/375-3367
SEATTLE	206/285-0109	206/281-7141
SPOKANE	509/624-1549	509/747-3011
TACOMA		206/572-2026
VANCOUVER		206/574-0427
YAKIMA		509/248-1462

WISCONSIN

City	300-1200	300-2400
APPLETON		414/730-8029
BELOIT		608/362-4655
BROOKFIELD	414/785-1614	414/785-0630
EAU CLAIRE		715/833-0121
GREEN BAY		414/432-3064
JANESVILLE/BELOIT		608/362-4655
KENOSHA		414/553-9044
LA CROSSE		608/784-9099
MADISON		608/221-0891
MILWAUKEE/BROOKFIELD	414/785-1614	414/785-0630
OSHKOSH		414/235-7473
RACINE/KENOSHA		414/553-9044
SHEBOYGAN		414/457-6128
WAUSAU		715/848-6171
WEST BEND		414/334-1755

WEST VIRGINIA

City	300-1200	300-2400
CHARLESTON		304/345-9575
HUNTINGTON		304/523-8432
MORGANTOWN		304/292-3092

Glossary of Terms

Append To make one file a part of another. In Workspace, a command that attaches one specified file to another specified file. In Mail, an optional qualifier used with the EXTRACT command.

ASCII Acronym for American Standard Code for Information Interchange. ASCII is a standard numeric code used by most computers for transmitting data. There are 128 standard ASCII code numbers, each of which is assigned a standard character, control character, or special character.

Backspace The action of moving a cursor one or more spaces to the left on the computer screen.

Backspace key The backspace key is a large left arrow key on most keyboards. The character sent by a backspace key is a Control-H.

Baud rate In common usage, a measure of the speed at which characters are transmitted from one computer to another. Baud rate is actually a measure of the number of times per second a signal from a modem changes; depending on the signal modulation technique in use, on baud can transmit 1, 2, 4, or more bits. The most common data transmission speeds are 300 (300 baud/1 bit per baud), 1200 (600 baud/2 bits per baud), and 2400 (600 baud/4 bits per baud) characters per second. (See BITS PER SECOND.)

Binary A system of counting that uses only two digits: 1 and 0. Many computer programs are stored in binary, rather than ASCII form, and text files may be transferred in binary form. (See ASCII, KERMIT, XMODEM)

Binary file A file in binary format. Binary storage is more space efficient than the 7-bit ASCII code.

Bit The smallest unit of computer information. A binary digit; its value is either 0 or 1. (See BYTE, DATA BITS, STOP-BIT)

Bits per second (BPS) A measure of the rate of data transmission.

Block A measurement of file size used by DELPHI. A block is equal to 512 bytes.

Buffer A section of a computer's RAM reserved by terminal software to temporarily store incoming data for display. Many terminal programs can open and close the buffer, and write its contents to disk when it becomes full.

Byte A computer character made up of seven or eight binary digits. (See BIT)

Capture Storing the contents of a computer's RAM buffer on disk or other media. (See BUFFER)

Carriage return The signal sent by a computer's «RETURN» key; normally a Control-M, or ASCII 13. (See RETURN KEY)

Carrier A tone transmitted over telephone lines by computers. The carrier tone is modulated to transmit data.

Character A letter, number, space, punctuation mark, or symbol; any piece of information that can be stored in one byte.

Character length A terminal software setting that determines the number of data bits in each character sent. Seven data bits make up each character in the ASCII character set; to send these characters in binary format, eight data bits are required per character. Also referred to as data word length. (See DATA BITS, ASCII, BINARY)

Command An instruction or set of instructions that tells a program to perform a specified function or functions. (See IMMEDIATE COMMANDS, INTERRUPTS, OPTION, QUALIFIERS)

Communications settings The parameter settings used by terminal software; the group of changeable settings available in a program. These settings determine how your computer will communicate with DELPHI, and include buad rate, parity, duplex, character length/data bits, and number of stop bits. (See PARAMETERS, TERMINAL CONFIGURATION)

Communications software (See TERMINAL SOFTWARE)

Control character A non-printing character generated by holding down the Control key and a letter key on a computer keyboard. Control characters are used on DELPHI to issue commands. Control characters are usually indicated online as Control-X, but may sometimes be indicated as CTRL-X or ^X.

Control key A special key on your computer keyboard marked CONTROL, CTRL, or [CTRL] (the down arrow on the TRS-80 Color Computer; shift key on some Commodore VIC-20's). The Control Key is designated as Control, CONTROL, CTRL, or ^ in computer software and hardware documentation. The Control Key is used with other keys to send special commands to DELPHI.

CRC Acronym for Cyclic Redundancy Check; an error-checking protocol for XMODEM transfer.

Cursor A small flashing block or bar that designates where the next character typed will appear, or prompts for input.

Data Information of any type. Addresses are data; so are names or groups of numbers. (Data is the plural of the Latin datum.)

Database An organized collection of related programs and/or information in the form of binary and/or ASCII files. DELPHI Group and Club databases are organized under various topics, and contain text, data, and program files. The files are searchable by various keywords, and may be downloaded. Members may submit files for inclusion in certain databases. Some databases contain files in which related information is organized into sub-groups, called fields. (See ENTRY, FIELD, FILE, KEYWORD, SEARCH, SUBMIT, TOPICS)

Data bits The number of all bits sent for a single character that represent the character itself, not counting parity or stop bits; normally seven or eight bits. (See BIT, BYTE, CHARACTER, PARITY, STOP BIT)

Default A setting, instruction, or data that a program uses unless you enter a different value. (See PARAMETER, PROGRAM)

Delete To erase or remove. In Databases, Forums, Mail, Workspace, other areas, a command that erases specified files or messages. In the EDT or OLDIE online editor, a command that erases a line or range of lines. (See FILE, MESSAGE, FORUM, MAIL, WORKSPACE)

Delete/Rubout key The backspace or large left arrow key on most computer keyboards; issues a Control-H, which tells DELPHI to move the cursor on your screen one space to the left.

Description In databases, the brief description of the contents of an entry. Also, a databases Action prompt command that displays the description of an entry. (See READ)

Directory A summary list of available files in a Database, Mail, and Workspace command that displays a summary list of available files. The summary may include file sizes, date and time of creation, and owner, where appropriate. In Workspace, Databases, Forum, and elsewhere on DELPHI, a command that produces such a summary listing (CATALOG command is synonymous with DIRECTORY). (See DATABASE, WORKSPACE)

Display To print to the computer screen. In Databases, a command that prints a text file to the screen using any special formatting commands in the file. Sometimes used to refer to the screen itself. Compare with LIST and READ. (See SCREEN, SCROLL)

Distribution list A file formatted with one membername per line, and with the filename extension .DIS. A distribution file is used as a source file for sending the same mail message to more than one DELPHI member.

Download To receive data from a computer. In Workspace, Databases, and elsewhere, a command that lists a file to your computer screen as an ASCII download, with a delay, Control-Z, and BELL (Control-G) at the end. (See TURNAROUND CHARACTER, UPLOAD)

Duplex A data transmission mode that determines whether another computer echoes characters typed at your computer's keyboard. (See FULL-DUPLEX and HALF-DUPLEX)

Echo (Character echo) To repeat. When character echo is enabled during data transmission, the receiving computer sends back characters it has received for display on the transmitting computer's screen. (See FULL-DUPLEX, HALF-DUPLEX)

Edit To alter a file. In Workspace, a command that invokes the EDT or OLDIE line editor to edit a specified file. In FORUM, EDIT allows you to edit the topic, subject, or text of a specified or the last read message. EDIT may also be used on messages you post elsewhere, such as on the Chatter Board. (See EDIT, FILE, OLDIE, WORKSPACE)

Emulation A mode of operation that enables a computer to function as if it were a specific type of terminal. Terminal emulation is an option included with some software packages. (See TERMINAL, TERMINAL EMULATION, VT)

ENTER key (See RETURN KEY)

Entry In Group or other databases, a file or group of files. The lists displayed by the DIRECTORY command consist of the names of entries. (See DATABASE, FILE)

Extension The categorizing portion of a filename following the period. This may consist of up to three digits or numbers. Example: NAME.EXT (See FILENAME)

Field A defined area containing a fixed number of characters. Fields can be found in online forms, and in some databases. You can fill a field in a form manually by entering characters from your keyboard, or it can be filled automatically by data from a file or with its default value.

File A collection of data stored as a discreet unit. A file may consist of text in ASCII format, or text or programs in binary format. Files can be found in databases and in Workspace. (See DATABASE, ENTRY, FILENAME, WORKSPACE)

Filename The identifying label given a file. DELPHI filenames consist of a filename of up to nine letters or digits, followed by a period, followed by an extension of up to three letters or digits, followed by a semicolon and a version number from 1 to 32767. Example: NAME.TYP;1 (See EXTENSION)

Filter To remove unwanted characters in a transmission. This is a function of terminal software.

Flow control A means whereby a receiving computer can signal a sending computer to pause and resume data being sent. With DELPHI, this is normally accomplished by having your computer sending a Control-S to pause the data transmission, after which sending is resumed with Control-Q. Many terminal programs automatically send commands to DELPHI to pause sending during a capture or download, to allow time for the data to be written to disk.

Folder In Mail, a subdivision of a mail file into which mail messages may be moved or copied.

Formatting commands "Dot" commands put into a file that cause it to be displayed with specified formatting, as dictated by the creator of the file. With these commands, headings may be centered, margins set, etc. Each dot command must be placed at the left margin of the document, on a line by itself.

Full-Duplex A communications mode in which DELPHI echoes characters you type back to your screen. (See DUPLEX, ECHO, HALF-DUPLEX)

Half-Duplex A communications mode in which DELPHI does not echo characters you type on your keyboard. In half-duplex mode, your software must handle the display of characters to your screen. (The recommended setting for communicating with DELPHI is Full-Duplex. At Full-Duplex, commands and other input you type will appear on your computer screen; at Half-Duplex, they will not.) (See DUPLEX, ECHO, FULL-DUPLEX, MODE)

Handshaking The mutually agreed-upon method by which the rate of data transmission is controlled during an ASCII Upload or Download. (See DOWNLOAD, FLOW CONTROL, UPLOAD)

Hardware The individual or collective physical components of a computer system, including but not limited to the keyboard, monitor, disk drives, and printer.

HOME In Workspace, a command that changes your default Workspace to your HOME (personal) Workspace. This command is executed automatically when you enter and exit your Workspace. Your personal Workspace, as opposed to the COMMON area.

Immediate Commands Also known as "slash commands" Immediate Commands are preceded by a slash (/) and may be executed from most prompts on DELPHI. A special set of Immediate Commands is available in Conference. (See COMMAND, INTERRUPTS)

Interface An electronic device that facilitates communication between a computer and a peripheral device like a modem.

Initialization string A character string that "wakes up" a modem; usually precedes dialing commands. A typical modem initialization string consists of AT (for "attention").

Input A command or data of any type supplied in response to a prompt.

Input file A file whose contents are copied to another file. (See COPY, OUTPUT FILE)

Internal modem A modem installed inside a computer, usually in the form of a printed circuit board or card.

Interrupts Systemwide commands that abort, stop, or pause a current activity. Interrupts consist exclusively of Control-key commands, such as Control-C and Control-Z. (See COMMAND,

CONTROL CHARACTER, CONTROL KEY, IMMEDIATE COMMANDS)

Item In Group databases, an individual file in a database entry. (See DATABASE, ENTRY)

KERMIT A special file-transfer format for ASCII and binary files, available in Databases and Workspace. In Workspace, a command that invokes the Kermit file transfer server.

Keyword A word used to label database files in DELPHI databases and the entries in People on DELPHI. The keywords attached to a file serve as references during database searches. (See DATABASE, PEOPLE, SEARCH)

Kilobyte (K) A unit of computer memory, normally referring to the number of bytes in RAM or the size of a file, equal to 1024 bytes. (See BIT, BYTE)

LENGTH (Line Length) A SETTINGS option used to specify the number of lines DELPHI displays on your computer screen before pausing and giving the More? prompt. Length can also be set using the Immediate command /L=x (where x is equal to the desired line length).

Linefeed A signal that causes the cursor to advance one line downward on the display screen. Sometimes sent after a carriage return during upload or download.

List To display the contents of a file. In databases, a command that causes the actual contents of a file to be printed to your computer screen, unformatted. In Workspace, a command that displays a file to your computer's screen, unformatted. (Compare with DISPLAY and READ)

Logon The process or event of connecting with and identifying yourself to DELPHI. Also referred to as "sign on" or "signon."

Macro Character strings or commands issued or sent with one keystroke. Macros are usually issued by a control-key combination or by a function key, and are created and stored by terminal software or a special keyboard macro program. (See CONTROL KEY)

Menu A listing of commands and/or options available in a particular area on DELPHI. (See COMMAND, SELECTION, SUB-MENU)

Message In general, any communication from one member to another, or to a group of members, delivered by DELPHI. Messages can be found in Mail, Forums, and on bulletin boards, or can consist of one-line "sends" from one user to another. (See FORUM, MAIL)

Modem A device used to translate binary signals from a computer into tone signals for transmission via telephone line, and vice-versa. (From modulate-demodulate device.)

Nickname In Conference, an assumed name selected with the immediate command /NAME nickname. (See CONFERENCE)

Offline Not connected to DELPHI.

Oldie An alternative editor to EDT. (See EDIT, EDT, WORKSPACE)

Online Connected to DELPHI.

Option In general, any menu selection that is not a command; a choice on a Selection menu. (See COMMAND, MENU, SELECTION MENU)

Output file A file to which the contents of another file are copied. (See COPY, INPUT FILE)

Packet switching network A communications service that provides a nationwide system of local telephone numbers and computers for connecting with DELPHI. Also known as a packet switching network. Datapac, Telenet, and Tymnet are packet switching networks.

Parameters The settings selected by a computer user, and/or included in a program, used as established values or defaults in program instructions or functions. (See DEFAULT, COMMUNICATIONS SETTINGS, PROGRAM)

Parity A method of data transmission error-checking in which the receiving computer periodically counts the number of bits transmitted and verifies this with the transmitting computer.

Portal A "shortcut" from a group or club to a merchant area or sub-group, or vice-versa. A portal appears as a selection on the group or merchant menu. Sometimes called a "Gateway."

Premium Service A DELPHI service for which there is an extra per-minute or flat-rate access charge in addition to normal connect charges.

Program A set of instructions that tells a computer how to perform a set task or tasks, and which processes commands and input in accordance with these instructions. (See COMMAND, DEFAULT, INPUT, PARAMETER)

Prompt A request for a command or information, in the form of word(s) or symbol(s) displayed on the screen. DELPHI command prompts consist of menus or one-word requests (such as MAIL] or ACTION]). DELPHI information prompts consist of Yes or No response requests (Y/N or More?), and "fill-in-the-blank" prompts (MM/DD/YY).

Prompt level The level of menu and option information displayed by DELPHI. Prompt levels can be BRIEF, VERBOSE, or consist of complete MENUs. (The prompt level is set in USING, but may be temporarily reset with the immediate command /PROMPT =)

Protocol Mutually agreed-upon "rules" or settings for data transmission.

Qualifiers Specifications or modifications that may be added to certain commands, usually preceded by a slash. Qualifiers limit or direct how a command is executed. Example: EXTRACT /NOHEADER (an Electronic Mail command where /NOHEADER is the qualifier). (See COMMAND)

READ A database command that displays the description of a file. READ does not display the contents of a file itself. (Compare with DISPLAY and LIST.)

Realtime (Real-time) Taking place at the present time; not delayed or recorded. "Live."

RETURN key The computer key used to send text or commands to software and to DELPHI. Marked RETURN on most keyboards, and referred to as «RETURN» in this book, this key is marked ENTER, NEW LINE, XMIT, <—', or CR on some keyboards.

Scroll The vertical movement of text on a computer screen display, normally in an upward direction. New characters appear at the bottom-most available line on the computer screen and "push" the lines above them upward. This movement is called scrolling. (See DISPLAY, SCREEN)

SEARCH A command used in Databases, PEOPLE, and elsewhere to find all files or entries meeting a specified criterion or criteria. (See DATABASE, KEYWORD, PEOPLE, MEMBER DIRECTORY)

Selection An item on a menu. Also, an item chosen from a menu. (See MENU, OPTION)

Selection menu An interim menu that lists only selectable options, and no commands. Selection menus are used to present a list of categories in Group databases, Group Announcements, and elsewhere. (Although not normally listed on Selection menus, Systemwide and Immediate commands operate at most selection menus.)

Settings A Using DELPHI Menu selection and a Groups and Clubs and Workspace option. The

Settings Menu in USING allows you to use the SETTINGS sub-menu to customize DELPHI to fit your individual requirements. Entering the selection SETTINGS in Workspace presents the same options, and selecting Set Preferences at a group or club menu displays a menu on which Settings is a selection.

Sign on (See LOGON)

Slash commands (See IMMEDIATE COMMANDS)

Software (See PROGRAM)

Stop-bits Data bits that mark the end of a transmitted character. Most terminal software packages offer the option of setting stop-bits at 1 or 2; DELPHI requires 1 stop bit. (See BIT, BYTE, DATA BITS, CHARACTER)

String A series of letters, numbers, or symbols to be input or output as data. Strings that cannot be used as numeric operands and whose values do not vary are character strings. "Wilson A. Tucker," "ALLIED PUBLISHING COMPANY," and "3-21-51" are all character strings. Strings with set numeric values are numeric strings. "451.50" and "910234" are numeric strings.

Sub-menu A secondary menu of commands displayed in response to a primary menu selection. (See MENU)

Submit In Workspace or group databases, the command that sends a file to a database or group manager for posting in a database. (See DATABASE)

Sub-sig A "group within a group," accessed via a group menu. (See GROUP)

Syntax A set of rules governing how commands, filenames, or data can be entered at a prompt.

Telecommunications Communication over telephone lines via computers and associated devices.

Telex An international telecommunications system that handles messaging to and from special Telex terminals anywhere in the world. Telex service can be accessed through the DELPHI Mail selection from the DELPHI Main Menu.

Terminal A device that displays and sometimes stores data received from another computer and can transmit data from a keyboard or mass storage. A dedicated computer that is capable of performing telecommunications and related tasks only. (See EMULATION, TERMINAL EMULATION, VT)

Terminal Configuration Collectively, the parameters established by your computer's terminal software. (See COMMUNICATIONS SETTINGS, PARAMETER)

Terminal emulation An option provided by some terminal software that allows a computer to emulate (imitate) a specific brand or type of computer terminal, such as a DEC VT100 or VT52. (See TERMINAL, EMULATION, VT)

Terminal settings The individual parameters selectable with terminal software.

Terminal software Software designed to allow a computer to emulate a terminal.

Text Any message or file composed of standard 7-bit ASCII characters. (See ASCII, CHARACTER)

Text file A file in ASCII format, as opposed to Binary format. (See ASCII, BINARY, FILE)

Thread In Forum, a group of messages, related by subject and other parameters, and accessible by special command DIR and READ commands. (See FORUM)

Topics In Groups and Clubs, the database and Forum message categories. Topics represent the major subjects of interest in a Group. (See DATABASE)

Turnaround character A pre-selected character or prompt for which a terminal program may wait before sending a line of text during an ASCII upload or receiving an ASCII download. No turnaround character is required for ASCII uploads to DELPHI. (See DOWNLOAD, UPLOAD)

Type ahead Type Ahead is a DELPHI feature that allows you to type several commands in succession without waiting for the commands to be executed. The commands (each should be followed by «RETURN») are stored in a "type-ahead" buffer. Type Ahead facilitates moving from one area to another on DELPHI, and decreases the time it takes to execute multiple commands.

Upload To send data to another computer. In Workspace, the command that initiates an ASCII file transfer from your computer to DELPHI. (See TURNAROUND CHARACTER)

Videotex A term applied to the transmission of textual data and/or text and graphics by an online information service like DELPHI.

VT (VT52 VT100) A type of terminal designed for use with Digital Equipment Corporation's Vax computers. Using or emulating a Vax Terminal allows you to take advantage of DELPHI's enhanced screens and some graphics, as well as full screen editing using the EDT line editor. (See EMULATION, TERMINAL, TERMINAL EMULATION)

Width (Line Width) A SETTINGS option used to specify the number of columns (characters) DELPHI displays across your computer before beginning a new line. Width can also be set using the Immediate command /W=x (where x is equal to a number between 16 and 132).

Workspace Your personal file storage, creation, and transfer area on DELPHI. In Workspace, you can create, edit, delete, upload, download, and otherwise manipulate and maintain text files. Program files may also be uploaded and downloaded in Workspace, and you may submit files of any type to Groups and Clubs from your Workspace. (See COMMON, CREATE, DELETE, DOWNLOAD, EDIT, HOME, OLDIE, UPLOAD)

XMODEM A special binary file transfer protocol that is virtually error-free.

XMODEM BLOCK One unit of data transmitted during an XMODEM transfer. In standard XMODEM transfer, one XMODEM block equals 128 bytes; a special 1024-byte XMODEM file-transfer protocol is available, called YMODEM.

XON-XOFF A standard type of flow control using CTRL-S to signal a sending computer to pause, and Control-Q to signal the sending computer to resume sending. This is the flow control used by DELPHI. (See FLOW CONTROL)

Index

C

D